THE **NEW** CULTURAL **HISTORY** OF **PERONISM**

Matthew B. Karush and Oscar Chamosa, eds.

THE NEW CULTURAL HISTORY OF PERONISM

....

Power and Identity in Mid-Twentieth-Century Argentina

Duke University Press   Durham and London   2010

© 2010 Duke University Press

All rights reserved.

Printed in the United States of America on acid-free paper ∞

Designed by Heather Hensley

Typeset in Arno Pro by Keystone Typesetting, Inc.

Library of Congress Cataloging-in-Publication Data appear
on the last printed page of this book.

CONTENTS

ACKNOWLEDGMENTS

This project began as a panel on Argentine cultural history at the meeting of the Southeastern Council of Latin American Studies in San José, Costa Rica, in 2007. As we editors exchanged e-mail messages in the months leading up to the conference, we realized that we had stumbled upon an important historiographical trend: a generation of young historians of Argentina had begun to produce exciting new work on the cultural aspects of the Peronist experience. Informed by recent trends in Latin American historiography, this research had the potential to transform our understanding of the period from 1946 to 1955, in many ways the key turning point in Argentine history. Since this new interpretation-in-progress was the work of several historians working independently, an edited volume seemed the best way to have these scholars engage in a dialogue and to introduce their work to a broad audience.

We would like to thank all the contributors to this book for their willingness to participate in an extremely productive process of give and take. We are grateful as well to Valerie Millholland at Duke University Press for her enthusiastic support of the project and for an unending stream of good advice. Both the University of Georgia and George Mason University provided research and travel support, and a "Creative Award" grant from George Mason University funded the translation of the three chapters originally written in Spanish. Beatrice D. Gurwitz produced excellent translations of these chapters under some very demanding time constraints. Two chapters were previously published in Argentina: chapter 6 in Anahi Ballent, *Las huellas de la política: vivienda, ciudad, peronismo en Buenos Aires, 1943–1955* (Buenos Aires: Universidad Nacional de Quilmes, 2006), and chapter 7 in Mirta Zaida Lobato, ed., *Cuando las mujeres reinaban: belleza, virtud y poder en la Argentina del siglo XX* (Buenos Aires: Biblos, 2005). By allowing us to republish these chapters, Mirta Lobato and Anahi Ballent helped us to present a more inclusive view of scholarship produced in North American and Argentine universities. John Chasteen and Mark Healey served as conscientious and creative readers for the press; their many useful suggestions improved the book immeasurably. We are also grateful to a third reader who served anonymously. Finally, we thank Alison Landsberg and Patricia Richards for their ideas and their inspiration.

Matthew B. Karush and Oscar Chamosa
....

INTRODUCTION

As we write this introductory essay, current events in Argentina have revealed yet again the enduring relevance of Peronism. On 10 December 2007 Cristina Fernández de Kirchner was sworn in as Argentina's thirty-fourth constitutional president, the second woman to occupy that office and the seventh Peronist. Returns from the previous October's general election show that Fernández's ticket lost in high- and middle-income urban districts, secured a strong advantage in the industrial belt and secondary cities, and won by a landslide in small towns and rural communities across the country. Despite Argentina's pronounced political instability over the last sixty years, these results suggest that underlying patterns of electoral preference have remained remarkably stable.[1] Peronism's most recent resurgence indicates that the movement is much more than the cynical electoral machine dismissed by many political analysts during the 1990s, when Carlos Menem engineered the party's embrace of neoliberalism. Not only has Peronism retained its electoral power, but many of its central images and rhetorical moves remain staples of political discourse. Throughout the winter of 2008 a conflict between the government and the agricultural sector dragged on for four months, producing massive street demonstrations, roadblocks, strikes, lockouts, and angry debates in the press and the National Congress. President Fernández denounced farmers who opposed her government's increase in the export tax as greedy enemies of the poor, while her pro-farmer foes charged her with trampling on democratic institutions. The verbal virulence of both camps shocked the country with words that seemed to have been taken directly from the political playbook of 1945.

Of course historians hardly needed current events to remind them of Peronism's significance. Virtually all accounts of Argentina's modern history have identified the first Perón regime, from 1946 to 1955, as the critical turning point. Latin America's prototypical populist government mobilized the nation's growing working class behind its project for rapid industrialization and corporatist political organization. Channeling export earnings into the industrial sector and into the pockets of workers, Perón transformed Argentina's economy, its social structure, and its political culture in ways that continue to shape Argentine reality. Unsurprisingly this experience has attracted a great deal of scholarly attention; certainly no other period in the nation's history has been the object of so much study. Nevertheless key questions remain. For decades the prevalence of top-down approaches and of certain forms of economic determinism inhibited an understanding of working-class, Peronist identity. Later works used classic social history methodology to illuminate the perspectives of rank-and-file Peronists, but they tended to oversimplify the interaction between popular consciousness and state action. With this book we hope to demonstrate the potential of a theoretically informed cultural history to chart a course that avoids these pitfalls and to produce a richer understanding of Peronism.

Like Luis Alberto Romero, the authors collected in this book view the struggle unleashed by Perón's rise to power as a "cultural conflict." Notwithstanding Peronism's initial attempts to build a multiclass alliance, the regime developed a deeply polarizing appeal that divided Argentina into two irreconcilable subcultures. But Romero describes the conflict as cultural in order to minimize it. In this view the dispute between Peronists and anti-Peronists was "cultural" rather than "real"; since Perón did not expropriate the means of production, fundamental interests were not at stake.[2] By contrast, we are more inclined to accept Tulio Halperín Donghi's assessment that the advent of Peronism amounted to a "social revolution . . . under the aegis of the Peronist regime, all the relations between social groups were suddenly redefined, and to see that, it was enough to walk the streets or ride a streetcar."[3] As Halperín suggests, the Peronist transformation was radical enough to sow the seeds of the brutal and seemingly unending conflict that marked the decades after Perón's fall. To define this process as cultural is not to downplay its significance but to reframe it as an object of historical inquiry.

Such a reframing implies the inclusion of new topics—such as commercial culture and ethnic identity—as well as the use of new methods.

Inspired by recent approaches to the cultural history of Latin America, the chapters that follow highlight the system of symbolic representations that transformed the collective identities of vast portions of the Argentine population. Yet they situate this cultural development within the process of state formation. In other words, this is a cultural history that is simultaneously a political history. It illuminates Peronism first by locating it in the longer sweep of Argentine cultural development: without downplaying the regime's innovations and impact, this book reveals how existing values, ideologies, practices, and traditions shaped the Peronist experience. Second, the book reconsiders the interactions between the regime and ordinary Argentines, revealing the mediating role of the capitalist marketplace and avoiding the facile binarism of resistance or domination. The chapters that follow show Peronist and anti-Peronist identities to have emerged from the complex negotiation between dynamic cultural traditions, official policies, commercial imperatives, and popular perceptions. By attending to this multilayered process, the book exposes the unintended consequences, contradictions, and ambivalences that have characterized Argentine populism.

In this introduction we begin by describing the emergence in recent decades of cultural approaches to the history of Peronism. Social history, Marxist ideological analysis, the "linguistic turn" in historical scholarship, gender studies, and finally cultural studies have debunked the determinist certainties of earlier structural approaches, even as they have expanded the scope of historical inquiry beyond labor politics and official policy. Next we will describe the methodological innovations of recent Latin American historiography, the "new cultural history" that we seek to bring to bear on the case of Peronism. In so doing we will further specify the precise contribution of this book to the study of Argentina's most important decade.

PERONISM STUDIES: FROM MODERNIZATION THEORY TO CULTURAL HISTORY

The academic study of Peronism began with the works of the sociologists Gino Germani, Torcuato Di Tella, and Miguel Murmis and Juan Carlos Portantiero, who sought to explain why the working class followed Perón and to define the political system that resulted.[4] Writing in the 1950s, Germani embraced the modernization theory then in vogue, explaining Peronism as a product of the asynchronies produced by the transition from a traditional to a modern society. According to Germani, Peronism recruited most of its initial following from among the industrial workers who migrated to Buenos Aires from the countryside in the decade before 1945. These workers were rapidly adjusting to an urban and industrial milieu but still belonged to a traditional society and were physically and culturally separated from the older, more self-conscious working class.[5] The new migrants sought to advance their political and economic claims by supporting an authoritarian project that resonated with their traditional values. Germani, an avowed anti-Peronist himself, emphasized the irrationality of the pre-modern masses who he claimed constituted the bulk of Perón's constituency. Di Tella strengthened this account by adding a different element: the support of the middle cadres of institutions such as the army, the press, academia, and the church. According to Di Tella these dissatisfied members of the intelligentsia found in Peronism a movement opposed to the status quo that satisfied their aspirations for upward mobility.[6] The presence of these middle cadres helped to explain some of Peronism's ideological ambivalence. However, once economic development allowed the middle class to meet its expectations, these sectors abandoned the class alliance.

Writing in 1971, Murmis and Portantiero examined the actions and organization of labor unions in the pre-Perón years to refute some of Germani's generalizations.[7] They found that much of the so-called new working class had already been incorporated into the labor union structure, and they argued that both internal migrants and established urban workers supported Perón not because of an atavistic attachment to authoritarianism but rather out of a rational calculation of their class interests. When Perón became secretary of labor in 1943 he encountered a well-organized working class long accustomed to negotiation with the state. He responded with a series of significant measures that advanced the interests of labor unions in concrete and measurable ways. In this context labor's responsiveness to Perón's overtures made perfect sense. Murmis and Portantiero turned Germani's modernization paradigm on its head: workers' decisions to support Perón were an expression not of their irrational traditionalism but of their class consciousness.

Despite their differences Germani and the revisionists shared a pronounced structuralism. Both accounts depicted Peronism as the result of a particular pattern of economic development rather than of a dynamic and contingent political process. Beginning in 1969, with the publication of Félix Luna's careful chronological reconstruction of the events of 1945, a new generation of historians paid closer attention to the complex conjuncture opened by the military coup of 1943.[8] This approach proved extremely fruitful, culminating in Juan Carlos Torre's *La vieja guardia sindical y Perón*, which stressed the contingency of Perón's dealings with labor as well as the key mediating role played by the existing union leadership.[9] According to Torre, union leaders recognized the danger of supporting an authoritarian project, but they saw little alternative given the extreme hostility to social reform that characterized the opposition to Perón. Torre's work complemented an extensive literature on the labor history of the pre-Perón era, which traced many of labor's strategies and predispositions to the struggles of the 1930s.[10] In a sense this new scholarship followed Murmis and Portantiero in describing organized labor's actions as rational, but not, as those authors had suggested, because they corresponded to workers' objective class interests. Rather, the working-class embrace of Peronism only made sense within the extremely fluid conjuncture of Argentina in the 1940s.[11]

From a very different perspective, the Marxist political theorist Ernesto Laclau also began to chip away at the economic determinism that had shaped earlier interpretations of Peronism. Seeking to define "populism" in general and Peronism in particular, Laclau criticized Germani and Di Tella for reducing the phenomenon to the political expression of a particular class or class alliance. Instead, he argued, class discourses are always articulated with cultural "raw materials" that have no necessary affiliation with any class. Populism occurs when these elements—what Laclau called "popular-democratic interpellations"—are presented as oppositional to the ideology of the dominant bloc.[12] In contrast to European fascism, Peronism empowered workers against the ruling class, and it did so by drawing on and rearticulating available discursive elements. Peronism's hostility to liberal democracy, for example, was not the product of traditional authoritarianism but the result of the crisis of the 1930s, in which the historic articulation between democracy and liberalism had been severed. Thus by 1945 Peronism could present liberalism as an ideology linked to elite class interests, while offering workers a more socially defined democracy, together with industrialism and nationalism, as an "antagonistic option" against the oligarchy.

In an early critique of this interpretation, Emilio de Ípola accused Laclau of focusing excessively on the "conditions of production" of Peronist discourse while overlooking the "conditions of reception." In so doing Laclau had implied that Peronist discourse constructed its subject —the Peronist working class—and denied any agency to workers themselves. De Ípola argued that the production and reception of discourse must be situated in its historical context. Much as Torre and other labor historians would do, he stressed the dynamic relationship between Perón and the unions from 1943 to 1946. In particular he emphasized the union leadership's failed attempt to retain a margin of autonomy from Perón's vertical leadership. It was the defeat of the "worker's populism (*populismo obrero*)" represented by the Labor Party that made possible Perón's national-capitalist version of populism.[13] In this way de Ípola accepted Laclau's focus on discourse but sought to make it less abstract by bringing politics back into the analysis.

By the late 1980s the classic structuralist accounts of Peronism had therefore been largely discarded in favor of studies that focused either on politics or on discourse. Labor historians had demonstrated that workers' support for the Peronist project reflected the strategic decisions of a union leadership in a rapidly changing political environment rather than a particular pattern of economic development. Meanwhile, Laclau and de Ípola had uncovered the importance of Peronist language: any explanation of rank-and-file Peronist identity needed to attend not just to the actions of union leaders but also to a longer discursive history. This attention to language, part of the larger "linguistic turn" in historical scholarship, prompted a shift in Peronism studies from socioeconomic analysis toward an emphasis on discourse.[14] Juan Perón's speeches, and Eva's to a lesser extent, previously dismissed as mere pandering, now attracted serious analysis. Beyond the presidential couple, scholarly attention extended toward a wide range of discursive production, including that of the opposition and of intellectuals of both camps. Most of these works combined a new attention to the linguistic aspects of speeches and written texts with the more traditional methods of intellectual history.

Still, these various approaches to politics and to discourse, focused as they were on intellectuals, government officials, and union leaders, shed very little light on what Peronism meant for workers. It would fall to the historian Daniel James to initiate serious analysis of this question. James's *Resistance and Integration* (1988) signaled an important departure from earlier scholarship.[15] Set in the larger chronological frame of 1946 to 1976, the book charts the interactions of the state and organized labor during the period, but it also devotes attention to the lives and actions of the Peronist rank and file. Drawing on a wide range of sources including personal testimonies and newsletters of local, often clandestine Peronist organizations in the industrial belts of Buenos Aires and Rosario, James reconstructs the "structure of feelings" that informed the behavior of Peronist workers in the face of repression. The book's examination of workers' initial support for Perón has been particularly influential. Instead of reexamining the political calculations of union leaders, James explores why Perón's rhetoric and political style appealed to the rank and file. Without denying the existence of a Peronist ideology, he highlights the performative aspects of Peronism, which included not only Juan and Eva Perón's speeches from the balcony of the Casa Rosada but also demonstrations, strikes, and, after the fall of Perón in 1955, acts of sabotage and other clandestine operations.[16] In a way James's bottom-up approach resurrected the pioneering research carried out during the 1960s by the sociologist Julio Mafud and the anthropologist Hugo Ratier, who had been interested in the constitution of a Peronist subjectivity.[17] James's emphasis on popular reception reinvigorated the study of Peronist discourse and revealed for the first time the enormous potential of a "culturalist" approach to the history of Peronism.

A recent summary of research on the "democratization of welfare" in the Perón years by Juan Carlos Torre and Elisa Pastoriza reminds us of the revolutionary impact of the regime, as the working class enjoyed dramatically expanded access to education, tourism, housing, and entertainment.[18] Following James, Torre and Pastoriza stress that although this transformation was engineered by the state, it was decisively influenced by rank-and-file workers, who were anything but passive recipients of official largesse. However, to date very few studies have emulated James's innovative reconstructions of popular reception. Rosa Aboy's study of Peronist housing policies, which uses oral history to assess individuals' responses to the houses they received from the regime, is an important exception.[19]

Since the earliest studies, scholars have recognized the importance of mass culture in preparing the terrain for Perón's political success and in communicating the regime's political message. Di Tella, for example, carved out a key role for radio and the cinema in creating a "revolution of rising expectations" that in his view yielded widespread support for populism: "The mass media raise the levels of aspiration of their audience . . . Yet economic expansion lags behind . . . with expectations soaring high above the possibilities of satisfying them."[20] De Ípola stressed the enormous success of Perón's discursive techniques and argued that scholars needed to pay careful attention to the communicative strategies of Perón and his team.[21] Once again, though, it was James who demonstrated the political significance of Perón's rhetoric, paying particular attention to his use of popular culture.[22] Perón borrowed liberally from the nineteenth-century epic poem *Martín Fierro*, as well as from tango lyrics and popular expressions in *lunfardo*, the "disreputable" argot of Buenos Aires, to make himself understood by his blue-collar audiences. Though many critics of Peronism saw this rhetorical strategy as condescending demagoguery, James found in it the seeds of an enduring Peronist identity. Likewise, in his more recent work James has pointed to the importance of popular melodrama in shaping the working-class consciousness that would prove so receptive to Peronism.[23]

The study of the Peronist propaganda machine has produced a growing and increasingly nuanced body of literature. The personality cult around Perón and Eva, the politicizing of the school curricula, the profusion of official advertising on the radio, in newsreels, and in printed media, as well as the regime's efforts to shape the contents of movies and radio programs, are among the practices that have drawn the most attention.[24] Within this literature the works of Mariano Plotkin and more recently Marcela Gené stand out. Plotkin's *Mañana es San Perón* carefully examines Peronist textbooks as well as the crucial role of the Eva Perón Foundation in generating support for the regime, but perhaps its most important contribution is its emphasis on the construction of Peronist power through massive political rituals.[25] A case in point is the annual October 17 celebration, the commemoration of Peronism's foundational moment in 1945, when Perón was ousted from his multiple offices in the military government, briefly detained in a military facility, and restored to power after massive demonstrations by workers. Though October 17 is a favorite theme in Peronist historiography, Plotkin shifts the spotlight from the historical episode to the political history of the public commemoration, showing, among other things, how the state wrested control over the meaning of the celebration from grassroots Peronist organizations such as the Labor Party and the unions. Plotkin describes October 17 as an annual ritual of communion between Perón and his followers, as important in consolidating both Perón's leadership and Peronist identity as the original act being commemorated. For her part, Gené offers a thick description of the visual representation of workers in Peronist propaganda.[26] Gené reveals that the propaganda machine was not limited to the state but involved other actors, including the Peronist Party, the labor unions, and the sympathetic media. Against the naïve notion that propaganda is only employed by totalitarian regimes, she demonstrates how Peronist publicists borrowed from Franklin D. Roosevelt's New Deal, especially in the crucial area of labor iconography.

Recent scholarship has pushed the study of Peronism in interesting new directions. Particularly noteworthy is a long-overdue corrective to the excessive focus on the national government and its policies. A new crop of studies on provincial Peronism reminds us that Peronism was born in the industrial corridor encompassing Greater Buenos Aires and La Plata, and that any study of the movement's origins and development should start there.[27] Expanding the geographical scope even farther, several scholars are now laying the groundwork for a truly national assessment of Peronism. These historians reject the image of the Argentine interior as a politically empty place that merely implemented policies designed in Buenos Aires.[28] Gustavo Rubinstein, for instance, shows how the rapid rise of the Sugar Workers' Union in Tucumán consolidated the Peronist presence in the interior and revolutionized the electoral politics of a province traditionally dominated by the planter elite. But far from being a docile labor branch of a centralized regime, sugar workers did not hesitate to go on strike against Perón's explicit orders when their interests conflicted with the agenda of policymakers in Buenos Aires.[29]

In addition to this geographic expansion, perhaps the most exciting recent development in Peronism studies is the widespread incorporation of gender as an analytical category.[30] While the prominent role of Eva Perón and the political role of women have long preoccupied historians, it is only recently that scholars have begun to focus on how Peronism may have reshaped gender roles and representations. In these new studies historians have found little evidence of a radical challenge to existing patriarchal norms. In fact the expansion of welfare during Peronism increased the burden on women by increasing their obligation to provide services and reinforcing their role as objects of state control. For example, Karina Ramacciotti and Adriana Valobra have demonstrated that Peronist health policies appropriated both traditional Catholic constructions of female domesticity and the modernizing discourse of hygiene in an effort to turn mothers into unpaid agents of a male-dominated public health system.[31] Although the best of this scholarship is sensitive to how women's demands prompted and conditioned state responses, it has fallen again to Daniel James to explore more fully the ways working-class women made sense of Peronism's gendered discourses. His *Doña María's Story* uses the life history of one Peronist activist to produce a rich account of the complex interactions between Peronist gender representations and the consciousness and practices of women.[32]

Despite the recent advances in Peronism studies, there is a great deal more to be done. The structural determinism of earlier scholarship has been largely discarded, and scholars now appreciate the contingent political dynamics that helped shape the movement in its early years. Likewise, historians now recognize that Peronism's impact cannot be reduced to its economic effects; the regime's discursive innovations helped produce new identities that have shaped the course of Argentine political history. Yet while the study of Peronist rhetoric and representations has grown increasingly sophisticated, most scholars continue to conceptualize the encounter between the state and the masses in reductive ways. The explorations of Plotkin, Gené, and others into what might be called the "cultural policies" of the Perón regime represent a crucial line of inquiry given Peronism's unprecedented use of these techniques to generate political support. But the production of discourse involves more than the intentions of policymakers. Juan Perón's political imagination, like that of any historical actor, was enabled and constrained by the cultural material available to him in the time and place in which he lived. At the same time, as James demonstrated twenty years ago, the study of official policy needs to be complemented by careful consideration of how rank-and-file workers understood Peronism. Under the influence of classic social history methodology and of Gramsci's understanding of hegemony, the dominant approach tends to reduce the role of subordinate groups to either resistance or acceptance. Workers in particular are still usually treated as a group with an objective class interest that the historian can deduce, and any transformation of their identity is generally attributed to Perón's top-down project. In other words, both the production and reception of Peronist discourse, to borrow de Ípola's formulation, need to be approached in more subtle ways. Popular consciousness is not determined by interests that are in some way prior to discourse, nor is the state an autonomous and omnipotent actor, able to shape popular identities as it wishes. Cultural history can and must reconceptualize this encounter.

Outside the field of history Peronism has long raised questions about the complex interconnections between culture and politics. Laclau, for example, used Peronism to generate a larger theory about how culture and class operate in political discourses. More recently the movement has continued to provide rich material for theoretical innovation. The sociologist Javier Auyero has examined Peronist networks in a shantytown in Buenos Aires in the 1990s to generate a new approach to the problem of clientelism.[33] Auyero treats the relationship between patron and client as a cultural phenomenon, emphasizing the production of meaning in addition to the exchange of favors. Similarly, the political scientist Pierre Ostiguy has studied Peronism to examine the role of culture in the process of political identification, positing a framework in which positions and identities are defined by the intersection of the axis of high culture and low culture with the left-right political spectrum.[34] As a result of the diffusion of Laclau's work, Peronism continues to occupy an important place in cultural studies as well. John Kraniauskas, for example, has found in the novels of Manuel Puig suggestive insights into the connections between melodrama and Peronism, particularly in the role played by Eva Perón.[35] But if these nonhistorical approaches to Peronism have produced theoretical innovation, their contributions have been weakened by their reliance on relatively simplistic historical accounts. Lacking sustained engagement with archival materials from the period, scholars in cultural studies have tended to produce simplistic interpretations of early Peronism. Not only can a new cultural history of Peronism provide a more satisfying account of this crucial period in Argentine history, but it can also provide the basis for more successful theory building.

THE NEW CULTURAL HISTORY

The phrase "new cultural history" by now has various referents. Lynn Hunt's *The New Cultural History* (1989) took stock of the influence of Foucault, Geertz, LaCapra, and others on contemporary historians of the United States and Europe. The essays in the book explored the promise and pitfalls of approaches that stressed the importance of language or discourse.[36] Ten years later a special issue of the *Hispanic American Historical Review* announced the arrival of "Mexico's New Cultural History." In this iteration the phrase indicated above all an effort to reconceptualize the political agency of marginalized actors; the dominant influences were Gramsci, subaltern studies, and the larger "linguistic turn" within the historical profession.[37] In fact this reconceptualization has not been limited to Mexicanists. Over the last fifteen years or so it has begun to transform the historiography of Latin America as a whole, even if its impact among historians of Argentina has been somewhat less pronounced.[38] By bringing to bear the methodological and theoretical insights of the new scholarship on the study of Peronism, we hope to demonstrate that this new approach to cultural history can transform our historical understanding of the period.

While this rich new scholarship resists any simple gloss, Steve Stern has usefully summarized its major innovation as "a transition from studies of 'politics and society' to studies of 'politics and culture.'"[39] The former approach, dominant among Latin Americanist historians writing in the 1970s and 1980s, explored popular agency as shaped by economic and political structures. Among studies of Peronism, James's *Resistance and Integration* is perhaps the best example of this approach. By contrast, the new work moves away from the model of "history from below," disavowing any attempt to locate the uncontaminated consciousness of subordinate groups. In Stern's words, it asks "how people constructed their political imagination *within* the process of state formation."[40] Informed by sophisticated cultural analysis, it understands individual subjectivities as culturally constructed and treats politics as an arena involving identities produced simultaneously from above and below. Rather than view the agency of subalterns as motivated by some set of objective interests that the historian can discern, it envisions these actors as engaged with multiple discourses in a struggle over meaning. It avoids imposing the simple framework of domination and resistance, opting instead for a more dynamic understanding of "hegemonic processes." In the best cases this approach also avoids the seductive pitfall of easy triumphalism, by exploring how culture constrains, as well as facilitates, individual agency.

Inspired by the recent historiography this book aims to do more than simply endorse the inclusion of cultural topics in studies of the period. As we have described, the study of Peronist cultural policy is already fairly well developed. Many of the chapters in this book contribute to this important project, describing for example the regime's sponsorship of folk music and beauty contests. Yet the cultural history proposed here goes beyond an analysis of official policy. As in the best recent scholarship on Latin American history, we conceive of cultural history as a way of studying politics. Our goal is to reimagine the encounter between the masses and the state. We hope to move beyond a voluntarist understanding of the state by revealing how large cultural and commercial processes shaped specific policies. At the same time, we do not intend to reconstruct an autonomous grassroots perspective. Argentines did not simply resist or adopt Peronist identities created for them by the regime. Nor did they manipulate the symbols and images provided by Peronism in defense of existing, socially determined interests. Rather, they constructed their own identities and interests through their engagement with the Peronist project, even as they pushed and pulled the regime's ideology in new directions.

While this book is not a comprehensive history of Peronism, it does touch on many of the central issues raised by the Peronist experience. Our emphasis is on the first Perón presidency, from 1946 to 1955, but one chapter considers the origins of the regime while two others explore Peronism's transformations in subsequent years. The book examines the experience and agency of women, indigenous groups, middle-class anti-Peronists, internal migrants, architects, and academics, in addition to those of urban, male workers. They assess not only class-based identities but also questions of race and gender. But although they cover a broad range of topics, each chapter explores the nexus between the state and popular consciousness and conceives of these two spheres as mutually constitutive. While popular consciousness is both enabled and constrained by official ideology, the converse is also true.

In her chapter on the image of the "cabecita negra"—or "little black-head"—an insult directed against internal migrants to Buenos Aires, Natalia Milanesio examines the discursive praxis through which anti-Peronists stereotyped their enemies. Middle- and upper-class opponents of the regime produced these stereotypes in response to two related threats: the massive invasion of the city by migrants from the interior and Peronism's challenge to traditional hierarchies. Milanesio explores the mechanisms through which opponents of the Peronist project elaborated a new identity in dialogue with official ideology. Analyzing the cultural conflict fought over attire, manners, and comportment, she reveals the struggles over meaning that took place in the streets, as Peronists and anti-Peronists used available categories to make sense of a world in flux. Like Milanesio, César Seveso explores how individuals made sense of and responded to a time of rapid change and rising anxiety. His chapter uses the history of emotions to illuminate the moment of Perón's overthrow in 1955. Facing the end of an era that they experienced as utopian, Peronists confronted the coup and the ensuing repression with shame and humiliation, emotions that paralyzed many in the short term. Eventually, however, memories of these emotions facilitated the recuperation and reinvention of Peronism's original heretical message.

The chapter by Mirta Lobato, María Damilakou, and Lizel Tornay explores one element of the Peronist regime's massive propaganda machine: the annual coronation of a Queen of Labor on May Day. The authors analyze photographs and accounts from the period in conjunction with a series of interviews they conducted with the queens themselves. The result is neither a vision of Peronist cultural practice as simply imposed from above nor the recuperation of an uncontaminated grass-roots perspective. On the contrary, the chapter, a newly translated excerpt from a recent book, provides a sense of the deep contradictions— the opportunities and constraints—that Peronism provided to these young women. This chapter exemplifies the gendered aspects of Peronist discourse, which dramatically recentered women in the national community.

Several of the chapters approach the dialectic between the state and the masses by examining a third register located somewhere in between, namely the capitalist marketplace. In these accounts Peronism emerges as the product not only of a give and take between official ideology and popular consciousness but of a larger cultural process shaped by attitudes and values disseminated in commercial culture. Here too this book follows trends in Latin American historiography, which has recently generated several sophisticated studies of the intersection between mass cultural capitalism and national politics.[41] Matthew Karush's exploration of Peronism's roots in the melodramatic mass culture of the 1930s suggests that commercial dynamics shaped the development of populism in Argentina even before the emergence of Juan Perón. From this perspective the consciousness of Peronist workers cannot be reduced either to official ideology imposed from above nor to a particular pattern of economic development or labor politics. Rather, mass culture disseminated certain discursive elements among popular audiences that the Peróns were able to repackage toward their own ends. Likewise, Oscar Chamosa's examination of folk music reveals that the popularity of this genre was the result of the complex interplay between official policy, market pressures, and consumer preference. His exploration of the commercial appeal of folk music reveals that national identity was not simply a unilateral creation of the state, nor could the regime control its meanings. Folk music retained its popularity and symbolic power for Peronists and anti-Peronists alike.

Like Karush and Chamosa, Eduardo Elena explores cultural history at the interface between state, market, and masses. His analysis of the cultural politics of the Peronist magazine *Argentina* reveals the way the capitalist marketplace constrained the ideological maneuvers of Peronist intellectuals. Building on his earlier work on Peronism and consumption, Elena's essay highlights the limits of Peronism's cultural populism in matters of taste.[42] Like Elena, Anahi Ballent takes a novel look at Peronist aesthetics. Ballent's chapter, taken from her recent book on Peronism's architectural policies and practices, examines the various construction projects associated with Eva Perón and demonstrates how these buildings helped constitute Evita's political iconicity. Taken together, the chapters by Karush, Chamosa, Elena, and Ballent situate the radical ruptures of Peronism within longer-term cultural continuities. Popular melodrama, *hispanista* versions of national identity, and bourgeois aesthetics, as well as rustic and neoclassical architectural styles, represented established elements of the Argentine cultural milieu before the emergence of Peronism. Rather than build the New Argentina from scratch, the regime redeployed these existing elements, transforming them for its own ends, but also producing a series of unintended consequences.

Among the more fascinating insights produced by this new cultural history of Peronism is an appreciation for the centrality of race in Peronist and anti-Peronist representations. Diana Lenton's chapter offers the most explicit analysis of Peronism and racial identity. She analyzes the "malón de la paz," a protest in Buenos Aires in 1946 by indigenous groups from the interior provinces Salta and Jujuy, to track the complex interaction between popular action and state policy in producing an indigenous political identity. The racialized aspects of the Peronist experience are visible as well in Milanesio's chapter on anti-Peronist stereotypes and in Chamosa's examination of folklore, which offered an alternative to Argentina's dominant white culture. Since official Peronism did not include race as an explicit component of its project, historians have tended to overlook its significance. Together these chapters reveal some of the ways that race did in fact structure the lived experience of Peronism.

What emerges most clearly from this new cultural history is a picture of the deep contradictions that characterized Peronism. Peronism toppled class hierarchies, yet often upheld bourgeois respectability and aesthetics. Its heretical message aimed to mobilize the masses, yet its efforts to institutionalize itself led to an official ideology that emphasized discipline and good manners. It embraced the *cabecitas negras* of the interior and promoted folk music as an alternative to the white nation envisioned by Argentine liberals. Yet Peronists, like conservative nationalists before them, stressed the Spanish roots of Argentine folk music, thereby reinscribing whiteness. Peronist nationalism was often at odds with the regime's promise of a comfortable, modern lifestyle—a promise largely fulfilled through foreign imports. If populism, as Laclau defined it, occurs when "popular interpellations" are directed against the dominant power bloc, then the contributors to this book suggest that this political strategy unleashes a complex process marked by contradiction, ambivalence, and conflict. These contradictions were the unintended consequence of Perón's appeal, and they reveal the cultural constraints within which the regime operated. Given the resilience and continuing power of Peronism in contemporary Argentina, a historical examination of these tensions is as urgent today as it was fifty years ago.

NOTES

1 República Argentina, Poder Judicial de la Nación, http://www.pjn.gov.ar.

2 Luis Alberto Romero, *Breve historia contemporánea de la Argentina* (Buenos Aires: Fondo de Cultura Económica, 1994), 157–63.

3 Halperín Donghi, *La larga agonía de la Argentina peronista*, 27. The translation is ours.

4 Comprehensive surveys of the literature on Peronism include de Ípola, "Ruptura y continuidad"; Buchrucker, "Interpretations of Peronism"; Plotkin, "The Changing Perceptions of Peronism"; see also the reaction to de Ípola's review by Jorrat, "Reflexiones sobre un balance de las interpretaciones del peronismo," and de Ípola's response in the same issue.

5 Gino Germani, *Política y sociedad en una época de transición* (Buenos Aires: Paidós, 1962).

6 Torcuato Di Tella, "Populism and Reform in Latin America," *Obstacles to Change in Latin America*, ed. Claudio Veliz (London: Oxford University Press, 1965), 70–78.

7 Murmis and Portantiero, *Estudios sobre los orígenes del peronismo*.

8 Félix Luna, *El 45: Crónica de un año decisivo* (Buenos Aires: J. Alvarez, 1969).

9 Torre, *La vieja guardia sindical y Perón*. On this historiographical trend toward an emphas on the "conjuncture" see Adelman, "Reflections on Argentine Labour and the Rise of Perón."

10 Key works include Horowitz, *Argentine Unions, the State, and the Rise of Perón*; del Campo, *Sindicalismo y peronismo*; Tamarin, *The Argentine Labor Movement*. For a recent summary of the scholarship on Peronist unions see Doyon, "La formación del sindicalismo peronista."

11 Proving that in the case of Peronism old conflicts are never truly resolved, Di Tella has recently taken issue with the views of Torre and many others, while resurrecting some aspects of Germani's long-discarded thesis. See Di Tella, *Perón y los sindicatos*.

12 Laclau, "Towards a Theory of Populism."

13 de Ípola, "Populismo e ideología," 946.

14 Buchrucker, *Nacionalismo y peronismo*; Sigal and Verón, *Perón o muerte*, 72–

74; Bianchi and Sanchís, *El Partido Peronista Femenino*; Plotkin, "La 'ideología' de Perón"; Walter, "The Right and the Peronists."

15 James, *Resistance and Integration*.

16 Also influential in this regard was James, "October 17th and 18th, 1945."

17 Mafud, *Sociología del peronismo*; Ratier, *El cabecita negra*.

18 Torre and Pastoriza, "La democratización del bienestar."

19 Aboy, *Viviendas para el pueblo*. See also Aboy, " 'The Right to a Home.' "

20 Di Tella, "Populism and Reform in Latin America," 49.

21 de Ípola, "Populismo e ideología," 951.

22 James, *Resistance and Integration*, 22–25.

23 James, *Doña María's Story*, 255.

24 On Perón's mass media policies see Ciria, *Cultura y política popular*; Sirven, *Perón y los medios de communicación*. On the expropriation of the newspapers see Cane-Carrasco, *The Fourth Enemy*. Several popular histories catering to a broader audience have also treated this subject. See for example D'Arino Aringolli, *La Propaganda Peronista*; Foss, "Selling a Dictatorship."

25 Plotkin, *Mañana es San Perón*.

26 Gené, *Un mundo feliz*.

27 See Aelo, "Apogeo y ocaso de un equipo dirigente"; Rein, "Preparando el camino para el peronismo"; Lobato, *La vida en las fabricas, trabajo, protesta y politica en una comunidad obrera*.

28 Silva, "Las políticas económicas y sociales del primer peronismo y sus repercusiones"; Kindgard, "Procesos sociopolíticos nacionales y conflictividad regional"; Healey, *The Ruins of the New Argentina*; Macor and Tcach, eds., *La invención del peronismo en el interior del país*.

29 Rubinstein, *Los sindicatos azucareros en los orígenes del peronismo tucumano*.

30 Guivant, *La visible Eva Perón y el invisible rol político femenino en el Peronismo*; Franco and Pulido, "¿Capitanas o guardianas del hogar?"; Di Liscia, *Mujeres y Estado en la Argentina*; Di Liscia and Rodríguez, "El cuerpo de la mujer en el marco del Estado de bienestar en la Argentina"; Ramacciotti and Valobra, eds., *Generando el Peronismo*; Milanesio, " 'The Guardian Angels of the Domestic Economy.' "

31 Ramacciotti and Valobra, " *. . . plasmar la raza fuerte . . .* Relaciones de género en la campaña sanitaria de la Secretaria de Salud Pública de la Argentina (1946–49)," *Generando el Peronismo*, 19–64.

32 James, *Doña María's Story*.

33 Auyero, *Poor People's Politics*.

34 Ostiguy, "Peronism and Anti-Peronism."

35 Kraniauskas, "Political Puig." For other cultural studies approaches that have highlighted the affinities between Peronism and mass culture see Beasley-

Murray, "Peronism and the Secret History of Cultural Studies and the Substitution of Culture for State." Tandeciarz, "Romancing the Masses."

36 Hunt, *The New Cultural History*.

37 See the essays collected in Gilbert Joseph and Susan Deans-Smith, eds., *Mexico's New Cultural History: ¿Una Lucha Libre?*, special issue of *Hispanic American Historical Review* 79, no. 2 (1999).

38 Classics of this new literature include Joseph and Nugent, eds., *Everyday Forms of State Formation*; Florencia Mallon, *Peasant and Nation: The Making of Postcolonial Mexico and Peru* (Berkeley: University of California Press, 1995). Recent works of Argentine history that deploy similar strategies of cultural history include de la Fuente, *Children of Facundo*; Salvatore, *Wandering Paysanos*.

39 Stern, "Between Tragedy and Promise," 41.

40 Stern, "Between Tragedy and Promise," 41. The emphasis is ours.

41 See for example McCann, *Hello, Hello Brazil*; Joseph, Rubenstein, and Zolov, eds., *Fragments of a Golden Age*.

42 Elena, "Peronist Consumer Politics and the Problem of Domesticating Markets in Argentina."

Matthew B. Karush

....

POPULISM, MELODRAMA, AND THE MARKET

The Mass Cultural Origins of Peronism

Our doctrine is simpler. I can now explain it with an example given to me by five boys in Paraná. Our doctrine embraces that first great humanitarian principle. They were in the port, and one of them had no boots. From on board, we threw him five pesos, which fell into the hands of one who was well-dressed. The four boys who witnessed the scene said: "No, that's not for you; that's for him, who's barefoot." And the boy gave the five pesos to the barefoot kid. This is our doctrine; we want one of those great gentlemen (*grandes señores*) to learn how to give to those who have no boots. We want that one day those who have everything sympathize with their fellow man, so that there are no more barefoot people and so that our children learn to smile from the moment they are born.

JUAN PERÓN, 10 FEBRUARY 1946[1]

You don't charge for such things. You do them for free, or you don't do them.

LUIS SANDRINI IN THE FILM *CHINGOLO* (DEMARE, 1940) AS THE HOBO CHINGOLO,
REFUSING COMPENSATION FOR HAVING SAVED THE LIFE OF A MILLIONAIRE'S SON

As historians have long recognized, Peronism cannot be understood on purely instrumentalist grounds. The movement's transformative impact on Argentine politics as well as its impressive longevity reflect the fact that it provided workers with much more than a higher standard of living; it offered them both an identity and a convincing interpretation of the society in which they lived. Thirty years ago Ernesto Laclau argued that the power of Peronism lay in its ability to mobilize already existing cultural elements and rearticulate them in defense of the class interests of Argentine workers. For Laclau, "populism starts at the point where popular-democratic elements are presented as an antagonistic option against the dominant bloc."[2] Yet we still lack a cultural history of these "popular-democratic elements," a convincing account of the ideological transformations that made Peronist consciousness possible for Argentine workers. In the now classic first chapter of his history of Peronism, published in 1988, Daniel James laid the essential groundwork for this project. Stressing Peronism's "heretical" meanings, James revealed how the movement enabled workers to contest traditional cultural hierarchies.[3] Historians now need to revisit the period before 1943 to uncover the cultural elements that provided the discursive material out of which this heretical appeal was built; they need, in other words, to write the cultural prehistory of Peronism.

Since most Peronist workers were not union members before the advent of Perón, any such prehistory will have to look beyond the realm of organized labor. A handful of scholars have called attention to Perón's debt to the tradition of popular melodrama, visible for example in his tendency to draw on the language of the tango.[4] This insight reflects a much deeper, more pervasive indebtedness. Peronism was built in large part out of discursive elements made available by the commodified mass culture of the previous period. The 1920s and 1930s saw the explosion in Argentina of mass culture on an unprecedented scale: it was in this period that the radio, the cinema, spectator sports, and mass-circulation journalism transformed daily life. Thanks to the recent work of scholars in cultural studies, anthropology, film studies, and other disciplines, we know a great deal about the cultural products disseminated by the new media. Tango songs, soccer, domestic films, the popular press, and pulp fiction have all been the object of sustained research and analysis.[5] Nearly all these mass cultural forms appropriated the generic conventions and narrative strategies of Argentine melodrama, a literary tradition with roots in the late nineteenth century. In this chapter I trace the connections between the melodramatic mass culture that thrived on the radio stations and movie screens of the 1930s and the political appeals crafted by Juan Perón in the period between 1943 and 1946, when the movement took shape. The focus here will be on the radio and cinema of Buenos Aires, since so much of Argentina's mass culture was produced there and introduced to the rest of the country by radio networks and cinema distributors.

My attempt at a cultural prehistory of Peronism is not a tautological quest for precursors. While the pervasive mass culture of the 1930s must have had a dramatic effect on popular consciousness, this effect was multivalent. It did not lead inevitably to any particular political outcome. Moreover, Perón did not simply adopt a philosophy already formed in the mass culture of the previous period. Rather, in the specific conjuncture opened up by the coup of 1943, Perón was able to appropriate discursive elements that circulated in mass culture and refashion them into a powerful political appeal. These existing elements represent what Laclau referred to as "the residue of a unique and irreducible historical experience."[6] They helped determine the universe of the possible within the political arena of the 1940s. Recognizing the central role of mass culture in producing this discursive universe sheds important new light on Peronism. Although the cinema, radio, and the press experienced significant government intervention during the 1930s, the content of mass culture reflected the logic of the marketplace rather than any official ideology. As this chapter will demonstrate, commercial imperatives —in particular the need to compete with North American imports like jazz and Hollywood movies—reinforced the heretical meanings implicit in Argentine melodrama even as they encouraged conformism and the quest for individual upward mobility. Both the powerful appeal of Peronism and its internal contradictions reflect its origins in mass culture. Populism in Argentina was not merely a byproduct of industrialization or a reflection of labor politics; it was also the outcome of a particular pattern of mass cultural development.

THE MELODRAMATIC TENDENCY IN EARLY PERONISM

Historical analyses of Peronist rhetoric have stressed the essential binarism at its heart. Juan and Evita Perón explained their political project through a series of basic oppositions: national versus antinational, pueblo versus antipueblo, workers versus oligarchs. The logic that the Peróns used to make these distinctions between us and them was always deeply moralistic; by opposing sacrifice to egotism, austerity to frivolity, solidarity to treachery, and hard work to idleness, Peronism depicted class struggle in essentially moral terms. Perón frequently denounced the exploitation of the working class, but he described it as part of a historic contest between good and evil.[7] In a speech before the railroad workers union in 1944, Perón, then labor secretary, described his agenda as a "revolution of the poor . . . The country was sick of important men; it is necessary that the days of simple, working men arrive." He then denounced his opponents as representatives of "the eternal forces of egotism and avarice, that make the pocket into man's only sentient organ."[8] The conflict between bourgeoisie and proletariat was initially described as a battle between rich and poor, "important men" and "simple, working men," before being boiled down to a struggle against a particular form of immorality, namely greed. As Eduardo Elena has recently demonstrated, Perón's promise to control the cost of living was central to his political rise in 1943–46. And when he turned from the sphere of production to that of consumption, Perón continued to operate within the discourse of moralism and binary oppositions. As he put it in another speech in 1944, "We are a dignified and proud country; and none of its children should have to tolerate ever again that Argentine workers be converted into shabby people [gente astrosa] so that a group of privileged individuals can hold onto their luxuries, their automobiles, and their excesses." According to Perón, rising prices, like capitalist exploitation, were the product of immorality, in this case the selfish greed of merchants and speculators.[9]

As many scholars have noted, Perón rejected class conflict and promised to achieve not the triumph of the proletariat but a state of harmony between labor and capital. Conflict and struggle characterized the past; Perón would bring about "the union of all Argentines so that that struggle is transformed into collaboration and cooperation, so that we can create new values and not destroy uselessly, in a sterile struggle, values and energies that are the only forces capable of making men happy and nations great."[10] To create this harmonious national unity, Perón promised to do two things. First, he aimed to reduce the gap between the haves and the have-nots or, as he put it in a speech in Rosario in 1944, to "equalize a little the social classes so that there will not be in this country men who are too poor nor those who are too rich."[11] But redistribution of wealth was not enough. Class reconciliation and social harmony also required a process of moral education and rehabilitation. The rich had to learn to behave morally, to renounce their greed and egotism and embrace the spirit of cooperation and solidarity. As Perón made clear in the speech quoted at the beginning of this chapter, the "grandes señores" had to learn to give to those in need, and this was a virtue they could learn from those beneath them on the socioeconomic ladder. Throughout Perón's speeches one finds constant praise for the noble, dignified poor as "simple," "humble" people without pretension. In this discourse the socially inferior are morally superior; national unity and class reconciliation can only occur when the rich learn to follow the example of the poor. The idea of the poor as teachers of the rich is one aspect of Peronism's heretical inversion of hierarchy and of a broader anti-intellectualism characteristic of the movement.[12]

If Perón's major goals included defending the poor and achieving national unity, he made those promises through a rhetoric filled with the vocabulary of work and production. According to a recent linguistic analysis, "politics is work" is the one "major metaphor" that Perón introduced to Argentine discourse. His repeated use of verbs such as to build, to construct, to employ, to produce, and to earn extended this basic metaphor.[13] This language clearly had resonance for those Argentines who earned a living through manual labor. It lent concreteness and familiarity to abstract concepts like progress and justice. But the power of this discourse lay above all in its moral connotations. Perón pledged to "humanize capital" and "dignify labor."[14] If the rich would be taught the virtues of solidarity and generosity, the poor would be publicly recognized as dignified, virtuous, and respectable. Honest, hard work was in fact the ultimate proof of moral superiority: "We struggle so that labor may be considered with the dignity that it deserves, so that we all may feel the desire and the impulse to honor ourselves by working, and so that no one who is able to work may live only to consume."[15]

The binary moralism of Peronist discourse is essentially melodramatic, and its roots, I would argue, lie in the mass culture of the 1930s. Argentina's radio programs and domestic movies, both major attractions during this period, were infused with the aesthetic conventions and narrative structures of melodrama. These conventions and narratives crossed lines of genre, informing tango lyrics, nativist dramas, urban tragedies, and comedies of all types. But although melodrama came in various forms, its distinctive hallmark was a particular vision of society. In all of its guises, melodrama presupposed a Manichean world in which poverty was a guarantor of virtue and authenticity, and wealth a moral flaw. Hundreds of songs, radio plays, and films presented Argentina as a nation irreconcilably divided between rich and poor. Perón's essentially moralistic view of class conflict had clear precedents in this mass culture, as did his utopian promise that class reconciliation could be achieved through the moral education of the rich. The moral categories that Perón deployed to distinguish poor and rich—us and them—are all integral to mass culture of the 1930s, in which the rich were almost unfailingly egotistical, greedy, and frivolous, while the poor were hard-working practitioners of sacrifice and solidarity.

Throughout the mass culture of the 1930s, wealth functioned as a sign of malice. The prototypical tango plot, revisited in dozens of songs, describes the tragic demise of the *milonguita*—the poor, innocent girl from the *barrios* who is tempted by the bright lights and wild life of downtown.[16] Seduced by a *bacán* (a wealthy playboy) or *niño bien* (a rich kid), the milonguita is usually abandoned once her looks have faded. A typical example is "Pompas de jabón" ("Soap Bubbles," Cadícamo, 1925), in which the singer sees a girl from his barrio riding in the car of a bacán and warns her that her luxurious lifestyle will not last long.[17] In "No salgas de tu barrio" ("Don't Leave Your Barrio," Rodríguez Bustamante, 1928), a female singer tells a young girl to marry someone of her class, using her own life as a cautionary tale:

Como vos, yo, muchachita	Like you, little girl, I
era linda y era buena,	was beautiful and good
era humilde y trabajaba	I was humble and worked
como vos en un taller;	like you in a workshop;
dejé al novio que me amaba	I left the boyfriend who loved me
con respeto y con ternura,	with respect and with tenderness
por un niño engominado	for a hair-creamed boy
que me trajo al cabaret[18]	who brought me to the cabaret.

Here, as in so many tangos, the journey from barrio to cabaret, from honest work to frivolity, results in the loss of goodness and love. The culprit—the rich kid with slicked-back hair—is such a familiar character that his class affiliation and lack of virtue can be evoked in just two words.

With the introduction of sound technology in 1933, the domestic film industry took advantage of the popularity that tango music had already achieved on the radio. Popular tango singers like Carlos Gardel and

Libertad Lamarque became stars in films that enabled them to showcase both their acting and their singing. Since many of these films lifted their melodramatic plots directly from tango songs, they often featured the same stock characters. The niño bien, for example, became a staple of the domestic cinema. A selfish, spoiled young man, he typically frustrated his parents by dedicating himself to drinking and dancing instead of working or studying. In films such as *Gente bien* (Romero, 1939), *Mujeres que trabajan* (Romero, 1938), *Chingolo*, and *La ley que olvidaron* (Ferreyra, 1938), a niño bien initiates the melodramatic plot or subplot by impregnating a woman and failing to take responsibility for the child. Other films used tango to figure class division in a different way. Argentine filmmakers often denounced class prejudice by depicting elite disdain for this allegedly disreputable, popular music. In *El alma del bandoneón* (Soffici, 1934), *Besos brujos* (Ferreyra, 1937), *Puerta cerrada* (Saslavsky, 1939), and *Yo conocí a esa mujer* (Borcosque, 1942), Libertad Lamarque plays a tango singer whose romance with a wealthy suitor is opposed by his élitist family.[19] These melodramas leveraged the popularity that Lamarque had already earned on the radio as a symbol of porteño popular culture. In this way they not only assured that the audience would identify with Lamarque but gave that identification an anti-élitist cast.

Even when it avoided tango, the Argentine cinema abounded in wealthy villains and humble heroes. As the film historian Domingo Di Núbila points out, Argentine movie makers in these years did not spend much effort fleshing out the characters of their villains: "it was sufficient that they be rich."[20] In addition to tango melodramas, this period also saw the emergence of a cinema of social critique. Films like *Maestro Levita* (Amadori, 1938), as well as the classic works of Mario Soffici— *Viento norte* (1937), *Kilómetro 111* (1938), and *Prisioneros de la tierra* (1939)—denounced the exploitation of poor Argentines in rural settings far from Buenos Aires. Soffici's films in particular depicted the life of the rural poor with realist detail, while using melodramatic narrative structures to highlight the contrast between rich and poor.[21] Even comedies tended to play out against a melodramatic backdrop. Luis Sandrini, one of the era's biggest comedic stars, played the same character in virtually every film he made, an essentially kindhearted simpleton prone to malapropisms. In films like *Don Quijote del Altillo* (Romero, 1936), *El cañonero*

de Giles (Romero, 1937), and *Chingolo*, Sandrini's character was positioned on the lower end of the class divide and forced to confront the
bad intentions of the rich and powerful.

The cinema of the 1930s elaborated a vision in which poverty and
hard work were ennobling. Like so many films in this period, *La vida de
Carlos Gardel* (de Zavalía, 1939), a fictionalized biography of the singer
made five years after his death, establishes the audience's identification
with its protagonist by depicting his humble origins and his resistance to
class prejudice. After being treated shabbily by a group of wealthy party-
goers, Gardel (played by Hugo del Carril) declares, "We may be poor,
but we have dignity." In addition to their commitment to hard work,
what makes the poor morally superior to the rich is their capacity for
solidarity. While the rich are selfish, the poor stick together; they take
risks and make sacrifices to help those in need. This message is nowhere
clearer than in the work of Manuel Romero, who made some thirty-four
films for the Lumiton company between 1935 and 1945. In this vast body
of work Romero offered a melodramatic yet optimistic vision of an
Argentina divided between rich and poor, in which unity could be forged
through interclass romance. Just as Perón would later insist that the
rich must learn the values of generosity and solidarity from the poor,
Romero's films repeatedly enacted this process of moral instruction. In
Gente bien, a community of working-class musicians come to the rescue
of the poor girl abandoned by the niño bien. In films like *Mujeres que
trabajan* (1938), *La rubia del camino* (1938), *Isabelita* (1940), and *Elvira
Fernández, vendedora de tienda* (1942), a spoiled young woman learns
both the value of hard work and the capacity to care for others under
the tutelage of working-class characters. Perón's insistence on the dignity and moral superiority of the poor echoes the central message of
these films.[22]

Mass culture also provided a great deal of source material for Perón's
depiction of the poor as the most authentic representatives of the nation.
In announcing his resignation from the army in the highly charged
atmosphere of October 17, 1945, Perón made this vision explicit: "I leave,
then, the honorable and sacred uniform given to me by the fatherland in
order to put on the coat of a civilian and join with that suffering and
sweaty mass that produces with its labor the greatness of the country . . .
This is the people; this is the suffering people that represents the pain of

the mother earth, which we must vindicate. It is the people of the fatherland [Es el pueblo de la patria]."[23] Perón's insistence on equating workers, pueblo, and nation reproduces mass culture's depiction of the hard-working, long-suffering poor as the authentic Argentines. The melodramatic opposition between rich and poor was often figured as an opposition between the foreign and the national. In film after film, well-to-do dancers prefer the foxtrot and shun the tango. In *La rubia del camino* the spoiled protagonist prefers the foreign name Betty to her given name, Isabel, and even more glaringly, she has never tried *mate*, the popular tea that symbolizes Argentine national identity. The association of Argentine authenticity with the poor was also visible in the popular fascination with the nation's rural past. Beginning in the early 1930s with the enormously successful show *Chispazos de Tradición*, radio stations endlessly revisited the days of the gauchos. These programs combined conventional, melodramatic plots with rural, pre-modern settings and featured frequent breaks for performances of folk music. Building on an old trope in Argentine culture that associated Buenos Aires with foreign influence, these programs implied a nationalist affiliation with rustic, plebeian culture, a preference for the authenticity of the countryside over the fanciness and foreign influence of the modern city. Likewise, the epic film *La guerra gaucha* (Demare, 1942) narrated Argentina's war for independence against Spain as a tale of anonymous heroism; as the film concluded, "Like this they lived, like this they died, the nameless, those who fought the gaucho war." Whereas the book upon which the film was based, an episodic account by the modernist poet Leopoldo Lugones, stressed the leadership of General Martín de Güemes, the film version imbued the story with a more democratic vision that emphasized the contribution of the poor in creating the nation.[24]

Even beyond his apparent debt to melodrama and his association of national identity with the poor, Perón's rhetoric bore the traces of mass cultural influence. Perón's famously lowbrow language—his use of lunfardo, the popular porteño slang, and his invocation of familiar tango tropes—expressed an overt affiliation with popular culture. This gesture of pride in the culture of poor Argentines was in itself a staple of mass culture in the 1930s. In the film *Los tres berretines* (Susini, 1933) an immigrant shop owner chooses Argentine popular culture over education and hard work when he embraces his sons' dreams of success as a tango composer and a soccer player. Throughout these years entertainment and sports reporters celebrated these cultural practices not just as Argentine achievements but as the achievements of working-class Argentines. Thus the fan magazine *Sintonía* emphasized the lower-class origins of the tango orchestra leader Francisco Canaro: "He represents the emotional superstructure of that human and grey, humble and combative belt that encircles our capital."[25] Similarly, the popular daily *Crítica* celebrated the soccer played by "our ordinary boys [nuestra muchachada vulgar]" as the nation's greatest export.[26] Coursing through mass culture was populist nationalism—a celebration of the achievements of authentic, plebeian Argentina.

In crafting his own version of populist nationalism, Juan Perón did much more than simply embrace a discourse provided by melodramatic mass culture; as I will argue, he appropriated and rearticulated discursive elements, and in so doing transformed them. Melodrama was hardly Perón's only mode. Still, when he celebrated the moral superiority, dignity, authenticity, and cultural inventiveness of the poor and attacked the egotism and avarice of the rich, Perón was drawing on the well-established melodramatic tradition that permeated mass culture in the 1930s. Of course the discursive affinities between Peronism and mass culture do not prove that Perón self-consciously imitated the movies and radio programs of the preceding decade. The moral superiority of the poor was an idea circulating in the larger cultural milieu that Perón shared with Argentine filmmakers and radio programmers. Catholic social thought in particular offered one possible source for this notion, as well as for Perón's rejection of individualism and bourgeois materialism. Catholicism experienced a resurgence in Argentina in the 1930s, and Catholic intellectuals played a prominent role in elaborating Nationalist ideology.[27] Further, melodramatic and quasi-populist cultural forms certainly existed in Argentina before the age of mass culture.[28] Yet it was in the cinema and on the radio that these forms were most widely diffused, and it seems likely that it was the mass cultural versions of popular melodrama that had the most direct influence on Peronism.

Perón clearly recognized the political potential of mass culture. Not only did he enable and encourage Evita, a radio and movie actress, to play a major public role, but his regime invested heavily in controlling the media. The Peronist state effectively expropriated the country's most important newspapers and radio stations, cultivated ties to celebrities, imposed censorship, and made extensive use of the radio and cinema for the diffusion of propaganda.[29] Many of the architects of Peronist cultural policy were men with extensive backgrounds in mass culture. Raúl Alejandro Apold, who as undersecretary of information and the press led the regime's massive propaganda efforts from 1949 on, had been a film critic and the publicity chief of one of Argentina's most important film studios. Eva Perón's speechwriter, Francisco Muñoz Azpiri, had written many of her scripts during her career as a radio actress. And while many artists were prevented from working during the Perón years because of their antipathy to the regime, others made key contributions to Peronism. Established filmmakers like Manuel Romero and Luis César Amadori thrived by producing movies that seemed to advance the government's ideological agenda. Within the world of tango, the long-time bandleader Francisco Lomuto was an outspoken Peronist, while the composer and lyricist Enrique Santos Discépolo applied his biting sarcasm to the vigorous defense of the regime on a recurring radio program.[30] Given Perón's obvious interest in the political utility of mass culture, the echoes of mass cultural melodrama in his rhetoric likely reflect purposeful borrowing. But regardless of his sources or intentions, Perón's message resonated with the meanings already made widely familiar by movies, music, and radio theater, and this resonance helps to account for the power of his appeal. In fact, the omnipresence of populist elements on Argentine radio waves and movie screens before the advent of Peronism suggests that populism was as much the result of mass cultural capitalism as of industrialization, political development, and labor history.

THE PURSUIT OF AN AUDIENCE:
MASS CULTURAL POPULISM AND THE LOGIC OF THE MARKET

If Argentine populism was built in part of mass cultural components, then its internal dynamics must have reflected the logic of the capitalist marketplace. Compared to the heavy-handed censorship of the military government after the coup of 1943 and the massive media apparatus built by Perón after 1946, the state played a much smaller role in shaping mass culture during the 1930s. The conservative governments of this period, particularly the administration of Agustín P. Justo (1932–38), did see the value of controlling the mass media. Justo secretly purchased the country's most important mass-market newspaper, *Crítica*, and exerted substantial influence on press coverage of his administration.[31] However, despite a series of campaigns for media nationalization, the vast majority of radio stations and film studios remained in private hands throughout the 1930s. While these media were subject to meddlesome regulations and to occasional censorship, they were not enlisted to serve an official propaganda campaign, as they would be under Perón.[32] On the contrary, commercial interests dominated both radio broadcasting and the cinema. It was the pursuit of profit, more than any overt political ideology, that shaped the decisions made by mass cultural entrepreneurs and artists.

Argentine film studios and radio stations, like mass cultural industries elsewhere, depoliticized earlier cultural traditions to make them acceptable to a broad, multi-class audience.[33] But Argentina's "peripheral modernity" lent this process some distinctive features.[34] Attempting to build a mass audience, cultural producers confronted a marketplace in which foreign imports enjoyed substantial popularity and prestige. This competition produced a dialectic of emulation and distinction. Argentine producers tried to live up to the high technical and artistic standards set by their North American and to a lesser extent European competitors. At the same time, they needed to distinguish their offerings, and they did so by appropriating existing popular culture and stressing its Argentinidad. The attempt to wrest wealthier consumers away from imported products encouraged producers to sanitize and "elevate" their offerings, to purge them of depictions of the urban working class, to emphasize the pursuit of upward mobility rather than the political potential of working-class solidarity. Yet the use of authenticity as a marketing strategy tended to deepen mass culture's affiliation with plebeian Argentina. These conflicting market pressures produced an ambivalent mass culture that transmitted both subversive and conformist messages. As a result, the elements that Perón would appropriate from mass culture contained deep and pervasive contradictions.

During the 1930s between nineteen and twenty-two radio stations broadcast simultaneously in Buenos Aires, the great majority of them commercial enterprises.[35] To a certain extent these stations distinguished themselves through specialization, with some variously offering mainly tango, opera and classical music, jazz, radio theater, and programming for the city's immigrant communities. But by the early 1930s one station owner dominated porteño radio: Jaime Yankelevich. In addition to his flagship station, Radio Nacional (renamed Radio Belgrano in 1934), Yankelevich ran three other stations from his studios in Buenos Aires, the so-called "Palacio de los Broadcastings," and he assembled Argentina's first and most important radio network so that he could sell advertising in the Argentine interior as well. To boost the size of their audience and attract advertisers, his stations specialized in all things popular: they emphasized jazz and other foreign music, but their prime time slots were reserved for tango and radio theater. It was on Radio Nacional that Chispazos de Tradicion had aired, earning opprobrium from critics who considered the program lowbrow and full of inaccurate caricatures, but establishing a model that dozens of other radio theater companies would imitate. Similarly, the station promoted its commitment to tango as a sign of its adherence to popular tastes. In 1937 Sintonía reported on a popular contest organized by Yankelevich, an "expert in popular psychology." Having asked listeners to select the best new tango song played on its airwaves, Radio Belgrano had allegedly received 1,835,235 votes through the mail.[36] Yankelevich's use of popular contests like this one continued a tradition that had begun in the early days of tango recording and helped cement the music's reputation as the people's choice.[37]

The success of Yankelevich's formula was ratified by the speed with which his competitors rushed to copy him. The entertainment magazines were filled with columns complaining about the legions of imitators who filled the airwaves.[38] While niche programming did exist, tango, jazz, comedy sketches, and radio dramas dominated on virtually every station. Tellingly, the one station that emerged in the 1930s with sufficient economic backing to challenge Radio Belgrano's dominance saw no alternative but to adopt its rival's approach. In 1935 Editorial Haynes, the company that owned El Mundo, one of the top-selling daily newspapers in Buenos Aires, launched Radio El Mundo with the intention of creating "the leading station in South America." Toward that end it named as its artistic director Enrique del Ponte, one of the founders of Radio Cultura, a station long praised by critics of Radio Belgrano's vulgar populism.[39] El Mundo bragged of del Ponte's commitment to the "constant improvement of the cultural and artistic level of the radio,"[40] and the director himself announced plans to assemble a house orchestra as skilled in symphonic music as those that played in the prestigious Colón Theatre in Buenos Aires.[41] Yet within a few weeks the station had reversed course, firing del Ponte and replacing him with Pablo Osvaldo Valle, the former artistic director of Radio Belgrano. For the rest of the decade Radio El Mundo employed an approach distinctly inspired by Yankelevich as it competed with Radio Belgrano. Through their emphasis on programming with mass appeal, these two stations dominated the radio market, absorbing some 60 percent of all the advertising revenue on Argentine radio by 1939 and alarming observers who worried that without state intervention, radio would become an effective monopoly.[42] The popularity of their programs crowded out alternatives. While critics continued to call for an improvement in the quality of broadcasts, and most program directors committed themselves at least rhetorically to that pursuit, all the major radio stations offered their listeners a steady diet of tangos and radio melodramas, while relegating more "serious" offerings to a subordinate role.

The predominance of tango and radio theater revealed the pressure on radio programmers to deliver a mass audience, but the competitive environment brought conflicting pressures to bear on the producers of these cultural commodities. Even as composers and performers aimed to give their listeners what they wanted, they also sought to attract more educated, higher-class consumers who might appreciate more "sophisticated" material. This tension affected all the major cultural products of the day, but it was particularly apparent in tango. Confronting extensive foreign competition, most tango performers, composers, and lyricists tried to elevate the genre while preserving its authenticity. They hoped to purge tango of its dangerous and immoral associations, without abandoning the music's ability to represent the nation.

Various foreign musics attracted popular interest and secured air time on Argentine radio stations in the 1930s, but tango's biggest competitor was undoubtedly American jazz. Already popular in the 1920s, jazz and the foxtrot, as porteños typically referred to the dance music played by jazz bands, gained a new prominence in the 1930s. Local tango bands— the so-called *orquestas típicas*—responded to this challenge in various ways. As early as 1920 the tango orchestra leader Roberto Firpo included several foxtrots in his repertoire.[43] But in the 1930s, the presence on the porteño airwaves of jazz bands like the Dixie Pals, the Santa Paula Sere-naders, and others inspired more defensive reactions from tango's defenders. A cartoon in *La Canción Moderna* in 1933, playing on the shared surname of Firpo and the great Argentine heavyweight Luis Firpo, depicted the bandleader as a boxer and proclaimed that he had launched "a bloody fight against the American fox trot."[44] And Firpo was not alone in his desire to see tango triumph over jazz. The letters-to-the-editor section of the radio magazine *Sintonía* was filled with diatribes against the omnipresence of jazz on the radio. As one tango fan put it, "I cannot conceive how eight of the ten stations currently broadcasting can simultaneously be playing fox-trots."[45]

Not all porteños saw jazz and tango as implacable antagonists, and the two musics coexisted in the same magazines and on the same radio stations and bandstands throughout the period. Still, the popularity of jazz encouraged tango artists to define themselves against the American import. And because jazz was foreign, proponents of tango boasted of its Argentinidad, its ability to represent the nation. In other words, the pressure to compete with jazz reinforced a discourse of tango authenticity. Thus the tango star Azucena Maizani was not just a talented singer; she was "the greatest, most exact and popular expression of porteño sentiment, which condenses the psychology of our race—sentimental, emotional and melancholy like no other on earth."[46] Depictions like this one celebrated tango stars as symbols of Buenos Aires and Argentina, and the music as the expression of certain essential qualities of Argentine national identity.

The discourse of tango authenticity involved three claims: tango was located in the past, it was melancholy, and it was rooted in popular rather than elite culture. All three of these elements were well established by the 1920s, when the advent of the phonograph and the radio turned Gardel and other singers into major stars. Tango's creation myth—its birth in the brothels and dance halls of the turn-of-the-century slums of Buenos Aires, or *arrabales*, were repetitively explored in the song lyrics. Tango singers always located themselves within this marginal, plebeian world, an affiliation made more explicit by the lyricists' extensive use of lunfardo, the popular porteño slang. The immortal opening line of Pascual Contursi's "Mi noche triste (1917)," "Percanta que me amuraste (Woman who abandoned me)," inaugurated tango's obsession with stories of romantic betrayal as well as its self-conscious break with proper Spanish and its explicit affiliation with the popular culture of the urban plebe. But all three elements of tango authenticity were reinforced by competition with North American popular music. Given its associations with the United States and in particular with Hollywood movies, jazz conveyed the promise of modernity.[47] At the same time, the many Argentine films featuring wealthy foxtrotters suggested that jazz and the swing dance that it accompanied were the frivolous pastimes of wealthy, happy-go-lucky partiers. In this context tango proclaimed its Argentine authenticity by insisting on its sadness, its resistance to modernity, and its affiliation with plebeian popular culture.

This discourse produced a contradictory populism. As I have suggested, tango musicians were often celebrated as working-class heroes, and tango lyrics proudly proclaimed the music's plebeian roots. But this populism hardly embraced progressive social change. Tango, like other melodramatic texts, systematically depoliticized social conflicts and contradictions by transposing them onto stories of frustrated love. In addition, the songs were essentially conformist, since they suggested that happiness could be attained so long as one avoided certain transgressions: "Don't leave your barrio," and all will be well.[48] In fact many tangos went well beyond this sort of conformism, expressing a fatalistic skepticism toward any possibility of improving one's lot in life: as the lyricist Francisco Bastardi put it, "to be poor is not a crime / And it is a glory to know how to suffer."[49] Further contributing to this conservatism was tango's persistent nostalgia, its evocation of a pre-modern golden age. In *Tango*, Argentina's first sound film, the final words belong to Azucena Maizani, singing "Milonga del novecientos," a song made famous by Gardel: "I do not like paved streets / Nor do I get along with the modern." Here, at the very moment when Argentine producers appropriated the sound cinema, that symbol of technological modernity, Maizani gave voice to tango's classic opposition to modernity.[50] Nostalgia was omnipresent in the mass culture of these years. Serialized radio dramas often set their stories of love and political intrigue among the gauchos of the preceding century, and recreations of the Rosas period of the early nineteenth century were extremely popular. This nostalgia neatly expressed the dislocations felt by those bearing the brunt of Argentina's rapid modernization, but it also suggested that these problems could be ameliorated not through social transformation but through an escapist recreation of a golden age.

Just as tango combined populism with fatalism and nostalgia, it expressed similarly conflicting attitudes toward the pursuit of upward mobility. As *La vida de Carlos Gardel* suggests, the enormous appeal of tango's biggest star was related to his personal rise from humble origins. That "El morocho del abasto" (the dark-haired kid from the modest Abasto neighborhood) was now an international celebrity who performed in black tie must have thrilled a working-class audience that dreamed of similar success.[51] And tango lyricists took explicit pride in the genre's popularity among sophisticated, international audiences. Yet tango also expressed suspicion about the pursuit of upward mobility, which many lyrics condemned as petty striving or even fakery.[52] To cite one example, the tango "Mala entraña" (Flores, 1927) criticizes a guy from the neighborhood for putting on airs:

¡Compadrito de mi esquina,	Tough guy from my corner
que sólo cambió de traje!	who only changed his suit
. . . .	. . . .
se murió tu pobre madre,	your poor mother died
y en el mármol de tu frente	and on the marble of your forehead
ni una sombra, ni una arruga	neither a shadow nor a wrinkle
que deschavara, elocuente,	which might eloquently reveal
que tu vieja no fue un perro,	that your mother was not a dog
y que vos sabés sentir.[53]	and that you know how to feel.

Here upward mobility is a perversion: the poor man who puts on a nice suit has lost the capacity to feel anything at the death of his own mother. Tangos like "Mala entraña" redirect the genre's fatalism toward a critique of upward mobility. This skepticism amounts to more than simple resignation. It is an explicit embrace of a set of values associated with the poor: solidarity, true feeling, honesty. It is for abandoning those values that social strivers are condemned. Thus while tango tended to discourage any attempt at social transformation, its discourse of plebeian authenticity did offer the elements of a populist critique of the status quo.

Market pressures pushed the tango in many directions at once. Even as the competition with jazz reinforced tango's claims of authenticity, the effort to make tango more acceptable for middle- and upper-class audiences led some lyricists to sanitize the genre in an attempt to elevate it from its humble origins. While Contursi's plebeian language remained the dominant model, it was not the only available tango aesthetic. During the 1930s a new type of tango became common, one that replaced lunfardo with a more universal, lyrical idiom and told stories of love and betrayal less rooted in the social world of the suburbios. This tendency gained prominence with the emergence of Alfredo Le Pera in 1931 as the screenwriter of Carlos Gardel's films. Produced by Paramount and marketed to an international, Spanish-speaking audience, these movies needed to avoid references that would be accessible only to Argentine viewers. Le Pera responded to the challenge by elaborating less localist and less insistently plebeian tango stories. Since Le Pera also wrote the lyrics to the tangos that Gardel sang on screen, his more universalist aesthetic had a major impact on the tango canon.[54] These countervailing tendencies produced an ongoing discussion about how tango could both preserve its authenticity and lift itself above its plebeian roots. The magazine *La Canción Moderna*, for example, attacked one radio station for playing classical music, fit only for "distinguished girls," instead of the more authentic and popular tango.[55] But the magazine also railed against tango lyricists who relied on "vulgarity and *lunfardismo*," praising Le Pera for writing tangos with a universal message and refuting critics who argued that he was "foreignizing" the genre.[56] The attempt to improve the tango without destroying its authenticity was widespread. Francisco Canaro, for example, was careful to qualify his praise for what he saw as the steady improvement in tango lyrics: "The primitive lyric has given way to the deeply poetic lyric . . . But with this I do not mean to praise pretentiousness, which is the worst vice of literature."[57] Tango's advantage over jazz and other imports was precisely its Argentine authenticity, and since that authenticity was bound up with the genre's plebeian origins, any effort at improvement faced the charge of élitism.

Similar efforts to reconcile authenticity with modernity and artistic improvement were visible in the case of Argentine folk music. Although not nearly as commercially viable as tango, several musical genres from the Argentine interior received air play on radio stations in Buenos Aires, which packaged them together under the rubric of "folklore." As a symbol of the nation, folk music enjoyed certain advantages over tango: since it came from the rural interior of Argentina, folklore was untainted by any association with either the immoral underworld or the immigrant culture of the big city. As with tango, however, folk music's claims of authenticity relied upon its roots among the suffering poor. Radio magazines celebrated folk musicians for their "humble" origins and lauded a music "in which each note is the expression of a thousand sacrifices."[58] Like tango, folklore was pushed in various directions at once. On the one hand folklore was even more backward-looking than tango. Proponents demanded that folk music be preserved as a bulwark against modernization, "the civilization that advances, represented by the locomotive, the automobile and the radio, destroying the past."[59] Yet on the other hand, critics insisted on the need for composers and lyricists to expand and improve the folk repertoire.[60]

The tensions visible in the realms of both tango and folklore—between nostalgia and modernity and between authenticity and improvement—revealed the deep contradictions that shaped the mass culture of these years. Themselves the product of the countervailing forces in the mass cultural marketplace, these contradictions were visible in the cinema as well. The domestic film industry, which had been virtually obliterated by Hollywood during the silent era, recovered impressively after the introduction of sound technology in 1933. Although Argentine film companies were small, undercapitalized firms lacking any significant protection from the state, they achieved success by responding to local tastes. Hollywood films were technically and artistically impressive, but they were for the most part spoken in English and set in remote locales. While the local studios could not hope to meet North American standards in production quality, their films featured local performers well known from their careers on the stage and the radio, speaking Spanish in Argentine accents and acting out stories in recognizably Argentine settings. Sensing their advantage, the first two modern film studios, Argentina Sono Film and Lumiton, pursued a strategy similar to the one that Jaime Yankelevich had used on Radio Belgrano. The first two domestic sound films established the formula. Lumiton's *Los tres berretines* was based on a popular *sainete*, or comic play, while Sono Film's *Tango* (Moglia Barth, 1933) featured many of the most popular radio stars of the day and a plot recycled from tango songs; both films included tango performances and plot elements drawn from the tradition of popular melodrama. For the next decade the local film studios appropriated existing popular culture to capture an audience willing to choose Argentine authenticity over Hollywood's technical virtuosity.

Through this strategy the Argentine cinema effectively acquiesced in the segmentation of the film audience. The insistently popular orientation of domestic movies—their inclusion of tango music and local radio stars—made them attractive to poorer Argentines, who preferred not to read subtitles and presumably enjoyed seeing their world depicted on screen. Meanwhile, as the U.S. Commerce Department put it, "The so-called better class Argentine . . . has a predilection for American films."[61] In Buenos Aires first-run North American and European films were shown for high prices at fancy downtown theaters, while dozens of more modest theaters in the barrios screened domestic films at prices that were accessible even to manual laborers. Ordinary Argentines still saw plenty of Hollywood movies, since the major studios continued to flood foreign markets with their products. But the disdain that elites showed for domestic films reinforced their popular orientation, leading the studios to specialize in films that the local trade magazine labeled as "suitable, preferably, for popular cinemas."[62] In the same way that competition with jazz deepened tango's claim to plebeian authenticity, the market power of Hollywood tightened the local cinema's embrace of Argentine popular culture.

Nevertheless, the same countervailing pressures that pushed tango lyricists to elevate their poetry and eliminate lunfardo encouraged Argentine filmmakers to moralize their offerings and purge them of threatening and lowbrow elements. Signs of these pressures were apparent everywhere. For one thing, even if movies celebrated the moral virtue of the poor, they tended to avoid depicting the struggles and challenges facing their contemporary working-class audience. With a handful of important exceptions—*Riachuelo* (Moglia Barth, 1934), *Chingolo, La maestrita de los obreros* (de Zavalía, 1942), and especially the urban realist films of José Agustín Ferreyra—the Argentine cinema rarely included the growing industrial workforce in its plots. The dignified poor who served as victims in the melodramas of the period were far more likely to be tango singers than factory workers. And while this tendency partly reflected the cinema's reliance on tango and popular melodrama for its source material, it also followed from the studios' marketing goals. For example, Ferreyra abandoned his realist explorations of working-class life in 1936 at the behest of the SIDE company, which preferred musical melodramas that would showcase the star power of Libertad Lamarque. In the words of Ferreyra's biographer, "the reality of a cinema with aspirations of industrialization was closing in on him."[63] The relative absence of the urban working class on Argentine movie screens was a byproduct of the local studios' pursuit of a mass audience.

Not content with being relegated to the inexpensive barrio theaters, Argentine film companies engaged in an intensive effort at market expansion targeted at wealthier moviegoers. The companies used various strategies to wrest these consumers away from Hollywood films. Argentina Sono Film specialized in "films for the family," pursuing middle-class audiences by avoiding or sanitizing the morally dubious, plebeian world of the tango. *La vida de Carlos Gardel*, a Sono Film product, carefully avoided any depiction of the gritty, working-class milieu in which Gardel was raised and focused instead on the singer's ascent to stardom.[64] Even Lumiton, the company most closely associated with films based on tango, sought to clean up its movies. Critics praised the studio's adaptation of the popular sainete *Así es la vida*, specifically for having eliminated its lowbrow jokes. In another effort to attract more affluent viewers, new film studios such as BAIRES and Artistas Argentinas Asociadas emerged in the late 1930s with the goal of making sophisticated films and raising the artistic level of Argentine cinema.[65] In their desire to compete for the higher-class audience that preferred North American films, the studios also engaged in open imitation. By the early 1940s films modeled on Hollywood's so-called white telephone comedies became increasingly common. With lighthearted stories set in luxurious interiors, these movies offered viewers the same escapist entertainment they had come to expect from Hollywood.

Yet despite all these efforts, the melodramatic tendency in Argentine cinema persisted. Throughout the 1930s most domestic films, regardless of genre, depicted a society divided between the selfish rich and the noble poor. To film critics who longed for an improvement in the quality of the local cinema, this melodramatic orientation was problematic not only because it was lowbrow but also because it had clear, populist implications. One critic denounced the enormously successful Manuel Romero as "an interpreter of the simple tastes of the masses that attend these homegrown productions . . . He has [not] tried to do anything other than to reach his audience directly, using elements of simple melodrama, in order to tip the balance in favor of the humble masses."[66] As this critic recognized, Romero's films used melodrama to appeal to the non-elite audience that filled the barrio movie theaters. The enduring commercial viability of his style indicated that even as the market encouraged the studios to try to pry well-to-do audiences away from foreign films, it also continued to reward filmmakers who remained loyal to their roots in local popular culture.

As with tango music, the conflicting forces at work in the mass cultural marketplace shaped a domestic cinema that sent contradictory messages. Competition with Hollywood encouraged both emulation of North American practices and the adoption of discourses of national authenticity. Filmmakers attempted to expand their audience into the middle and upper classes while holding on to their base in the barrios. Romero's films in particular reveal the effects of these conflicting pressures. Often borrowing quite openly from Hollywood hits, Romero transformed class conflicts into morality tales, but he insisted on identifying national authenticity with the poor. His interclass couples model national unity, but it is a unity that is only possible when the rich character adopts the moral virtue and cultural practices of the poor. As a result, the happy endings and moral resolutions offered by these films often fail to silence their critique of class prejudice and persecution.[67] Yet perhaps betraying his roots as a tango composer, Romero's vision of Argentinidad was fundamentally nostalgic. Films like *Los muchachos de antes no usaban gomina* (1937) imagine an Argentine identity rooted in the tango golden age and threatened by North American influence. In *La rubia del camino* a working-class truck driver resists the efforts of his wealthy girlfriend to incorporate him into the modern, cosmopolitan world of elite Buenos Aires. In the end their romance is saved when she turns her back on that world to join him in his authentic, rustic, traditional milieu. In Romero's cinematic universe the poor represented the nation, but they also represented the past.

Like tango music, the Argentine cinema expressed contradictory attitudes toward upward mobility. Films like *Los tres berretines* and *La vida de Carlos Gardel* peddled rags-to-riches fantasies, yet as *La rubia del camino* shows, national authenticity often required that the poor reject social striving. In *Chingolo* Sandrini's character refuses a life of leisure and privilege because it would require him to adopt the selfish, hypocritical, and exploitative practices of the rich. More broadly, by setting so many of their movies in the luxurious homes and fancy cabarets of the rich, Argentine filmmakers, like their Hollywood counterparts, offered their audiences a chance to indulge their envy for elite lifestyles. Yet even the most benign white telephone comedies often trafficked in the populist messages of melodrama. In *Soñar no cuesta nada* (Amadori, 1941) a poor girl, played by Mirtha Legrand, gets to experience how the other half lives for a day. Legrand's character is an innocent who poses only mild critiques of the rich around her, yet since she is the only available object of identification, she is a sort of proxy for the audience. Her innocence and moral virtue—among other accomplishments, she teaches the niño bien to appreciate the opportunities that his class position affords him—are possible precisely because she stands outside the moral universe of the wealthy. This film, like the Argentine cinema more generally, allowed popular audiences to fantasize about wealth even as it reinforced the idea that we, the poor, are morally superior to them, the rich. The persistence of these elements in the mass culture of the 1930s undoubtedly had many causes. But in large part they responded to the logic of the market. With foreign cultural imports marked as the preference of elites, it made good commercial sense to embrace the populist discourses that circulated in vulgar tangos and popular films.

FROM THE COMMERCIAL TO THE POLITICAL: THE TRANSFORMATION OF POPULISM

As Juan Perón began building his mass movement in the wake of the coup of 1943, he confronted a public that had been shaped by the explosion of mass culture in the previous couple of decades. Needless to say, other developments had been important as well: industrialization, migration, the resurgence of the labor movement, the political frustrations of the década infame. But the entertainment offered on the radio and in the movie theater had by this time become a significant part of the everyday lives of Argentines of all classes. It would be an exaggeration to say that this mass culture had prepared working-class Argentines for populism. As I have tried to show, mass culture was ideologically ambivalent, oscillating between conformist and heretical messages. Neither can one claim that Peronism was a straightforward case of selective appropriation, that Perón simply adopted the subversive elements circulating in mass culture while leaving aside its conservative aspects. On the contrary, Perón's political success was due to his ability to overcome some of the central contradictions reproduced by mass culture in the 1930s. To do that he could not take mass cultural populism as he found it; in politicizing commercial culture, he transformed it. At the same time, Perón did not manage to overcome all of mass culture's contradictions. As the remaining chapters in this book will make clear, Peronism was a profoundly ambivalent movement, its discourse marked by numerous points of tension. Many of these ambivalences originated in the commercial culture of the previous period.

Among the most persistent tensions in Argentine mass culture was the apparent contradiction between the goal of individual upward mobility and the celebration of working-class solidarity. Rags-to-riches fantasies thrived alongside melodramatic narratives that contrasted the generosity and self-sacrifice of the poor with the egotistical greed of the rich. Carlos Gardel was a hero for having achieved fame and wealth, yet tango lyrics condemned social climbing as petty and doomed to fail. In this way mass culture promoted both the pursuit of individual achievement and the defense of collective interests. Perón appropriated this discursive material but introduced new elements that enabled him to overcome the contradiction. In particular, by introducing a novel conception of the state as the ultimate guarantor of social justice, he was able to reconcile the quest for upward mobility with an insistence on collective solidarity. In Daniel James's words, Peronist rhetoric envisioned the state as "a space where *classes*—not isolated individuals—could act politically and socially with one another to establish corporate rights and claims."[68] Perón constantly trumpeted the state's capacity to provide the poor with a comfortable standard of living and to enable them to enjoy material benefits previously reserved for the rich. The upward mobility he offered was fundamentally collective. Thanks to the intervention of the state— and of Perón himself, as the personification of the state—the poor could attain concrete improvements without acting selfishly. Perón thus appropriated both the dream of upward mobility and the celebration of the generosity of the poor, but his capacity to use these discourses toward political ends entailed substantial innovation.

Another of Peronism's key innovations was to place workers, and particularly urban workers, at the center of its melodramatic vision of Argentine society. As we have seen, the mass culture of the 1930s tended to erase urban workers. The cinema of social critique concentrated on the plight of the rural poor, while popular melodramas often cast tango singers in the role of victim. Perón appropriated melodrama's Manichean depiction of a society divided between noble poor and hateful rich, but he applied this vision to the travails of actual, contemporary workers. By persistently invoking the suffering and pain of Argentina's workers he lent greater specificity and relevance to mass cultural melodrama.

More important, though, Perón managed to overcome the fatalism of melodrama, suggesting that workers need not accept the status quo. Perón appropriated the discourses of authenticity that made the poor central to Argentine national identity. Yet in mass culture this vision of authenticity tended to lock the poor in a position of stasis. Since poverty was a sign of moral virtue and true Argentinidad, upward mobility and progress were problematic goals. Both the absence of factory workers in the movies and the omnipresence of nostalgia reflected a deep disjuncture between authenticity and modernity. If jazz was the music of modernity, then tango was authentic to the extent that it remained focused on the past. Argentine mass culture depicted the poor as authentically Argentine by virtue of their affinity with either the rural past of the gauchos or the turn-of-the-century urban underworld of the tango. This authenticity compensated the poor for their fatalistic acceptance of subordination.

Perón overcame this fatalism by articulating mass culture's discourses of authenticity with a modernizing discourse of industrialization and economic nationalism. These commitments were hardly unique to Peronism. Calls for economic independence were central to both left- and right-wing nationalism in the 1930s, and by 1943 virtually every political party accepted the need for a state-led program of industrialization.[69] But by combining these arguments with the melodramatic vision that he drew from mass culture, Perón positioned the poor as the primary beneficiaries of industrialization. Economic nationalism and the promise of industrialization gave him a way of connecting the poor to a particular vision of modernization. He could appropriate melodrama's Manichean worldview without its fatalism. In effect, by fusing these very different discourses, drawn from very different sources, Perón managed to articulate authenticity and modernity.[70]

By overcoming these various contradictions, Perón built a political appeal that successfully mobilized thousands of Argentine workers. Nevertheless, several of mass culture's other contradictions persisted within Peronism. One example is the tension in Peronist discourse between the critique of elite greed and the expression of working-class envy. James has suggested that one of Peronism's advantages over traditional leftist parties was its ability to express workers' desires for expensive consumer goods. In particular, he argues, the figure of Evita provided working-class women with a model that legitimized their feelings of envy and resentment.[71] Yet the contradiction persisted, coming to the fore in moments when the state was unable to deliver on its economic promises to workers.[72] Perón's attacks on greed and his endorsement of the working-class desire for material goods were both drawn from mass culture. In film after film and song after song, it was greed, along with frivolity and hypocrisy, that defined the moral shortcomings of the rich. Yet at the same time, the cinema's tendency to revel in the luxurious interiors of elite mansions undoubtedly played to the audience's envy. In fact, poor people's resentment of the rich—visible in the tango singer's complaints about the bacán whose wealth enables him to steal the singer's girl— drove much of Argentine melodrama. It was Perón's debt to this tradition that distinguished his brand of populism from a more orthodox leftist appeal. This debt also helps to explain why, as Eduardo Elena's chapter in this book demonstrates, official Peronism often endorsed bourgeois standards of propriety and taste even as it celebrated working-class culture, offering its followers both "cultural orthodoxy" and heresy. Perón appropriated mass cultural discourses that expressed both popular resentment over social inequality and popular desires for the trappings of wealth. This discursive framework imposed limits on the utopias that Peronism might imagine. In a sense these limits were the consequence of having built his movement out of melodrama rather than Marxism.[73]

At the heart of Peronism was the contradiction between liberation and control, between mobilization and authoritarianism. Peronism invited workers to play an active role in history, but it also asked them to obey their leaders and stay off the streets. It represented both a heretical challenge to hierarchy and a self-conscious attempt to discipline the masses. Obviously these different faces of the movement responded to the exigencies of different historical moments. When he was seeking power, Perón emphasized mobilization and heresy. Once in control of the state, he reverted to discipline and social control. Yet here too one finds the traces of mass culture. It seems plausible that the contradiction between conformism and populist heresy so central to the cinema and radio of the 1930s is one source of Peronism's fundamental ambivalence. Argentine mass culture articulated a visceral anti-élitism, even as it de-politicized class conflict and suggested the futility of social transformation. Peronism's simultaneous commitment to a frontal assault on the oligarchy and to social harmony and class reconciliation betrays its origins in melodramatic mass culture.

NOTES

I would like to thank Oscar Chamosa, Eduardo Elena, and the anonymous readers for their many useful suggestions.

1 Juan Domingo Perón, *Obras completas*, vol. 8 (Buenos Aires: Fundación pro Universitaria de la Producción y del Trabajo y Fundación Universidad a Distancia "Hernandarias," 1998), 24. All translations are mine unless otherwise noted.

2 Laclau, "Towards a Theory of Populism," 173.

3 James, *Resistance and Integration*, 7–40.

4 Once again Daniel James has led the way. See James, *Resistance and Integration*, 26–27. To a great extent the present chapter is a response to James's recent suggestion that "in order to understand the sources of Peronist discourse's power and resonance we should pay more attention to its use of melodramatic form." James, *Doña María's Story*, 255.

5 A small sample of the best of this scholarship would include Archetti, *Masculinities*; Armus, "Tango, Gender, and Tuberculosis in Buenos Aires"; España, ed., *Cine argentino*; Saítta, *Regueros de tinta*; Sarlo, *El imperio de los sentimientos*.

6 Laclau, "Towards a Theory of Populism," 167.

7 Sigal and Verón, *Perón o muerte*, 72–74; Bianchi and Sánchis, *El Partido Peronista Femenino*; Caimari and Plotkin, "Pueblo contra antipueblo."

8 Juan Perón, *El pueblo quiere saber de qué se trata: discursos sobre política social pronunciados por el secretario de Trabajo y Previsión durante el año 1944* (Buenos Aires, 1944), 238.

9 Elena, "Peronist Consumer Politics and the Problem of Domesticating Markets in Argentina," 118 (translation by Elena).

10 Quoted in Sigal and Verón, *Perón o muerte*, 66.

11 Quoted in James, *Resistance and Integration*, 24 (translation by James).

12 On Peronist anti-intellectualism see James, *Resistance and Integration*, 22.

13 Berhó, "Working Politics."

14 Perón, *El pueblo quiere saber de qué se trata*, 10–11.

15 From Perón's speech on Labor Day, 1 May 1944. Perón, *El pueblo quiere saber de qué se trata*, 49. On the centrality of working-class respectability within Peronism see Gené, *Un mundo feliz*.

16 Armus, "Tango, Gender, and Tuberculosis in Buenos Aires," 112–22; Ulla, *Tango, rebelión y nostalgia*, 33–44.

17 Eduardo Romano, ed., *Las letras del tango: antología cronológica, 1900–1980* (Rosario: Fundación Ross, 1998), 84–85.

18 *Canción Moderna* 1, no. 9 (21 May 1928).

19 Diana Paladino, "Libertad Lamarque, la reina de la lágrima," *Archivos de la filmoteca* 31 (February 1999), 69.

20 Di Núbila, *La época de oro*, 305.

21 On Mario Soffici's films see Tranchini, "El Cine Argentino y la construcción de un imaginario criollista"; Falicov, "Argentine Cinema and the Construction of National Popular Identity."

22 Some scholars have gone so far as to describe Romero's films as precursors to Peronism. See Donatello, "Manuel Romero y el peronismo."

23 Quoted in Sigal and Verón, *Perón o muerte*, 50.

24 Maranghello, *La epopeya trunca*, 67. On Lugones's hierarchical and aristo-cratic vision of patriotic heroism see Fürstenberger, "Güemes y los de abajo."

25 *Sintonía* 6, no. 298 (4 January 1939).

26 *Crítica*, 29 May 1928, 12.

27 On the Catholic Nationalist intellectuals of the 1930s see Spektorowski, *The Origins of Argentina's Revolution of the Right*, 109–23; Zanatta, *Del Estado liberal a la nación católica*. On the influence of Catholic Nationalists on Peronism see the chapters by Chamosa and Elena in this volume.

28 The popular poetry of Ernesto Carriego, the *sainetes* of the Argentine the-ater, the *circo criollo*, and the *criollista* pamphlets that narrated tales of gaucho heroes for a popular audience all contained melodramatic elements that were reconfigured in the mass culture of the 1920s and 1930s.

29 On Perón's mass media policies see Ciria, *Cultura y política popular*; Sirven, *Perón y los medios de communicación*. On the expropriation of the newspapers see Cane-Carrasco, *The Fourth Enemy*.

30 On Apold see Sirven, *Perón y los medios de comunicación*, 122–31. On the efforts of Amadori and Argentina Sono Film, the studio that had employed Apold, to ingratiate themselves with the Perón regime see Ricardo Manetti, "Argentina Sono Film: más estrellas que en el cielo," *España* 1, 189–205. On Discépolo's radio program see Pujól, *Discépolo*, 366–85.

31 Cane-Carrasco, *The Fourth Enemy*, 58–93.

32 On the rise and fall of projects to nationalize the radio see Gallo, *La radio*, 62–71. On the dominance of commercial radio stations see Claxton, *From Parsifal to Perón*, 26–73. On official censorship of the cinema see César Maranghello, "Cine y Estado" and "Orígenes y evolución de la censura," *España* 2, 24–183. The dominant role of the market may not in fact distinguish Argentine populism from other Latin American cases. Bryan McCann's recent study of Brazilian popular music demonstrates that even under the Estado Novo dictatorship of the late 1930s and early 1940s, commercial imperatives shaped the music far more decisively than did direct ideological manipulation by the state. See McCann, *Hello, Hello Brazil*.

33 For an account of this process of depoliticization in the development of Hollywood cinema see Steven J. Ross, *Working-Class Hollywood: Silent Film and the Shaping of Class in America* (Princeton: Princeton University Press, 1998). Ross argues that in 1910–30 a working-class cinema gave way to one that fostered class reconciliation and an inclusive middle-class identity.

34 "Peripheral modernity" is Beatriz Sarlo's suggestive and influential phrase. Sarlo, *Una modernidad periférica*.

35 Dirección General de Correos y Telégrafos, *Reorganización de los servicios de radiodifusión* (1939), 91.

36 *Sintonía*, 23 September 1937.

37 The most important of these contests were those organized in the 1920s by Max Glucksmann's record label Nacional-Odeon. Even before this the popular theater in Buenos Aires was a testing ground for new tangos; those that impressed the audience earned the right to be published and recorded.

38 One magazine, for example, argued that the single-minded pursuit of profit had led stations to imitate any popular program, resulting in a lack of variety and originality for listeners. *Caras y Caretas*, 28 December 1935.

39 De Paoli, *Función social de la radiotelefonía*, 22.

40 *El Mundo*, 29 November 1935, 10.

41 *Sintonía* 3, no. 135 (23 November 1935). For a description of the station's programming plans see *El Mundo*, 28 November 1935, 8.

42 *Sintonía* 6, no. 298 (4 January 1939), 38.

43 Pujól, *Jazz al sur*, 20–21.

44 *La Canción Moderna* 7, no. 289 (2 October 1933).

45 *Sintonía* 3, no. 91 (19 January 1935).

46 *La Canción Moderna* 7, no. 295 (13 November 1933).

47 See Pujól, *Jazz al sur*.

48 On the fatalism of tango lyrics see Matamoro, *La ciudad del tango*, 117. Beatriz Sarlo has stressed the conformism of the sentimental pulp fiction of

the 1920s. See Sarlo, *El imperio de los sentimientos*, 176–78. Many scholars of Latin American film melodrama have pointed out its conservative implications. See Jesús Martín-Barbero, *Communication, Culture and Hegemony: From the Media to Mediations*, trans. Elizabeth Fox and Robert A. White (London: Sage, 1993), 167. See also Oroz, *Melodrama*; Monsiváis, "Se sufre, pero se aprende."

49 "Muchachita loca" (1923), cited by Ulla, *Tango, rebelión y nostalgia*, 39.

50 Adrián Gorelik has commented on the irony that tango, whose immense popularity was enabled by the emergence of the modern mass media, retained this hostility to modernity. See Gorelik, *La grilla y el parque*, 361–73.

51 Savigliano, *Tango and the Political Economy of Passion*, 65–66.

52 Matamoro, *La ciudad del tango*, 124; Ulla, *Tango, rebelión y nostalgia*, 33–44, 92.

53 Romano, ed., *Las letras del tango*, 111–13. For another tango expressing the same sentiment see "Niño bien" (Fontaina and Soliño, 1927): Romano, ed., *Las letras del tango*, 110–11.

54 Ulla, *Tango, rebelión y nostalgia*, 76–79.

55 *Canción Moderna* 7, no. 295 (13 November 1933).

56 *Canción Moderna* 7, no. 289 (2 October 1933). Five years later the magazine, now renamed *Radiolandia*, reiterated the point: "The author has a responsibility: to write seeking to improve. Those who do not fulfill this obligation are attacking popular song." *Radiolandia* 11, no. 545 (27 August 1938).

57 *Radiolandia* 11, no. 541 (30 July 1938).

58 *Sintonía*, 26 April 1939.

59 *Sintonía* 1, no. 22 (23 September 1933), 7.

60 *Radiolandia*, 16 April 1938. For more on folklore see Oscar Chamosa's chapter in this volume.

61 Nathan D. Golden, *Motion Picture Markets of Latin America* (Washington: U.S. Department of Commerce, 1944), 24.

62 See for example the descriptions of *Riachuelo* (Moglia Barth, 1934) and *Ayudame a vivir* (Ferreyra, 1936) in *El Heraldo del Cinematografista*, 11 July 1934 and 2 September 1936.

63 Jorge Miguel Couselo, *El Negro Ferreyra: un cine por instinto* (Buenos Aires: Freeland, 1969), 76.

64 This sanitizing of the Gardel myth drew praise from reviewers. See *La Razón*, 25 May 1939, 15. For Sono Film's commitment to family films see Ricardo Manetti, "Argentina Sono Film," 167.

65 See Félix-Didier, "Soñando con Hollywood"; and Maranghello, *La epopeya trunca*.

66 *La Razón*, 29 June 1939, 13.

67 I make this argument in more detail in "The Melodramatic Nation."

68 James, *Resistance and Integration*, 18 (emphasis by James).

69 Spektorowski, *The Origins of Argentina's Revolution of the Right*, 128–32, 181–83.

70 Nevertheless, Mariano Plotkin's analysis of Peronist textbooks reveals the persistence within Peronism of a tension between tradition and modernization. Plotkin, *Mañana es San Perón*, 189–92.

71 James, *Doña María's Story*, 240–41.

72 See Elena, "Peronist Consumer Politics and the Problem of Domesticating Markets in Argentina"; and Milanesio, "'The Guardian Angels of the Domestic Economy.'"

73 Elena's chapter reveals that the Peronist magazine *Argentina* catered to workers' interest in "window shopping," or indulging the fantasy of luxury and wealth, in much the same way as the mass culture of the 1930s.

Natalia Milanesio

....

PERONISTS AND *CABECITAS*

Stereotypes and Anxieties at the Peak of Social Change

In 1967 the social psychoanalyst Alfredo Moffat wrote: "The 'line' that separates the *cabecita* from other more urbanized groups is comprised of several elements whose identification and denomination is mainly taken on by the middle class: 'using poor people's clothes,' 'not being clean,' 'being ignorant,' 'behavior based on instinct,' etc. However, there is one feature that succinctly defines the *cabecita*: the fact of 'being a Peronist.'"[1] As Moffat's analysis attests, the Argentine middle classes continued to associate the *cabecitas negras* with Juan Domingo Perón's followers, even twelve years after he was overthrown. The term *cabecita negra* (little blackhead)—originally an Argentine bird—emerged in the popular vocabulary in the mid-1940s to denominate the recent migrant from the provinces to the major cities, especially Buenos Aires. Internal migration was the result of the process of import substitution industrialization initiated during the crisis of the 1930s and then accelerated with the Second World War. By 1947 some 17 percent of the national population had migrated from the provinces where they were born, and 68 percent of these migrants had settled in Buenos Aires.[2] The number of internal migrants to Buenos Aires went from 400,000 in 1935 to 1.5 million in 1947. That same year 73 percent of urban workers living in Buenos Aires were migrants from other provinces.[3]

In the 1960s and 1970s the role of internal migrants as the social base of Peronism was the first topic to spark fervent debate among researchers. Scholars were curious about the support that migrants gave to Perón, both as individual voters and as part of the unionized industrial working class. They were also interested in the relations between internal migrants and urban workers of European descent.[4] At the same time, anthropologists began to study the *villas miseria*, the shantytowns where migrants settled.[5] Their studies overlooked all issues related to identity construction, including the object of my analysis: the representations of the anti-Peronist middle and upper classes. These representations adopted the form of stereotypes: imprecise, protean, and reductive characterizations of behavior, inclinations, and taste as well as physical features and temperament. As a way of dealing with the instabilities of the perceived world and the inability to control it, stereotyping is a major discursive device in the ideological construction of social groups. A collective process of judgment, stereotyping renders everyone associated with the stereotyped group uniform through the arbitrary attribution of features that are considered essential to the group. Stereotypes externalize and exclude those who fall under the stereotyped profile, perpetuating a sense of difference between the "self" and the "Other."[6]

This chapter examines the construction of stereotypes of the popular classes during Perón's government. It attributes the representations of Peronists as violent, uneducated, vulgar, and criminal cabecitas negras to middle- and upper-class anti-Peronists.[7] Broadly, these social sectors encompassed people of diverse levels of affluence—from factory and landowners to small business owners, university graduates, clerks, and housewives—who opposed Peronism both from competing political parties and based on personal, noninstitutional stances. My analysis begins with the idea that anti-Peronism is central to a comprehensive understanding of Peronism. In contrast to most studies, which approach Perón's opposition by examining rival political parties, this chapter considers anti-Peronism a constructed ideology that operated through stereotypical representations of its political opponent grounded in cultural bias.[8]

As a starting point, the chapter addresses the identification among Peronists, cabecitas, and internal migrants that dominated the social imaginary in the 1940s and 1950s. In fact, although internal migration began in the mid-1930s and increased by the end of the decade, the term *cabecita* is absent from dictionaries of idioms published in the early 1940s. It appears in later editions that defined the cabecita as both an internal migrant and a follower of Perón.[9] My analysis examines the meanings and effects of each component of the conceptual triangle as well as the symbolic foundations of the relationship among the three. I show that stereotyping was more than a consequence of the political divide between Peronists and anti-Peronists. It channeled the prejudices of middle- and upper-class Argentines against the poor and of urban dwellers against lower-class, dark-skinned internal migrants. I argue that stereotypes emphasized "cultural inadequacies" such as ignorance, vulgarity, appearance, and incivility, and operated as a mechanism for maintaining and reinforcing forms of behavior, cultural norms, and social conventions. Stereotyping was a maneuver of the urban middle and upper classes when they found themselves in an unsolicited encounter with lower-class migrants triggered by urbanization, industrialization, mass consumption, and Peronism. The stereotypes of the popular sectors were responses from the middle and upper classes to what they perceived as a threat to urban lifestyle, class identity, and social status. Anxieties over an "invasion" of the cities, interclass coexistence in public spaces, safety and property, loss of exclusivity, and the inability to command respect combined with portrayals of the lower classes as aggressive, criminal, ignorant, intruding, and insolent. This analysis also demonstrates that Peronists manipulated anti-Peronist stereotypes for their own propagandistic purposes while creating their own stereotypes of their opponents. In addition, it shows that in some instances Peronists and anti-Peronists represented Perón's constituency in a strikingly similar manner, though they assessed and interpreted their portrayals in radically contrasting ways.

CLASS, RACE, POLITICS, AND CULTURE IN
THE STEREOTYPES OF RURAL MIGRANTS

The term *cabecita negra* refers to the subject's dark skin and black hair. The hair also inspired the term *pelo duro* to refer to the thick mane usually associated with indigenous people.[10] A typical description depicted the cabecita "with dark olive green skin, prominent cheekbones, straight, black, indigenous hair."[11] While some attributed the coinage of the term *cabecita negra* to the upper classes or the left, others claimed that Eastern European immigrants working in the industrial sector coined the offensive term to refer to factory newcomers.[12] More generally, *negro* (lit. black), usually used as *negro peronista* (black Peronist) or *negro villero* (shantytown black)—extremely class-prejudiced terms still very common in contemporary Argentina—was interchanged with the term *cabecita* and became predominant in the 1970s when *cabecita* increasingly fell into disuse.[13]

The adoption of the term *cabecita* by anti-Peronists suggests a racialization of Perón's followers that was loosely defined. Cabecitas could be either pure indigenous or criollos—understood as both people of Spanish descent and mestizos born from one white and one indigenous parent. The concept of the cabecita was also homogenizing in terms of ethnicity. In general neither popular nor academic writers expressed any interest in differentiating between the cultural particularities of the criollos and the diverse aboriginal groups. The anti-Peronist racialization of Perón's followers openly contrasted with Peronist discourse. As Oscar Chamosa points out elsewhere in this volume, Peronism avoided ethnic or racial language when addressing the working class, subordinating ethnic specificity to class consciousness and loyalty to the Peróns.

Even though anti-Peronist prejudice against the cabecita had an unmistakable component of racism, racist sentiments were subordinated to a strong classism. Discrimination was directed against poor and working-class people who were considered to be Peronist and happened to be dark-skinned and recent arrivals to the city. According to this form of classism, low social status was intrinsically related to specific racial features and a particular political ideology. However, it expressed itself by downplaying these aspects and emphasizing culture—defined as proper social conduct, deference, and civility—as the main class division. This is evident in a study of 106 members of the anti-Peronist elite from Buenos Aires conducted three years after Perón's overthrow. Interviewees chose culture and family origins as the most important factors in determining to which social class an individual belonged. When specifically asked about the cabecitas—a term that 55 percent of the informants did not consider derogatory but "the reflection of a social reality"—49 percent thought that cabecitas had no chances of social mobility and mentioned their lack of culture and education as the main reasons.[14]

Since anti-Peronists reinterpreted the cabecitas' class, political affiliation, and race in cultural terms, bias against this group took the form of accusations of vulgarity and socially unacceptable behavior. This explains the widespread adoption of the deprecating term *grasa* (greaser) as synonymous with the Peronist *cabecita*. *Grasa* was generally applied to the humble, and although it may merely evoke the dirt and oil on the workers' overalls, the term connotes someone of very cheap and bad taste. Peronists countered its negative connotations by embracing the diminutive form of the word. Eva Perón popularized the term *grasita* to affectionately refer to the poor.[15] The opposition severely criticized Peronists for publicly using a term that in their view infuriated real workers while psychologically preparing them for further subjugation and exploitation. Nevertheless, *grasa* became a common insult in the anti-Peronist vocabulary.[16]

Expressions of fear, disgust, and condemnation directed toward cabecitas' tastes, manners, morals, and habits were convenient vehicles for classism, racism, and anti-Peronism. This much is evident from one of the "black legends" of Peronism, according to which internal migrants who had been relocated from shantytowns to public housing pulled up parquet floors to use as firewood for barbecues and turned bathtubs into flowerpots. The story conveys how unprepared internal migrants were for urban life, their incapacity to live in a modern house, and their destructive behavior. The legend, a bizarre mockery and sordid critique of Peronism and Peronists in a cultural key, filtered the classist and racist presumptions behind it when people explained the "predictable" and "inherent" conduct of the new neighbors by pointing out that they were *coyas*,[17] migrants, *negros*, and the poor.[18]

The "cultural reinterpretation" of racist and classist arguments became an appropriate strategy in mid-twentieth-century Argentina for several reasons. First, the denunciation of cultural practices camouflaged racist thinking at a time when the unveiling of Nazi atrocities against the Jews made racial ideologies illegitimate. Second, concealing a class bias against the poor and the working class seemed like a sound strategy given the Peronist state's declared commitment to protecting the unprivileged and the defense of workers. Third, condemning the internal migrants' lifestyle translated prejudices against the interior as a backward place into a more legitimate argument to defend modern civilization. It also concealed feelings of frustration provoked by the crisis of the agro-export economy, which was losing workers to the urban factories in accordance with the Peronist industrialist project. Finally, scornful disapproval of cabecita culture was the safest way to express anti-Peronism even as the government was tenaciously persecuting every form of opposition and silencing all critical voices.

Porteños, the inhabitants of the capital city, stereotyped the internal migrant as a fool and simpleton.[19] Unimportant incidents such as a clumsy crossing of the street led urban dwellers to draw conclusions about rural migrants' inability to adapt to city life. By contrast, porteños represented themselves as savvy and sophisticated, while revealing "a humiliating fear of being confused" with the newly arrived: "Those of us from downtown must even walk differently. Or at least we have a 'debonair' way of crossing the streets, making our way through traffic with that haughty tranquility and arrogant indifference that we have cultivated over many years of repeating this suicidal act."[20] Some porteños further thought that Buenos Aires was "becoming a province," since the presence of the cabecitas in the city was demolishing the cultural barriers between "the cosmopolitan metropolis" and "the *mestizo* regions." In fact some observers believed that the massive popularization of folklore music and dances from the interior was proof that a city known for its taste for European culture was being transformed.[21]

The media echoed the distress over the dissolution of porteño identity in nostalgic articles on such quintessential Buenos Aires "institutions" as Florida Street, Avenida de Mayo, and the Obelisco. Numerous pieces longed melancholically for the *bar de la esquina* (the corner café) that once had hosted the ritualistic practices of everyday male sociability.[22] In the 1950s porteños felt alienated in cafés overcrowded with unfamiliar faces, and mistreated by bad-tempered waiters recently arrived from the provinces. The essayist Juan José Sebreli argued, "The *porteño* has now begun to miss the tranquility of his café table, because at the next table, a group of *cabecitas negras* is noisily becoming inebriated."[23]

This longing for the past reflects the perception that internal migration amounted to a disruptive "invasion" of the cities. The figure of the invasion was already present in interpretations of October 17, 1945, when thousands of people marched on the Plaza de Mayo to demand Perón's freedom after his incarceration by the military regime. Accounts of the event—which Peronists canonized as the foundational act of Peronism—stress how on that day the suburbs "had taken" the center.[24] Thus as social actors, Perón's followers burst into history as a crowd. According to Peronists, they were a devoted multitude: Perón's "suffering and sweating masses."[25] For anti-Peronists, whom the Chilean journalist Carlos Morales Salazar called "the anti-multitudes," they represented a "violent horde."[26]

In this way the *montonera*—a group of mounted gauchos, the traditional nomadic inhabitants of the Argentine countryside who fought in the wars of independence and in the civil wars preceding the national organization of the country—became a powerful analogue. The association revealed one central feature of Peronists: their rural origins and their status as the heirs of the country's traditional inhabitants. In the anti-Peronist interpretation, Perón and his followers were the last expression of a social phenomenon first recognizable in the nineteenth-century governor of Buenos Aires Juan Manuel de Rosas and his plebe,[27] and later in the Radical president Hipólito Irigoyen and his *chusma*.[28] In the three historical expressions of the montoneras the anti-Peronists saw an outrageous combination of barbarism, demagogy, violence, and uncouthness—the pre-modern rural leftovers of colonial times.[29]

During Perón's administration the "invasion" of large cities became massive and enduring. Buenos Aires experienced a population boom of enormous proportions, growing from 3,457,000 inhabitants in 1936 to 4,618,000 in 1947.[30] For the upper and middle sectors that lived and worked in the inner city, the arrival of migrants meant the loss of their monopoly over Buenos Aires. In a mea culpa for the porteños' conception of the city as "a walled fief," the writer and journalist Rodolfo Taboada explained: "Those of us from downtown began to feel as if we were being pushed out. And we began to experience jealousy. As if these streets of 'ours' were being invaded by foreigners. We felt like we were drowning in a human tide that was erasing us from the national map. That we were being diluted in the ever-changing multitude."[31]

These fears were more severe on weekends and in the downtown area, where the vast majority of theaters, cinemas, department stores, restaurants, cafés, and dance halls were located. Statistics help to explain that feeling. In January 1935 theaters and cinemas had a combined audience of 1,363,182 people; five years later that audience had increased to 1,607,392. In January 1947 audiences reached an impressive 3,147,473 people. In 1952 the monthly average of movie theater audiences alone was around 4,851,000.[32] These numbers illustrate a change that was also affecting boxing and soccer matches, concerts, and dance halls. Migrants from La Rioja argued that the lack of well-paid jobs was the first reason to migrate to Buenos Aires. Disappointment with a humdrum existence in their uninteresting rural towns and the resulting idealization of the city as a place of dazzling entertainment came in second.[33] Admission to this world of amusement was affordable thanks to full employment, rising wages, rent freezes, price ceilings, and the reduction of work time in many occupations. Equally important, the Peronist government recognized having time and money to devote to entertainment as a legitimate right and transformed recreation from a privilege limited to a select few to a luxury for everybody.[34]

There were several causes for the visceral rejection of the "unrecognizable faces" from the suburbs who "seized" the city.[35] For urban dwellers everyday life was becoming increasingly inconvenient, chaotic, and unpredictable: long waits in restaurants; endless lines to get in jam-packed subways, trains, and buses; congested streets; dangerous traffic; mobbed sidewalks; overcrowded stores, parks, and public swimming pools; food shortages and rising prices. In 1945 one author comically described a Saturday night in Buenos Aires as "the *porteño's* martyrdom." The hassle began immediately upon arrival at a movie theater in the downtown area: "You dive heroically into the stormy human sea that is fighting to buy tickets at the box office. You push, pull, attack, defend yourself, grunt, sweat, advance, swear, fight, make yourself thinner, squeeze in, and you're there! And when you get there, the show is sold out." Annoyed, one left the movies to "go on a pilgrimage" that involved fighting for room on the sidewalks and visiting dozens of restaurants with no tables. Tired and hungry, the last stop on "the Saturday calvary" was the subway station, where "if you are not lucky enough to get the right spot on the platform, you will not get in the next car, or in the ones that follow."[36]

Typically frustration over the growing inconveniences of urban life took on a less humorous tone. For the political opposition public transit represented the deterioration of urban living, the collapse of socially acceptable conduct, and the state's incompetence in the face of uncontrolled urban growth. Socialists argued that public transportation was "terribly insufficient," prices exorbitant, and service and schedules appalling. This forced people to travel like animals and risk their lives crammed in ramshackle train cars. Women bore the worst, suffering attacks on their intimacy and honor because of unsolicited flirtations and pawing. Massiveness and impersonality encouraged violence, individualism, and selfishness to the detriment of consideration and good manners.[37]

Critics slipped from blaming "indolent" and "ambitious" cabecitas for the mounting hardships of city life and the depopulation of the countryside to accusing the Peronist administration of promoting a poorly planned process of industrialization and urbanization.[38] The socialist newspaper *Nuevas Bases* argued: "This population has become a mass that does not hear or see or feel; it lives beneath the crushing weight of countless inconveniences and difficulties, risking at every turn its physical integrity and chipping away at its spiritual life."[39] Some observers perceived coming to the cities as the decay of social status, an impression largely based on the idealization of country life. In one account a young woman leaves the "paradisiacal" countryside to work as a housemaid in Buenos Aires because she finds her small town "too boring." The journalist who wrote the story described it as the reverse of the famous children's story: the princess became Cinderella. Women were especially identified as "enemies" of the countryside because they were said to believe that rural life threatened femininity and coquetry.[40]

For the upper classes the effects of the "invasion" further exceeded the new structural inconveniences of urban life. These groups felt threatened by a forced "social mingling" with people of lower status, an experience that they considered the triumph of social disorder. Teobaldo Altamiranda recalled that while working as a technician at the airbase of El Palomar, an upset captain expressed his disbelief at having seen the airbase garbage collector at the prestigious Opera movie theater in downtown Buenos Aires. When Teobaldo said he was glad that a humble worker could enjoy a night at the movies, the captain exclaimed: "But don't you get it? How can a garbage collector be on the same level as we are? The Peronists are going to drive us into anarchy."[41]

Mar del Plata further exemplified the impression of a loss of exclusivity. The traditional tourist bastion of the national elites, it became the most popular destination of hundreds of thousands of people who had never before left their home town for a vacation. While in the summer of 1940 Mar del Plata had welcomed 380,000 tourists, it witnessed the arrival of one million people in 1950 and 1.4 million five years later.[42] To make this possible the Peronist government mandated annual paid vacations, built inexpensive hotels and nationalized existing ones, helped unions to construct their own hotels, and set affordable train and bus ticket prices.[43] These measures, among others, transformed Mar del Plata into "a modern Babylonia, where the rich mingle with the poor."[44] In spite of such claims the upper classes still retained a firm monopoly over exclusive and expensive clubs, associations, restaurants, stores, and neighborhoods that workers could not afford, were not allowed to enter, or had no interest in joining.[45]

Whether the upper classes really shared the beach with the workers is less interesting than the perception that the presence of workers on the beach was an alarming threat to a beloved social order in which the poor crossed paths with the privileged only to serve them. The widespread nature of social integration and the active role of the government in manipulating it toward propagandistic ends probably contributed to the perception that the transformation was much more disruptive than it was in reality. Indeed, official propaganda celebrated the new experiences of the popular classes as evidence of Peronism's assault on privilege. To transmit the message more efficiently, the Peronist media ridiculed the upper classes by depicting them as spiteful and bitter. A cartoon in *Descamisada* shows a restaurant in which two angry, well-dressed, and very fat men stare hatefully at a nearby table where two men dressed in working clothes are happily toasting while enjoying the same meal. One of the corpulent men says to his companion: "Have you seen, Mr. Chanchiz, what this dictatorship is doing? Right there at the next table, the riffraff, drinking sparkling wine! And then they deny that they're fascists!" The cartoon mocks the elite's accusation of the Perón government as an authoritarian regime by showing that the allegation was a strategy to oppose social egalitarianism. It suggests the blurring of class identities that might occur when indicators that previously revealed one's membership in a specific social class—the practice of dining out, the taste for a certain meal, access to a particular restaurant—no longer conveyed this meaning.[46]

FROM *DESCAMISADOS* TO HOUSEMAIDS DRESSED LIKE "US": FEARS OF MISTAKEN CLASS IDENTITIES AND STATUS PANIC

In an article about how workers were now enjoying weekend excursions to parks and the countryside, *Mundo Peronista* claimed: "It has now become difficult to know the social class of those who head out with

picnic baskets on Sunday morning."[47] The alleged difficulty of distin-
guishing among members of different social classes represented a striking change from the society that Peronists and anti-Peronists left behind,
a society in which there were no ambiguous signs of class identity. The
Peronist union leader Angel Perelman recalled that in the 1940s, "at dusk,
on Callao Street, Avenida de Mayo and other downtown streets, people
were divided into two social classes that were easily differentiated: those
who walked along the street in a shirt and those who watched from the
sidewalk in full suits. The latter were fewer, the representatives of the
oligarchy and the middle class."[48]

For Peronists and anti-Peronists alike, dress was one of the earliest and
strongest elements in constructing a differentiated class and political
identity and a fundamental component of stereotypes.[49] After Peronists
took to the streets shouting, "*Alpargatas*, yes! Books, no!" the espadrille
became an enduring symbol of Perón's sympathizers. While Peronists
shouted out for basic needs over scholarly learning, anti-Peronists criticized the dichotomy, arguing that it was an absurd negation of education,
workers' ultimate aspiration, fueled by a demagogue.[50] Peronists appropriated the *alpargata*, an inexpensive rope-soled canvas shoe, from
lencinismo, a populist movement in the province of Mendoza that had
employed it as an emblem of its humble constituency.[51] Traditionally
linked to rural inhabitants, the shoe came to represent the urban industrial worker, the rural laborer, and the poor. After October 1945 it
also symbolized the Peronist cabecita. An anonymous anti-Peronist pamphlet mocking an invitation to a Peronist rally reported that the only
requirements for attendance were "*alpargatas*, a loud voice and plenty
of sweat."[52]

Peronists, for their part, marched on the streets chanting, "No top hat
and no cane, we're Perón's boys all the way!" to distinguish themselves
from the *galeritas*, as Peronists called the opposition, in an allusion to
turn-of-the-century symbols of social prestige.[53] At the same time, socialist and conservative newspapers used the term *descamisado* (shirtless) in
their accounts of October 17, 1945, to disdainfully refer to Perón's followers congregated in Plaza de Mayo.[54] Although the term could refer to
both men and women, and anti-Peronists and Peronists occasionally
used it as a feminine noun, *descamisado* carried unmistakably masculine
connotations.[55] For the opposition it referred to people who were ideo-

logically close to the blackshirts, Benito Mussolini's paramilitary groups. However, *descamisado* also gave Perón's newborn political movement a name that unintentionally recalled the sans-culottes of the French Revolution, the most powerful icon of republicanism, egalitarianism, and popular political extremism.[56]

On 15 December 1945 Perón used the term *descamisado* in public for the first time and appropriated it by arguing, "While they may insultingly refer to us as shirtless riffraff, we believe it is an honor to have our hearts in the right place beneath a simple shirt instead of a fancy jacket."[57] Perón also took physical possession of the symbol when he untied a national flag from its pole and fastened a shirt that he flew above his followers. This provoked an outcry among his opponents, who first accused Perón of disrespecting the Argentine flag and afterward ridiculed the event as an example of the impropriety of Peronism.[58] That day Perón also began a tradition of taking off his coat at rallies. By talking to the crowds in his shirtsleeves, Perón set himself apart from national political tradition.[59]

The opposition criticized and mocked Perón's followers because coming downtown without a jacket was a violation of a consuetudinary norm of fashion that was also legally enforced. Buenos Aires had a municipal bylaw that mandated wearing a jacket in public places.[60] Even newspaper accounts for foreign audiences stressed this characteristic of the Peronist constituency. The correspondent for the *New York Times*, an extreme anti-Peronist, wrote: "Judging for the appearance of the crowds that turn out for Perón, his appeal seems to be mainly to the humblest and poorest strata of the population. They almost invariably were hatless, coatless and tieless."[61] Some anti-Peronist representations went beyond noting the lack of a jacket by emphasizing the outlandish clothes and especially the miserable and filthy aspect of Perón's supporters.[62] The association of Perón's sympathizers with scruffiness was so pervasive that according to the socialist newspaper *La Vanguardia* Peronists insulted and mocked people who wore polished shoes and clean shirts.[63]

Peronists emphasized the shabbiness of Perón's followers congregated in the Plaza de Mayo instead of challenging these images. Also, Peronist accounts portrayed men in labor clothes.[64] This reaffirmation of the working-class identity of Peronists contradicted claims that Perón represented "the lumpenproletariat" or "the scum of society," an underclass of beggars, gangsters, the unemployed, crooks, and petty criminals.[65] An anonymous anti-Peronist humorous poem entitled "To Perón's Sympathizers," which circulated in pamphlet form, mocked the imagined Peronist audience as penniless and incapable of keeping a job:

If you've never made a dime
and never even found one by mistake
sing along with us
one hundred times: Long live Perón!
If you've never lasted two days
in any job at all
Keep those spirits up
And yell: Long live Perón!"[66]

However, numerous accounts, photographs, and personal testimonies suggest that the great majority of *descamisados* did wear jackets at that time. The three young men soaking their feet in a fountain in the Plaza de Mayo and immortalized in the most famous photograph of October 17 might have been giving evidence to the elite that Peronists were ill mannered, but they were certainly wearing suits. In 1996 Celso Pivida, one of those workers, remembered: "Back then, people from Greater Buenos Aires who went into the city put on a jacket and tie; otherwise, they were considered riffraff. In fact, that day I went home to change because I had my work clothes on."[67] In 1947 an American reporter recalled that "even the newspaper vendors on the streets of Buenos Aires worked with ironed suits, clean shirts and sometimes even ties."[68] Whether or not working-class men wore jackets in public, both Peronists and anti-Peronists constructed an image of Perón's followers as people in rags. For the elite the attire of the descamisado revealed Peronists' cultural inability to follow the rules of etiquette, demonstrating their troubling adaptation to urban space and exposing their uncouth tastes. In Peronist accounts worn-out clothing was proof of the poverty and marginalization endured by the workers before Perón's government. Written after 1945, these descriptions were perfectly in tune with official propaganda showing that in Perón's "New Argentina," good salaries allowed people to frequently buy new clothes of high quality.[69]

In the Argentina before Perón, clothing made people recognizable and easy to classify because they dressed according to how their social class was expected to dress. In 1946 anti-Peronists in charge of polling places did not let men in their shirtsleeves vote because they thought that such attire was evidence of their political sympathies.[70] Style was considered a sign of status that unmistakably conveyed to others what one did for a living and one's political affiliation. With Perón in power, both Peronists and anti-Peronists radically changed this perception. When the descamisado went from being a member of "the ragged poor" to a "well-dressed worker," physical appearance became a less reliable sign of class identity and more an artifice for disguise.[71] Comments such as "At a glance, who could tell which is the rich girl and which is the simple employee?" in the fashion section of a magazine not only revealed the progress of the workers' living conditions but also implied the fall of middle- and upper-class status.[72] *Rico Tipo* echoed this perception of a leveling between popular and upper sectors in a cartoon in which two gentlemen in tuxedos admire a stylishly dressed young woman. One of the men exclaims: "What an elegant girl! Imagine what she spent on that dress!" The friend answers: "Oh, nothing at all! Her maid lent it to her!"[73]

Since attire plays an important role in constructing a differentiating social identity, the risk of wearing clothes similar to those of the popular sectors provoked acute anxieties among the middle classes. In numerous interviews with Peronists and anti-Peronists, the story of the domestic servant who dressed as nicely as her employer surfaces as by far the most pervasive example of growing social equality during Peronism. The story conveys a sense of extreme social polarization, with class division not confirmed through the uniform of the subaltern. It also recycles a popular belief about feminine concern with clothing and appearance as constituent of women's identity. Most significant, interviewees referred to the anecdote to illustrate how the middle classes had lost a traditional sign of prestige and, as a consequence, fervently opposed the Peronist government. Violeta Benvenuto, born in Rosario in 1922, told me: "The hatred of the oligarchs was very profound. For example, I had an aunt who was very anti-Peronist and I said to her: 'Auntie, why are you so anti-Peronist?' And she answered: 'Because my maid dresses just like I do.' "[74]

As the working class was improving its standard of living and the elites still enjoyed an uncontested monopoly over expensive goods and exclusive places, the middle classes perceived as extremely real the threat of being unable to distinguish themselves from the popular sectors. The rising inflation of the Perón years, especially after 1950, significantly affected the middle class. Small merchants suffered government price controls and price ceilings while public servants and independent professionals witnessed in frustration a severe reduction in their salaries as prices rocketed. In contrast, the standard of living of the working classes was protected through the periodical renegotiation of wages by the unions, while the government monitored factory owners to ensure that they honored collective labor agreements. In 1950 a study of the middle sectors showed that in the previous years working-class wages tripled and white-collar employees' salaries doubled, while independent professionals' income remained unchanged. For the middle sectors the feeling of class belonging remained, but the economic and material indicators of that class position were increasingly deteriorating.[75]

Consequently, the middle sectors developed fears of undifferentiated social identities with the popular classes. To prevent confusion a manual for domestic workers recommended that maids avoid vanity, dress modestly, and never wear face cream or makeup. The author thought that makeup on women from the popular classes—and especially servants— had a "bad connotation" and could lead to "misunderstandings." The manual stressed: "Never try to imitate the lady of the house."[76] *Clase Media* (1949), a theatrical play about an impoverished middle-class family, shows how personal appearance was a weapon in the struggle for social status. In the play the anti-Peronist Elvira complains about her son's old and ragged jacket, calls Carlos *desharrapado* (shabby)—a term commonly used in anti-Peronist portrayals of the *descamisados*—and urges him to buy an elegant overcoat:

ELVIRA: Buy it on credit and then pay it off gradually. Why go around wearing the clothes the workers wear?
CARLOS: I am a worker, too.
ELVIRA: You're an engineer.[77]

Peronists ridiculed white-collar employees who put on airs and considered themselves "the new oligarchy" but suffered severe economic hardship to buy clothes they otherwise could not afford: "Composed and elegant, his attire is one of his most legitimate reasons for feeling proud. To perfect it, he forfeits—oh, the cost of vanity!—dire household needs, and credit payments cause him terrible monthly pains!"[78] In the mid-1960s an anthropological study argued that the middle classes' obsession with body cleanliness and impeccable clothing was the consequence of their longing for control and prestige and the overestimation of personal appearances, a conclusion that synthesized arguments about the middle classes already made by sociologists in the 1950s.[79]

Beyond the middle-class anxiety of looking similar to workers, both the middle and popular sectors found ways to express their distinct styles and to categorize people accordingly. To differentiate oneself from subaltern groups, some recommended paying close attention to shoes, the crease of one's pants, and the quality of women's stockings.[80] The writer Ernesto Goldar's description of *petiteros* and *divitos* shows the stereotyped stylistic polarization between middle- and popular-class men in the early 1950s. *Petiteros* took their name from the Petit Café in the élitist Barrio Norte, an institution they regarded as a social and cultural mecca. Petiteros did not belong to the elites but to the anti-Peronist middle classes. Unable to reproduce the economic status of the upper sectors, petiteros imitated their style inexpensively and with second-rate results. They commonly wore a very short, close-fitting, single-breasted blue jacket they never took off; straight, tight, gray pants; a tie with a traditional knot; and moccasins. Finally, they always used hair cream. *Divitos* took their name from the cartoonist Guillermo Divito, editor of the popular humoristic magazine *Rico Tipo*. Divitos wore brown or blue suits. The jacket was very long, fitted, double-breasted, and with a very wide and long lapel. The pants were also very long and narrow. Divitos wore a waistband and suspenders, a gaudy tie with a wide, heart-shaped knot, high-heeled shoes, and a visible handkerchief in the breast pocket. They had long hair, sideburns, a quiff, and a low ponytail.[81] Goldar argued that *Rico Tipo* targeted a middle-class readership who could never identify with the divitos, because the characters ridiculed fashion norms to make well-dressed readers laugh. It is uncertain whether Divito's characters were modeled on real men; according to the magazine he was the creator of a style that the popular sectors rapidly adopted. *Rico Tipo* criticized those who adopted a style created by a cartoonist rather than a fashion designer, as this endangered the international fame of porteños as elegant men.[82]

The Divito was the stylistic remnant of a culture that was disappearing. He was anachronistically inspired by tango characters and by the *compadrito*—"the tough guy," a lower-class man, quarrelsome and arrogant—the quintessence of the porteño outskirts. That a great majority of the lower-class men developing this style were migrants from the provinces shows an attempt at acculturation, at integration in the big city, by the adoption of an intrinsically porteño style, albeit one that was outdated and stereotyped. Such an attempt might have been a reaction to the porteños' astonishment at being in Buenos Aires and seeing men in *bombachas* (traditional gaucho pants) and women wearing long skirts in strident colors, traditional rural outfits that porteños considered "exotic."[83] Moreover, some members of the upper sectors interpreted the lack of "urban clothing" among recently arrived cabecitas as a sign of misery and backwardness comparable with rural people's lack of electricity and gas.[84]

Female fashion also shows that women of the popular classes abandoned their rural outfits but did not always adopt the trends followed by the middle class. As it did for men, *Rico Tipo* popularized a particular style of working-class women. The *chicas Divito* (Divito girls) became famous for their curvy, exuberant bodies and extremely small waists, sensually exalted by body-hugging tube skirts. A monopoly of popular-sector women in the early 1950s, tube skirts are a rare example of a fashion style that moved upward from working-class women to middle- and upper-class women later in the decade.[85] In addition to the tube skirts, women from the popular sectors in the early 1950s generally wore pants in public.[86] Some observers argued that these women "disguised as men" were renouncing their feminine identity and making their bodies look ugly in clothes at odds with the female anatomy.[87] In contrast, while commenting on the outfits of elite women, the fashion expert for the magazine *Rosalinda* noted that the extreme femininity of the designs was a tendency observed "during difficult times," a euphemism for the situation of the elites during the Peronist regime.[88] Regardless of the extent to which these stereotypical stylistic icons were adopted by lower class men and women, their very existence casts doubt on whether middle-class anxieties about social leveling were entirely justified. Also, the existence of such icons of popular fashion challenges traditional accounts of popular consumption as the uncreative emulation of the upper classes.[89] In addition, these icons question official claims of egalitarianism based on undifferentiated representations of unequal classes. Likewise, they problematize the success of Peronism in acculturating the popular sectors through the adoption of middle-class values and aesthetics.[90]

Some observers feared that acculturation was running in the opposite direction: lower-class values and aesthetics were rapidly spreading throughout society. Anti-Peronists claimed that "immense multitudes, politically empowered by the government, thrilled by their victory, move into all fields."[91] Consequently the popular crowd was imposing a downgraded standardization of culture. A journalist complained: "The book that everyone now carries is not the one previously read by a select minority, but that generically written for doormen."[92] Rather than "purifying" their taste—critics affirmed—the popular sectors were increasingly "contaminating" the taste of the elites—an argument difficult to accept after looking at magazines dedicated to the social events, fashion, and vacations of high society. Some other observers thought that with government having made the oligarchy its designated enemy and having held it responsible for the country's poverty, the rich "work hard at mimicry and try to lose themselves in the drab of the multitudes; they prefer to remain unnoticed and aspire to being ignored." How different from a time—an editorial in the magazine *Orientación: Modas y Mundo Social* lamented—when affluence was the measure of good taste and the privileged spared no expense to set the standards of refinement through lavish parties and ostentatious clothing. The author of the editorial expressed a frustrated nostalgia for a "golden era" of strident flamboyance when the rich "did not have to defend themselves the way they now do against the threats and dangers of having a fortune."[93]

VIOLENCE, INSOLENCE, AND REVENGE

As much as this situation disturbed the urban upper and middle classes, it was far less frustrating than "the alarming wave of uncouthness" that they believed *cabecitas* and Peronism had unleashed in Buenos Aires. The "rude jeers, cowardly provocations, scandalous catcalls and obscene gestures" that the media denounced in innumerable editorials damaged the prestige of porteños as a polite people and corroded the foundations of civilized social interaction.[94] In a veiled tone of opposition to the government, *Noticias Gráficas* argued: "We don't want a city that only improves in terms of its level of modernity and comfort"—two leitmotifs of Peronist propaganda—but a cultured city of prevailing good manners.[95]

Anti-Peronist portrayals of Perón's followers as violent, rude, and unruly were common after 1945. Enrique Mosca, vice-presidential candidate from the Unión Democrática, the coalition of political parties that competed with Perón in 1946, argued: "As a threat to civility, unconscious hordes, inebriated by their bullying tactics, have taken the streets of the metropolis, sowing fear, reaping terror, undermining peace, causing destruction and disorder that offend one's morals and inspire collective condemnation and repudiation."[96] Anti-Peronists used violence to differentiate between the "authentic workers" who "always act with respect and dignity" and Peronists.[97] These, according to Perón's adversaries, were a mob armed with rocks, sticks, guns, knives, and homemade bombs, vandalizing public monuments, private residences, social clubs, banks, anti-Peronist newspapers, schools, and universities. According to this view, Peronists robbed stores and factories, stole from innocent bystanders, and insulted, mocked, and attacked men and women alike in all major cities of the country. Newspaper articles frequently compared bands of Peronists who chased down and beat up students and communists, or entered restaurants and stores, forcing people to cheer the name of their leader and hitting those who refused, with the brutal mazorca, a paramilitary organization that persecuted and assassinated Rosas's opponents.[98] In the anti-Peronist imagination Peronists came to embody a form of impulsive, largely unrestricted, and chaotic violence. It was a violence that as a political expression disrespected urbanity and transgressed cultural norms, and as a social expression manifested criminality. The Peronist as a criminal is a recurring figure among Perón's adversaries. Even humorous images of the descamisados depicted Peronists as large, potbellied, hairy, bearded men with rough features and scarred faces, wearing the striped t-shirt traditionally associated with prisoners.[99] The communist newspaper Orientación referred to the "thugs" and "delinquents" that followed Perón as the "malevaje peronista," linking the Peronists to a popular term describing a group of evil, rebellious, and violent ruffians.[100]

In the early 1950s anxieties over the invasion of inner cities by thugs were evident in the obsession of the popular press with the patota (street gang), a group of men identified as young, dark-skinned, working-class, and living on the city's outskirts—a social profile suspiciously similar to that of the Peronist cabecita. The patoteros insulted pedestrians, upset strollers in the parks, beat men, molested women, wrecked public and private property, mistreated passengers in trains, subways, and buses, and sometimes stole and raped.[101] One year after Perón was removed from power, an anti-Peronist newspaper accused the deposed government of aiding and abetting bands of criminals who had seen in their leader an example of criminality. When arrested, these men continued to claim they were affiliated with the Peronist Party, believing that this gave them carte blanche. When they realized that their invocations were futile, they "mourned the absence of their protector, whom they had fervently supported at the cost of collective peace."[102] The media stressed the difference between the patota and the harmless *barra*, a group of well-behaved workers who gathered at bars, on corners, and in soccer fields to enjoy a good time. The press also distinguished between the current gangs and the nineteenth-century patotas of "well-to-do boys" who raided poor neighborhoods looking for a vulnerable lower-class girl to harass or an exhausted worker to beat. In the 1950s the media depicted men from the outskirts as inverting the roles and bringing back to the inner cities the disorder and aggression that the oligarchy had inflicted on working-class neighborhoods with impunity for decades.[103]

Still, denunciations of a broad array of antisocial behavior including impudence, vandalism, and physical and verbal aggression went beyond accusations against the patota. "Antisocial, aggressive and insulting behavior" was considered a "collective phenomenon" that was expanding throughout society.[104] For the anti-Peronist middle and upper classes, this represented the arrival of the "aluvión zoológico" (zoological alluvion). Coined by the Radical congressman Ernesto Sanmartino, the term synthesized the critique of the barbaric horde present in the *montonera* for widespread public consumption.[105] It likened the unexpected and overwhelming arrival of the popular sectors to a high tide flowing onto streets, factories, stores, and government institutions.[106] "Alluvion" also connoted a process of historical sedimentation: the popular sectors had settled for decades at the bottom of the social pond, out of sight, waiting to come to the surface. From a sympathetic perspective, the journalist and writer Raúl Scalabrini Ortiz applied another geological metaphor to describe the public emergence of the unnoticed popular sectors: "It was the subsoil of the country coming to the surface. It was the very foundation of the Nation that emerged, just as ancient earth emerges in the commotion of an earthquake."[107]

Among anti-Peronists these sectors, ignored by those in power and thus filled with disillusion and distrust, had been preparing their masterly entry on the scene with resentment, the most dangerous of feelings. Present in the media during the electoral campaign of 1946, this idea was fully articulated after Perón's overthrow by the writer Ernesto Sábato, who explained the emergence of Peronism as the "history of the resentful and the disbelievers." Sábato expressed the distress of the upper and middle classes upon realizing that the formerly marginalized would turn rancor into revenge soon after taking power. This realization awakened feelings of remorse, but even more powerfully it led to anxieties and prejudice.[108] For anti-Peronists, Evita was the ultimate example of this story of bitterness and retaliation.[109] A child born out of wedlock—the most famous, orthodox, anti-Peronist version goes—Evita attempted to escape poverty by leaving her small home town and pursuing a mediocre acting career in Buenos Aires, a time of humiliation and failure. A life of suffering and embarrassment fired Evita's hatred of the rich, especially the aristocratic women with whom she waged duels fueled by contempt and snubbing.[110]

Finally, "zoological alluvion" portrayed the popular sectors as both caged racial inferiors and mindless, uneducated creatures driven by their primary needs, basic instincts, and predatory appetites. Animalization differentiates adversaries from ordinary people and removes them from the moral community. In one cartoon, above a caption that reads, "You just smile, I'll hold you up," a small absentminded chimpanzee—an animal characterized by its clownish and unruly behavior—carries, like a beast of burden, a voluminous and smiling Perón over his shoulders while the two hold hands. Committed to the arduous task of supporting the figure from below, the undersized, dehumanized (social) base is subservient and secondary to Perón's leading role.[111] The socialist cartoonist José Antonio Ginzo, known as Tristán, stereotyped the Peronist as a shirted, robotic pig—a symbol of filthiness and gluttony—with a hollow head. A pig wearing a wristwatch, with a money box as its head and a wind-up key with the monetary symbol stuck in his back, revealed an enduring assumption among socialists that the working classes had sold their freedom in exchange for material benefits. On the flagpole the shirt was replaced by a slip, an emasculating version of the Peronist shirt and flag but also a subtle depiction of the popular classes' gratitude toward Evita and her predominance over Perón in commanding their loyalty.[112]

Cartoons also implicitly addressed the social consequences behind the public emergence of the Peronist popular sectors. In the anti-Peronist *Cascabel* an elephant painted with inscriptions such as "Hurrah!" and "Die!" and peculiar, lascivious eyes chases a panicky, well-dressed woman while two men in suit and tie comment: "This policy of letting the animals loose on Florida St. is getting a bit heavy." The inscriptions on the elephant suggest that this is a Peronist campaigner, while its weight and size evoke a crowd. The witness's use of the word "heavy" refers both to the animal's weight and to how dangerous the streets were becoming with the presence of "the animals." The metaphor of an elephant running free in a traditionally fashionable commercial street of Buenos Aires suggests the complete geographical misplacement, cultural awkwardness, and social ineptness of the Peronist crowd. The female victim reveals the anxieties about sexual propriety and women's safety and respectability when groups of rowdy men have taken control of the streets. These groups were represented as a menace to upper-class masculinity as well. In the cartoon the men do not intervene to defend the woman. Instead they merely make their comments from across the street.[113]

For anti-Peronists animalistic representations contributed to a resilient stereotype of the Peronist cabecita as ignorant and uneducated, also present in the infamous *"Alpargatas*, yes! Books, no!" This stereotype took forms that ranged from stressing his illiteracy—in sarcastic visual representations where he writes graffiti with spelling mistakes or "reads" a newspaper while holding it upside down—to condemning his inappropriate manners in public.[114] Among anti-Peronists ignorance and lack of education functioned as an automatic disqualification of the Peronists' ability to make adequate choices, while expressing the elite's suspicion that the popular classes were not entirely able to exercise political rights.[115]

Anti-Peronists always mocked and ridiculed their opponents but rarely parodied themselves. In contrast, Peronists scorned their adversaries but also caricatured themselves by using the same features that anti-Peronists employed to scoff at them, especially in humorous contexts. The Peronist magazine *Descamisada* offers an excellent example. Its section "Letters from a *descamisado*" is a hilarious mockery of anti-Peronists. Written by Juan Fabriquero, it is a note to the magazine's editor full of spelling mistakes, incoherent phrases, colloquialisms, and invented words. In a typical phrase Juan tells of infiltrating the opposition by traveling in the train used in its campaign: "We had a whoopin' time in the train, what's with eatin' and drinkin' to our heart's content and even some 'champ-pain,' which I drunk for the very first time!" By embracing the same stereotypical characters that the opposition ridiculed, *Descamisada* turned these figures against their creators. Juan Fabriquero was endowed with enough intelligence and wit to make fun of his opponents while offering revealing readings of current events. For example, he noticed how the oppositional press belittled the Peronists and exalted the Unión Democrática by the way they characterized them: "Youth groups be the big boys out yellin' Long live the union! But the big boys be the young ones shoutin' Long live . . . you-know-who."[116]

The rudeness and vulgarity of the zoological alluvion were less alarming as behavioral problems than as signs of the collapse of the social hierarchical system. What made uncouthness an unprecedented threat to the social order was that the offender was perceived as a social inferior. What made it even more alarming was that the wrongdoings went well beyond the fortuitous, unplanned, and almost impersonal misconduct of groups of the lower classes that took advantage of opportunity and anonymity. The most disturbing offense was the systematic, intentional, and face-to-face disrespect of the social class that was expected to serve and behave deferentially. The Radical congressman Reynaldo Pastor argued: "In the deepest depths of Peronism, arrogance, vulgarity and overconfidence extended the same way an oil stain spreads across a marble shelf. A wave of misconduct and brutality covered even the most remote locations of the country, with no respect for moral and no chance to stop it. Field hands, maids, delivery boys, taxi drivers, streetcar guards, telephone operators, government employees and shop and industry employees in both large and small cities acted with unheard-of haughtiness and insolence; their language was uncouth, their gestures awkward, unfriendly and arrogant."[117]

Customers and passengers became a group "humiliated, jeered, demeaned, begging instead of ordering, smiling at those who had always smiled at them."[118] Waiters as well as streetcar, bus, and train conductors —socially perceived as the quintessential male cabecitas—especially attracted public attention for recurring episodes of vulgarity and rudeness frequently denounced by the media. The newspaper *El Mundo* complained of the unpleasantness of eating in a restaurant: "There is no way to get the waiter to respond to our requests. He moves from table to table, pretending not to hear or see us. If we raise our voices too high, he will return to insult us."[119] Several newspapers launched a campaign against the rude misconduct of transit conductors, who were accused of using vulgar language, yelling at passengers, addressing them as *vos* (you) instead of the formal *usted*, and bothering and flirting with women.[120]

For some critics structural reasons such as full employment and increasing consumer demand were partial explanations for the coarseness of employees who were tired of crowds of demanding patrons and knew they would easily find a new job in the unlikely case they were fired for responding rudely. More visceral anti-Peronist arguments echoed Ernesto Sábato's contention that Peronists were a resentful and vindictive mass. In these interpretations mistreatment of the middle- and upper-class public and aggression toward it revealed the workers' longed-for revenge against snobbish patrons for real and imagined offenses. The class politics behind the condemnation of popular misbehavior became evident in arguments that stressed how the government was fervently controlling, persecuting, and incarcerating merchants, store owners, and industrialists for charging high prices while the employees abused the public with impunity in "moral" rather than economic ways. Peronism, anti-Peronists affirmed, ultimately provided the political context in which rude misbehavior was socially accepted and went unpunished.[121]

While industrialization, urbanization, and migration started a few years before Perón's government, the reaction against the social subjects associated with them and against their consequences became especially manifest during Peronism. This was the result of the impressive increase in the number of internal migrants arriving in the cities and consequently gaining higher visibility during the years when Perón held power. Most significantly, it is connected to the tendency of anti-Peronists to view the

Peronist government as the planner and promoter of the socioeconomic structural changes that transformed mid-twentieth-century Argentina and threatened the privileges historically enjoyed by the middle and upper classes. Peronism came to be seen as an advocate of the newly incorporated social sectors and as their channel for acquiring social and political benefits. The Peronist government, for its part, proudly recognized the inexorability of the transformation it was leading. Official propaganda confirmed the success of the "New Argentina" with statistics that showed impressive levels of urbanization and industrialization and a high standard of living. This is why anti-Peronists stereotyped internal migrants as Peronist cabecitas—in spite of their actual political affiliation—and identified Peronism with these social sectors. For anti-Peronists the cabecitas incarnated a new political system based on empowerment of the labor unions and a form of politics embodied in a charismatic leader who charmed lower-class people with grandiloquent promises. Prejudice against internal migrants was born of an anti-Peronist sentiment that identified cabecitas as Perón's supporters. In this regard stereotyping was a weapon in the struggle against Peronism, since it attacked the legitimacy of the government by condemning the character of its constituency.

However, the disruptive nature of migrants extended well beyond the political realm of the divide between Peronists and anti-Peronists. Whether or not they were perceived as Perón's followers, migrants embodied a process of transformation that changed the rhythms and appearance of the principal cities, redefined social manners and codes of urban civility, broke with traditional standards of deference and respect, and liberalized norms of appropriateness and taste. Frequently voiced as symptoms of conflict between contrasting political groups, stereotypes ultimately exposed anxieties and concerns about a process of social, economic, and cultural change. Internal migrants to the cities became the expression of a society that was increasingly metropolitan, massive, industrial, democratic, and consumerist. For the urban upper and middle classes, the rural worker of indigenous features whom they viewed as vulgar, impertinent, and enjoying what urban life had to offer seriously challenged the legendary image of an entirely white, urban, modern, socially exclusive, and Europeanist Argentina epitomized in Buenos Aires and other major cities. Accordingly, stereotyping became a mechanism to cope with the perceived threat of disruption to safety, well-being, exclusivity, deference, and prestige as well as to the set of norms and behaviors that protected these values.

NOTES

For their useful comments, my thanks go to César Seveso, Daniel James, Jeffrey Gould, Peter Guardino, Konstantin Dierks, Arlene Díaz, Donna Guy, Matt Karush, Oscar Chamosa, and the anonymous reviewers.

1 Moffat, *Estrategias para sobrevivir en Buenos Aires*, 13.

2 Torrado, *Estructura social de la Argentina*, 86.

3 Germani, "El surgimiento del peronismo," 452.

4 Germani, "El surgimiento del peronismo"; Smith, "The Social Base of Peronism"; Tulio Halperín Donghi, "Algunas observaciones sobre Germani, el surgimiento del peronismo y los migrantes internos," *Desarrollo Económico* 14, no. 56 (1975), 765–81; Murmis and Portantiero, *Estudios sobre los orígenes del peronismo*.

5 Moffat, *Estrategias para sobrevivir en Buenos Aires*; Margulis, *Migración y marginalidad en la sociedad argentina*; Ratier, *El cabecita negra*; Mafud, *Argentina desde adentro*.

6 Sander L. Gilman, *Difference and Pathology: Stereotypes of Sexuality, Race and Madness* (Ithaca: Cornell University Press, 1985), 15–35; Michael Pickering, *Stereotyping: The Politics of Representation* (New York: Palgrave, 2001), 1–46.

7 Throughout the chapter I use *cabecita negra* to refer to the stereotype, not to name the subject.

8 Spinelli, *Los vencedores vencidos*; Sebastiani, *Los antiperonistas en la Argentina peronista*.

9 Roberto Arrazola, *Diccionario de modismos argentinos* (Buenos Aires: Colombia, 1943); José Gobello, *Diccionario Lunfardo* (Buenos Aires: A. Peña Lillo, 1975).

10 Other names were *payuca* and *yuca*, the name of a vegetable that grows underground as the root of a plant cultivated in the northeast of Argentina, and *20 y 20*, the price that the popular sectors paid for a glass of red wine and for a record of the popular singer Antonio Tormo. Mafud, *Sociología del peronismo*, 63; Goldar, *Buenos Aires*, 168.

11 "Los cabecitas negras," *El Laborista*, 27 October 1948, 11.

12 "Impresiones sobre el 17 de octubre del historiador José María Rosa," *El 17 de octubre de 1945*, ed. Michelini, 93; Ernesto Sábato, *El otro rostro del peronismo* (Buenos Aires: López, 1956), 41.

13 Ratier, *El cabecita negra*, 81. On racial and social stereotyping in present Argentina see Margulis and Urresti, *La segregación negada*; Grimson and Jelin, eds., *Migraciones regionales hacia la Argentina*.

14 Imaz, *La clase alta de Buenos Aires*, 53–55; Ezequiel Martínez Estrada, *¿Qué es esto? Catilinaria* (Buenos Aires: Lautaro, 1956), 277.

15 Gobello, *Diccionario Lunfardo*, 100.

16 Reynaldo Pastor, *Frente al totalitarismo peronista* (Buenos Aires: Bases), 117; "Los descamisados," *Propósitos*, 3 November 1955, 1; "Primero los llamaron trabajadores, más tarde 'descamisados' y muy recientemente, 'grasas,'" *El Socialista*, 11 January 1949, 1.

17 Indigenous people from northwest Argentina.

18 Ratier, *El cabecita negra*, 47–48; Aboy, *Viviendas para el pueblo*, 123–36.

19 "Los cabecitas negras," *El Laborista*, 27 October 1948, 11; "Ingenio barato," *Fortaleza*, 28 October 1949, 3.

20 Rodolfo Taboada, "Turismo al centro," *Rico Tipo*, 31 July 1947, 12.

21 "Buenos Aires se provincializa," *Continente*, 15 October 1947, 154.

22 "La verdad sobre el café," *Continente*, 15 November 1947, 29; "Buenos Aires, 1952: La Avenida de Mayo," *El Hogar*, 9 March 1952, 22; "Buenos Aires, 1952: Una calle cualquiera," *El Hogar*, 18 July 1952, 78–79.

23 Sebreli, *Buenos Aires*, 102.

24 Plotkin, *Mañana es San Perón*, 31–32; James, "October 17th and 18th, 1945," 456.

25 "Las manifestaciones del General Farrell y del Coronel Perón desde la Casa de Gobierno," *La Prensa*, 18 October 1945, 7.

26 Carlos Morales Salazar, *Cuatro años de justicialismo observados por el periodista chileno Carlos Morales Salazar* (N.p.: N.p., 1953), 149.

27 *Plebe* (plebeian people) insultingly refers to people of the lower social classes and frequently stresses their coarseness.

28 *Chusma* (lit. the lowly ones) was originally used to refer to groups of women, the elderly, and children of the indigenous population, that is, those who did not participate in war. In its most frequent use it is an offensive term to designate the lower classes and to especially emphasize their vulgarity.

29 Martínez Estrada, *¿Qué es esto?*, 28; Américo Ghioldi, *La Argentina tiene miedo* (Montevideo: La Vanguardia, 1954), 39–47; "El método del 17 y 18 de octubre," *La Vanguardia*, 6 August 1946, 1.

30 Torre and Pastoriza, "La democratización del bienestar," 262.

31 Taboada, "Turismo al centro," 12.

32 *Revista de Estadística Municipal de la Ciudad de Buenos Aires* vol. 48, nos. 1–3 (January–March 1935), 108, vol. 53, nos. 628–30 (January–March 1940),

99–101, vol. 60, no. 670 (January–March 1947), 76; "Cuando se divierte el pueblo," *Mundo Peronista*, 15 December 1953, 39.

33 Margulis, *Migración y marginalidad en la sociedad argentina*, 78, 127.

34 "Cuando se divierte el pueblo," *Mundo Peronista*, 15 December 1953, 39; "Un privilegio de algunos que ahora es de cualquiera," *Mundo Peronista*, 15 January 1954, 26–30.

35 "La ciudad se ahoga en el centro," *Continente*, 15 May 1947, 182.

36 "La noche del sábado," *Rico Tipo*, 23 August 1945, 4–5.

37 "Vivienda y Transporte en Argentina," *Nuevas Bases*, 15 July 1950, 6; "Desastrosa situación del transporte," *Nuevas Bases*, 15 November 1950, 7; "Las tarifas y el servicio ferroviario," *Nuevas Bases*, January 1955, 2.

38 "Éxodo provinciano a la capital," *Aquí Está*, 12 January 1948, 6–7; "No dejeis el campo," *Vea y Lea*, 13 November 1947, 4.

39 "Planteos y soluciones para un gran problema nacional," *Nuevas Bases*, 5 August 1952, 1.

40 "De cada cinco habitantes que tiene el país, uno vive en la capital," *Mundo Argentino*, 14 November 1945, 5.

41 Interview with Teobaldo Altamiranda, 12 December 2001, Memoria Abierta Archives, Buenos Aires, interview 155A.

42 Torre and Pastoriza, "La democratización del bienestar," 301.

43 On popular tourism during Peronism see Scarzanella, "El ocio peronista"; Pastoriza, ed., *Las puertas al mar*.

44 "Mar del Plata: moderna Babilonia del verano," *Caras y Caretas*, February 1953, 83.

45 "Carta de un costumbrista a Bermudez," *La Prensa*, 15 March 1947, 9.

46 "Democracia y dictadura . . . o estamos todos locos," *Descamisada*, 22 January 1946, no page.

47 "Un privilegio de algunos que ahora es de cualquiera," *Mundo Peronista*, 15 January 1954, 26.

48 Angel Perelman, *Como hicimos el 17 de octubre* (Buenos Aires: Coyoacán, 1961), 77.

49 On dress and identity construction see Joanne Finkelstein, *The Fashioned Self* (Philadelphia: Temple University Press, 1991); Fred Davis, *Fashion, Culture, and Identity* (Chicago: University of Chicago Press, 1992). For a seminal interpretation see Georg Simmel, "Fashion" (1904), *American Journal of Sociology* 62, no. 6 (1957), 541–58.

50 "¡Viva la alpargata!," *Unión Ferroviaria*, January 1946, 1; "Reivindicación de la alpargata," *La Hora*, 26 November 1945, 4.

51 "La auténtica clase trabajadora," *El Mundo*, 26 October 1945, 4; "Hubo

manifestaciones en La Plata y diversos puntos de Buenos Aires," *La Prensa*, 18 October 1945, 7.

52 Anonymous pamphlet, Hoover Institution Archives, Argentine Subject Collection, box 3, file 4.

53 "Impresiones sobre el 17 de octubre del historiador José María Rosa," *El 17 de octubre de 1945*, ed. Michelini, 93; "Los 'galeritas' son racistas . . . ," *Descamisada*, 10 April 1946, no page.

54 *Descamisado* was initially used in the title of an anarchist newspaper published in the late nineteenth century. "El tango de la candidatura," *La Vanguardia*, 23 October 1945, 8; Félix Luna, *El 45* (Buenos Aires: Jorge Alvarez, 1969), 513; "Las patas en la fuente," *El 17 de octubre de 1945*, ed. Santiago Senén González and Gabriel Lerman (Buenos Aires: Lumiere, 2005), 279.

55 On the use of *descamisada* to refer to women see Eva Perón, *Discursos completos, 1946–1948*, vol. 1 (Buenos Aires: Piscis, 2004), 73. On visual representations of the *descamisado* by the Peronist government see Marcela Gené, *Un mundo feliz: imágenes de los trabajadores en el primer peronismo, 1946–1955* (Buenos Aires: FCE, 2005), 65–83. On the descamisado as a symbol of Peronism see Pittelli and Somoza Rodríguez, "Peronismo."

56 Juan Pérez, *Radiografías de una dictadura (por Argentino Cantinflas)* (Buenos Aires: La Vanguardia, 1946), 32; Eduardo Colom, *El 17 de octubre: la revolución de los descamisados* (Buenos Aires: La Época, 1946), 87; Luna, *El 45*, 513.

57 "El Partido Laborista realizó ayer un mitin inaugural de su campaña," *La Prensa*, 15 December 1945, 7.

58 "El Colegio de Abogados protesta por un agravio a la bandera argentina," *La Prensa*, 18 December 1945, 9; "Se juntaron lo muchacho . . . ," *Cascabel*, 19 February 1946, 5.

59 "La bandera y la camisa," *La Época*, 3 January 1946, 8.

60 "Los descamisados reclamamos el derecho a andar sin saco por las calles de la ciudad," *La Época*, 18 January 1948, 5.

61 Arnaldo Cortesi, "Portrait of a Rabble-Rouser," *New York Times Magazine*, 3 February 1946, 8.

62 James, "October 17th and 18th, 1945," 450; Martínez Estrada, *¿Qué es esto?*, 28, 34.

63 "Plan estratégico del Coronel Perón," *La Vanguardia*, 23 October 1945, 3.

64 Colom, *El 17 de octubre*, 87; "Impresiones sobre el 17 de octubre del historiador José María Rosa," *El 17 de octubre de 1945*, ed. Michelini, 93; Raúl Scalabrini Ortiz, *Los ferrocarriles deben ser del pueblo argentino* (Buenos Aires: Reconquista, 1946), 60.

65 Santiago Nudelman, *El radicalismo al servicio de la libertad* (Buenos Aires:

Jus, 1947), 252; "Proletarios y descamisados," *La Vanguardia*, 11 March 1947, 8; Martínez Estrada, *¿Qué es esto?*, 27–37. Interestingly, lumpen originally means "rags" and has been used to refer to "people in rags."

66 Anonymous pamphlet (poem), Hoover Institution Archives, Argentine Subject Collection, box 3, file 4.

67 "Las patas en la fuente," *El 17 de octubre de 1945*, ed. Senén González and Lerman, 279.

68 "El obrero tiene en la Argentina comida barata y buenos jornales," *Democracia*, April 9, 1947, 5.

69 "Postales estadísticas," *Mundo Peronista*, 15 September 1953, 2.

70 "Salúdelo," *Democracia*, 23 May 1946, 8.

71 "Nuestro hogar obrero," *Democracia* (Rosario), 25 January 1954, 2, 1.

72 "Las pieles," *Argentina*, 1 June 1949, 56.

73 *Rico Tipo*, 11 April 1946, 16.

74 Interview with Violeta Benvenuto, Rosario, 5 December 2005.

75 Alfredo Poviña, "Concepto de clase media y su proyección argentina," *La clase media en Argentina y Uruguay: materiales para el estudio de la clase media en América Latina*, ed. Theo Crevenna (Washington: Unión Panamericana, 1950), 68–75, 73.

76 María Gallia, *Trabajar con amor: manual de instrucción para mujeres del servicio doméstico* (Buenos Aires: Difusión, 1943), 114–15.

77 Jorge Newton, *Clase Media: el dilema de cinco millones de argentinos* (Buenos Aires: Municipalidad de Buenos Aires, 1949), 33.

78 "El nuevo oligarca," *Fortaleza*, 21 December 1949, 2.

79 Moffat, *Estrategias para sobrevivir en Buenos Aires*, 50.

80 "La raya del pantalón," *El Mundo*, 10 October 1945, 6; "Contrapeso de chiquizuela," *El Mundo*, 24 October 1945, 4.

81 Goldar, *Buenos Aires*, 50–60.

82 "Modas," *Rico Tipo*, 30 January 1947, 3; "Sastres," *Rico Tipo*, 13 May 1948, 3.

83 "Ingenio barato," *Fortaleza*, 28 October 1949, 3; James, "October 17th and 18th, 1945," 451.

84 Mafud, *Argentina desde adentro*, 183.

85 Saulquín, *Historia de la moda argentina*, 149.

86 Goldar, *Buenos Aires*, 49.

87 "Carta de un costumbrista a Bermudez," *La Prensa*, 15 March 1947, 9.

88 "Apuntes porteños," *Rosalinda*, May 1950, 42.

89 Thorstein Veblen, *The Theory of the Leisure Class* (New York: Macmillan, 1899).

90 Gené, *Un mundo feliz*; Torre and Pastoriza, "La democratización del bienestar."

91 "Claudicación de las 'elites,'" *El Mundo*, 1 April 1948, 4.

92 "Claudicación de las 'elites,'" *El Mundo*, 1 April 1948, 4.

93 "Cuando los ricos gastaban . . . ," *Orientación: Modas y Mundo Social*, March 1946, 56.

94 "Falta de civilidad intolerable," *La Nación*, 6 March 1948, 4.

95 "Buenos Aires se defenderá de la ola de incultura que afecta su prestigio," *Noticias Gráficas*, 3 January 1949, 13; Eduardo Elena, "Justice and Comfort: Peronist Political Culture and the Search for a New Argentina, 1930–1955" (Ph.D. diss., Princeton University, 2002), 170–221.

96 Enrique Mosca, *Unión, democracia y libertad* (Buenos Aires: Juan Perrotti, 1946), 48.

97 "La Mesa Directiva de la Unión Cívica Radical formuló una declaración," *La Prensa*, 30 October 1945, 10.

98 "Dirigió un manifiesto a los trabajadores un organismo político," *La Prensa*, 25 October 1945, 11.

99 *Cascabel*, 12 February 1946, 6.

100 Luna, *El 45*, 380.

101 "Mal año para las patotas," *Aquí Está*, 23 January 1951, 2–3; "Represión de la incultura callejera," *Crónica* (Rosario), 28 August 1952, 2; Pedro Casazza, *El patotero y la ley de profilaxis social* (Buenos Aires: N.p., 1952).

102 "La delincuencia actual es el triste resultado de 12 años de demagogia," *El Gorila*, 13 December 1956, 4.

103 "No confundamos barras con patotas," *Aquí Está*, 19 February 1950, 12–13.

104 "Falta de civilidad intolerable," *La Nación*, 6 March 1948, 4.

105 Ernesto Sanmartino, *La verdad sobre la situación argentina* (Montevideo: N.p., 1951), 152.

106 Francisco Sanchez Jauregui, *El desaliento argentino* (Buenos Aires: Jorge Alvarez, 1968), 27.

107 Scalabrini Ortiz, *Los ferrocarriles deben ser del pueblo argentino*, 61.

108 Sábato, *El otro rostro del peronismo*, 11–19.

109 Sanmartino, *La verdad sobre la situación argentina*, 138–39; Mary Main, *The Woman with the Whip* (Garden City, N.Y.: Doubleday, 1952).

110 On Eva Perón see Fraser and Navarro, *Evita*.

111 *Cascabel*, 19 February 1946, 16.

112 Tristán, *150 caricaturas* (Buenos Aires: Gure, 1955), 84. On humor and violence see Anton Blok, *Honour and Violence* (Cambridge: Polity, 2001), 29.

113 *Cascabel*, 3 September 1946, 2.

114 *Cascabel*, 12 February 1946, 6; Bernardo Rabinovitz, *Lo que no se dijo, 1943–1956* (Buenos Aires: Gure, 1956), 62.

115 Caruso, "El año que vivimos en peligro. Izquierda, pedagogía, y política," 91.

116 "Al tren no la pasamo mal porque morfe y chupi hay en forma y chanpán, que al fín probe," "Jumentud son lo muchachone que gritan viva la unidad, y muchachone la jumentud que grita viva el que te dije," "Cartas de un descamisado," *Descamisada*, 30 January 1946, no page.

117 Pastor, *Frente al totalitarismo peronista*, 119.

118 "Cuestión de proponérselo," *El Mundo*, 7 April 1948, 4.

119 "Cuestión de proponérselo," *El Mundo*, 7 April 1948, 4.

120 "La población desea que alcance a los guardas atrevidos la campaña contra la guaranguería," *El Líder*, 25 January 1950, 4; "Buenos Aires se defenderá de la ola de incultura que afecta su prestigio," *Noticias Gráficas*, 3 January 1949, 13.

121 "Cuestión de proponérselo," *El Mundo*, 7 April 1948, 4.

Diana Lenton

. . . .

Translated by Beatrice D. Gurwitz

THE *MALÓN DE LA PAZ* OF 1946

Indigenous *Descamisados* at the Dawn of Peronism

Peronism did not generate a particular policy to address the needs of Argentina's indigenous peoples. Instead, under Peronist rule indigenous policy was the result of the broader extension of social justice and civic rights to previously marginalized groups. Peronist discourse did praise the pre-Hispanic "ethnic elements" of descamisados and cabecitas, but this rhetorical vindication of indigenous roots did not accompany efforts to address the specific needs of the contemporary indigenous population. As I have argued elsewhere, any improvements that the indigenous communities experienced under Peronism were the result of general social and labor reforms and not of policies specifically designed for the indigenous population.[1] Nevertheless, the Peronist period today holds a prominent place in the collective memory of indigenous communities.[2] The years of Perón's rule are remembered as a foundational moment in indigenous people's transformation from "pariahs" to "citizens" as well as the period during which these groups began to mobilize politically in defense of their interests.

The "Malón de la Paz" (Raid for Peace) of 1946, also known as the Caravan for Peace,[3] occupies a special place in this collective memory as the first social movement for indigenous rights in Argentina. Moreover, the expropriation of latifundia in the Northern provinces of Jujuy and Salta after 1949 is celebrated as a reaction to the Malón of Peace three years earlier.[4] But while this narrative has become dominant within indigenous collective memory, the origins of the Malón, and especially its bitter ending, continue to provoke discussion and debate among scholars.[5]

Members of the Malón de la Paz marching on the outskirts of Buenos Aires, August 1946.
COURTESY OF ARCHIVO GENERAL DE LA NACIÓN (ARGENTINA).

Members of the Malón de la Paz entering Buenos Aires, August 1946. COURTESY OF
ARCHIVO GENERAL DE LA NACIÓN (ARGENTINA).

Members of the Malón de la Paz meet members of the National Congress, Buenos Aires, August 1946. COURTESY OF ARCHIVO GENERAL DE LA NACIÓN (ARGENTINA).

Members of the Malón de la Paz stand in line outside the Hotel de Inmigrantes, Buenos Aires, August 1946. COURTESY OF ARCHIVO GENERAL DE LA NACIÓN (ARGENTINA).

In this chapter I contextualize the Malón of Peace within the ethnic and demographic politics of Peronism to offer some hypotheses that would explain the discrepancy between collective memory and scholarly accounts. Unlike other scholars, I contend that during the period of Peronist hegemony the indigenous communities were not the object of novel measures nor the agents of any major changes.[6] Instead, the relationship between the Peronist government and indigenous communities developed within the new framework of relations between the state and "civil society," or in Peronist discourse the "pueblo."[7] One component of this new framework was the assumption by the state of certain aspects of Latin American indigenism, a movement initiated in the 1920s and canonized at the Congreso Indigenista Interamericano held in Pátzcuaro, Mexico, in 1940. Considering the ideological stance of Perón and his followers, it was no accident that the Peronist government should have preferred the style of indigenism associated with the Cárdenas government in Mexico to the Marxist version elaborated by the Peruvian intellectual José Carlos Mariátegui.[8] Given the regime's use of indigenism within its larger state-building project, the Malón of Peace must be analyzed as one aspect of the Peronist effort to establish a new "governmentality," to borrow Michel Foucault's concept.[9]

Academic accounts of the indigenous experience under Peronism have typically relied on the written press and on President Perón's speeches. Only very recently have studies begun to focus on the indigenous movement's participants and to analyze earlier incidences of indigenous militancy as important precedents.[10] This chapter explores these earlier episodes and the subjectivities of those involved, as well as the tensions that arose between Peronist efforts to create a hegemonic understanding of indigeneity and the agency that the indigenous people themselves exercised at the dawn of the Peronist era.

WELFARE STATE AND POLICIES OF INCLUSION

Hegemonic state practices not only justify strategies of domination and control over populations but also fundamentally prescribe the kinds of demands that minority groups are able to make.[11] The tendency to assign to certain political expressions a "cultural" character, thereby encouraging certain identities and forms of collective mobilization while neutralizing others, is a recurring feature of Latin American processes of negotiation between collective subjects in asymmetrical power relationships. As other chapters of this book have suggested, Peronism was a political rupture, characterized in part by the simultaneous "explosion" of popular culture and the rising hegemony of the mass media. Peronism always presented itself as a complete rupture from the past, emphasizing the novel relationships that it had facilitated within and between the classes, and depending on the context, between different ethnic groups as well. This self-presentation is apparent in the Constitutional Reform of 1949: the new "Justicialist Constitution" was the first Argentine constitution to explicitly denounce racial discrimination. The Law of Constitutional Reform, approved by the High Council of the Peronist Party in 1949, clearly disavowed article 67–15 of the National Constitution of 1853, which had stipulated that the National Congress would "provide security of the frontiers, maintain peaceful trade with the Indians and seek their conversion to Catholicism" for the sake of "providing security on the frontiers." Peronist leaders argued that the reference to peaceful trade with the Indians and their conversion to Catholicism "were anachronistic . . . because it is *prohibited to establish racial distinctions, and class distinctions, among the inhabitants of the nation.*"[12]

The Argentine constitutional reform of 1949 incorporated some of the ideas that had already been assimilated by European social constitutionalism and that had been incorporated into the Universal Declaration of Human Rights of 1948 and invoked at the IX Inter-American Conference of Bogotá that same year. Peronism also expanded the notion of rights to include the rights of workers, the elderly, and the family, as well as the right to education and to culture. It emphasized the "social function of property, capital, and economic activity" and the preeminence of "the common good and social welfare over private profit.[13] These collective rights were expressed so as to define the groups that deserved the state's protection. For indigenous people Peronism adopted a policy that I will call "protected incorporation."

PERONIST INDIGENISM IN GOVERNMENT AGENCIES

Under the military government of 1943–46 (which preceded Perón's rise to the presidency) the National Congress was dissolved, and the executive branch offered only a few decrees to regulate the agendas and internal organization of the agencies in charge of indigenous affairs, as well as their place within the structure of the state. While these decrees did establish indigenous peoples as a clear subject of state policy, they did not give any specific content to this policy. Still, the decrees did declare emphatically that relations between the state and indigenous people should reflect the norms applied to all citizens.

Along these lines, when the military government created the Secretariat of Labor and Welfare in 1943 it incorporated into it the Honorary Commission of Indian Reservations (Reducciones de Indios) among other agencies.[14] This initiative was an important effort to institutionalize the "indigenous problem." In synthesizing the "indigenous problem" with the "labor and social problem," the reorganization was the culmination of a process under way since the beginning of the century.[15] But while health and hygiene concerns had motivated attempts to unify indigenous and labor policy at the beginning of the century, the motivation behind the internal reorganization of 1943 was political centralization. It should be noted that Coronel Perón was the first secretary of labor, and thus also responsible for indigenous policy under the military government.

Another presidential decree under the military government created the Department of Aboriginal Protection within the General Department of Social Security—itself part of the Secretariat of Labor and Social Security—to replace the Honorary Commission of Indian Reservations.[16] As president, Perón created the National Department of Migrations, placing the Department of Aboriginal Protection under its auspices along with the National Ethnic Institute, the Argentine Delegation of Immigration in Europe, the General Department of Migrations, and the Commission for Reception and Channeling of Immigrants.[17] While the church supported the concentration of all these offices under the direct supervision of the president, the opposition repeatedly denounced it, distrusting the racial policy of the government.[18]

The creation of a single National Department of Migrations to oversee migration, ethnic policy, and indigenous policy occurred during a moment when many *democratic* states—France, Belgium, Switzerland— were also demonstrating explicit concern for the ethnic composition of their nations.[19] The concern for ethnicity in Argentina as well as in these European countries reveals a rupture in the perception of the national population. Republican definitions of the citizen—according to which ethnicity is invisible, given the presumption of state neutrality—were no longer deemed sufficient. Cultural aspects, including identity, performance, and loyalties, now became significant for both authoritarian and democratic regimes, which increasingly had a similar governmentality.[20]

The decision to move oversight of indigenous policy from the direct purview of the Secretariat of Labor and Social Security to the National Department of Migrations (which was itself subordinated to this secretariat) reflected the effort to centralize Peronist policymaking regarding the population's subgroups (both immigrant groups and indigenous ones). The names of the institutions under the National Department of Migrations reveal contrasting attitudes toward indigenous people and immigrants: the aborigine must be "protected," while the immigrant must be "channeled," suggesting that the aborigine was a vulnerable piece of the nation's heritage while the immigrant was a renewable resource that could be administered strategically.

The Argentine state bureaucracy's explicit attention to policies relating to these subgroups was expressed not only in Perón's speeches as the secretary of labor and social security and, after 1947, in support of his government's "Five-year Plans," but also in the creation of the National Ethnic Institute (IEN) as an agency especially dedicated to ethnological studies. This institute, a subsection of the Ministry of the Interior, was created in 1946 to replace the National Ethnographic Office, which President Farrell had created by decree a few months earlier and placed under the control of the General Department of Migrations. The movement of the IEN between different governmental agencies reflected a growing perception of the problematic legitimacy of state intervention in selecting immigrants and in determining the composition of the native population.[21]

Despite Peronism's attempt to maintain its centralized control over ethnic policy, both Peronist and opposition legislators in Congress continued to propose various state agencies to address the indigenous problem, indicating that the state was unable to establish a single credible agency from which to extend "social justice" to the indigenous population. Beyond these parliamentary initiatives, the executive branch would continue to promote greater intervention in the policies relating to particular groups, suggesting that traditional disciplinary methods were no longer sufficient to guarantee social peace. What was required was a greater concentration on what Foucault called "biopolitics." Biopolitics, characteristic of modern governmentality, involves the use of numerous technologies for the control of diverse populations.[22] Within Peronist biopolitics, culture would be a central factor.

In 1945 the military government had adopted some symbolic measures toward the indigenous population. For example, following the recommendation of the Pátzcuaro Congress of five years earlier, the government established 19 April as the Day of the Indian.[23] In this way the Argentine government adopted, at least symbolically, the new pan-American approach to the indigenous question. It mandated commemoration of the Day of the Indian in schools, an advance over the government's existing commemorative policy.[24]

On a more practical level, the Peronist government provided indigenous people with national identity cards, a measure that implicitly recognized their right to vote. Some indigenous people remember the time when they were first allowed to obtain these documents—the same ones carried by non-indigenous citizens—as the moment when they were elevated to the status of full, dignified members of the national community. In the words of some indigenous families, by making them eligible for the cards, "Perón *made us people*."[25]

More generally, Peronist discourse emphasized the erasure of differences within a collectivity struggling to declare itself homogenous after the decades-long hegemony of racialized representations of society and history. All members of "the organized community," as Perón described it, were considered "equal" by definition; the only exceptions were those who decided to alienate themselves from the community by opposing the Peronist project.[26] The hegemonic discourse thereby sought to establish the homogeneity of the "people," even if there were some Peronists who, while agreeing on the importance of legal equality and the incorporation of indigenous people into the labor force, also saw the validity of ethnic categories.[27]

Peronist indigenous policy aimed at applying social justice, but indigenous demands would only be channeled insofar as the petitioners were previously defined as preferential subjects of Peronist justice. Thus while Peronist discourse shared a rhetoric with the positions of contemporary Latin American indigenism, these ideas were filtered and relativized to adapt them to a political project that granted rights under the assumed homogeneity of *the people.*

A POLITICAL READING OF "THE UNFORTUNATE MALÓN OF PEACE"

In mid-1946 a large group of Kolla people living in the northwestern provinces of Salta and Jujuy marched toward the city of Buenos Aires to demand the return of lands they believed rightly theirs. They also sought the assignment of new officials to lead the Department of Aboriginal Protection because the sitting authorities had not been replaced since Perón's presidential inauguration.[28] Others have described the events of the Malón, and space here does not permit a detailed recounting.[29] Instead, to understand the development and outcome of the Malón, I will highlight its effects in the political arena as well as the challenges that it posed to Peronist indigenous policy.

Land possession in the northwestern provinces was already a prominent political concern before Perón rose to power. In the province of Jujuy the most popular wing of the Radical party, in power throughout the 1920s, sought the subdivision of latifundia and the end of mandatory rents. Though the party continued this struggle from the opposition in the following years, the initiatives never succeeded. Jujuy Radicals often expressed explicit sympathy for the region's indigenous people in their campaign slogans.[30] In Salta meanwhile, the San Andrés Estate and the Santiago Estate had become prime examples of the tensions between indigenous communities and large landowners. The Patrón Costas family controlled both estates, and the family's best-known member, Robustiano Patrón Costas—governor of Salta, national senator, presidential candidate before the military coup of 1943, and local member of Standard Oil—was the most vilified representative of Argentina's conservative elite.

Before Patrón Costas acquired it in 1930, the San Andrés Estate in northwestern Salta belonged to the provincial state, and the nearby Kolla communities enjoyed the use of it, subject only to lax regulations. After the privatization the Kolla communities were forced to pay rents and to pay for the rights to continue cultivating the land. The owners forced them into labor at the San Martín del Tabacal sugar mill, also the property of the Patrón Costas family. The year 1930 brought a major change in labor policies at the sugar refineries of Salta and Jujuy, as the managers began to replace indigenous laborers from the Chaco region with workers from the altiplano.[31] Some sugar mills—particularly San Martín del Tabacal—bought land in heavily populated areas not suitable for sugarcane cultivation, with the goal of coercing the residents into becoming manual laborers dependent on the refinery.[32] Owing to these practices the San Martín del Tabacal mill became a recognized example, along with the Ledesma mill in Jujuy, of the mistreatment of labor—indigenous labor in particular. Moreover, the extreme antisocial nature of the Patrón Costas strategy lent a potent symbolism to the protest initiated by the Kolla.[33]

Meanwhile in Jujuy, Kolla families that had been displaced from their land during the governorship of Benjamín Villafañe in the 1920s began their struggle again.[34] According to Luis Zapiola and Eulogio Frites, on 31 August 1945 a group of "indigenous leaders of la Puna" in Jujuy submitted a written solicitation to the National Agrarian Council (CAN) requesting that land be returned to the aboriginal communities.[35] The CAN lobbied the Secretariat of Labor and Social Security for support and funds to carry out studies regarding the potential expropriation. On 17 January 1946—coinciding with decree 1594, which created the Department of Aboriginal Protection—President Farell ordered the expropriation, but the decree was never executed.

On 15 May 1946 a contingent of indigenous people left the town of Abra Pampa in the department of Cochinoca, Jujuy, passing through Casabindo, Colorados, Tumbaya, Volcán, and Yala. Days later they joined a group of Kollas from Salta who had marched from the San Andrés Estate in Orán and from the Santiago Estate in Iruya, as well as from San Antonio de los Cobres. An oral tradition maintains that there were also people from Amaicha del Valle in Tucumán, although I have not been able to confirm their participation. In all the caravan comprised 174 people, among them 9 women; the youngest of the participants, Narciso López, was eight years old. Kolla collective memory, supported by some contemporary newspaper accounts, describes the enthusiastic reception and solidarity that the caravan received as it passed through different cities.

The first hint that the protest might have national repercussions came at the beginning of August before the caravan even reached Buenos

Aires: in the National Congress legislators struggled to offer "adequate" political interpretations of the caravan, which struck them as both abnormal and foolish. César Guillot, a Peronist deputy from Buenos Aires, suggested that the lower House create a commission to receive "this strange caravan of *our coya [kolla] brothers* [and] to embrace them in a brotherly manner, because they and we, we and they, *are the synthesis of this nation* to which we are all proud to belong."[36] Note that the idea of common belonging does not obscure the fundamental cleavage between "they" and "we." While he described the Kolla as "our brothers," Guillot still called the caravan "strange," using language meant to highlight the picturesque character of the kollas' homeland ("where two chains of mountains open in the mother's womb to amass people of greatness") as well as of the people themselves ("with that bustle so peculiar of the colla . . . In quaint uniformity . . . they come to the beat of a strange orchestra").[37] Even as he distanced the deputies from "them," Guillot attempted to imitate the style of regional folk music, which the folklore movement had generalized and disseminated as performance: "from there in the northern North . . . they come down, señor, they come down . . . at night gazing at the sky señor."[38]

Guillot's use of language to achieve some sort of symbolic union with certain cultural sectors while simultaneously maximizing his distance from them was a contradiction in the aesthetic field, one that foreshadowed what would happen between the representatives and the represented in the political field. In his description of those who participated in the caravan, Guillot revealed the most conventional understanding of indigenous people: "They do not understand juridical principles . . . they have not read anything; but they know that in the beginning of time, by divine mandate, God put their ancestors on the earth to give them a piece of land for them to cultivate. Coming in this way, *they do not want* to see the president of the Republic. They are more simple *in their childlike mentality.* They come to the pyramid on the Plaza de Mayo, because they know that humble monument symbolizes the true sovereignty of the Nation. And standing before the sovereignty of the Nation, they come to ask for the recognition of their ancient lands."[39] Guillot also felt the need to mention that a non-indigenous person was traveling with the caravan: "a strange criollo fellow that, tired of the hum of the metropolis, sought the peacefulness of a primitive environment, and has as his only ideal the recognition of that original race." He was referring to a lieutenant in the Army Corps of Engineers, Mario Augusto Bertonasco, who was participating in the march. Bertonasco's experience with the indigenous communities had begun only two years earlier. In 1944 the Commission of Indian Reservations, under the control of Coronel Perón, had sent Bertonasco to resolve an issue concerning indigenous families who had been evicted from the Mapuche reserve in Boquete Nahuelpan, Chubut. His orders were to "control and thoroughly analyze the ancestry of all of the people who invoked their right to return to the lands . . . thereby avoiding the admittance of foreigners to the reserve."[40] One can assume either that Bertonasco was chosen to represent the national government in Nahuelpan because he was already familiar to Perón, or that the two became familiar over the course of Bertonasco's tenure. In either case the relationship between Perón and Bertonasco leads us to suppose that Bertonasco's involvement in the indigenous movement in 1946 had not been as spontaneous or as innocent as Guillot's speech suggested.

According to an oral tradition from Abra Pampa, it was the "Southerner" Bertonasco's idea to call the indigenous protest a "Malón," a term that carried explicitly warlike symbolism and that would make clear to audiences in Buenos Aires that the protest was indigenous in nature. In contrast, to other participants the caravan was a movement of Argentine citizens, as indicated by the icons of the nation (Argentine flags) and Christianity (saints, crosses, virgins) carried by the protesters.[41] The press noted that Bertonasco "had been in contact with the northern aborigines for fifteen years."[42] But this assertion is contradicted by the oral testimonies of some involved in the beginning of the protest,[43] who claim that the residents of Abra Pampa and Deputy Vivanco had sent for Bertonasco "because he had been with the Mapuches during the expropriation of their land," even though many others distrusted him because he was in the military. In any case, Bertonasco's brief intervention in the former Nahuelpan Reservation as well as his involvement in the Malón of Peace attracted significant public attention. Deputy Guillot's stylized description stripped Bertonasco of his military rank to reveal him as a liminal figure (*a strange fellow*). As the days wore on, this liminality generated growing suspicion among Peronists and the opposition alike.

Legislators from the Radical party adhered to Guillot's proposal for a warm welcome—Guillot in fact had been a Radical before the advent of Peronism. The Radical deputy Nerio Rojas argued that the ceremonial reception should be followed by a legislative commitment to "solving the drama of the *Argentine Indian*." Yrigoyen himself had often emphasized the historical debt owed to indigenous people and the need to repay them through education. Nerio Rojas capitalized on this Radical tradition and reminded his audience that the Argentine state was "in debt to the Indian" for what he "did for the formation of the nationality."[44]

Rojas's speech received such acclaim that Deputy Eduardo Beretta, a Peronist from the province of Buenos Aires, began his own by apologizing for reaching a different conclusion, "precisely due to the profound love that I have for the Indian." He affirmed that despite being familiar with "the Indian problem and how it had been neglected by previous governments," it was necessary to find out "how this caravan is managed, organized, and financed; what the Indians' purpose is, what they have come for, and what they are doing on their trip."[45] Beretta expressed the fear that this was merely an "exhibition of Indians" like others that had occurred in the past, and that the indigenous participants were in reality being exploited. He said that before making a decision, Congress should ascertain whether the "Honorary Commission of Indian Reservations had adopted any measures."[46]

The Chamber of Deputies was divided between the Radical-led opposition, joined by Justicialists like Guillot, who supported a formal reception for the caravan in the name of the struggle against latifundism, and official Peronism, which displayed a certain fear of the unknown. The Peronist deputy from Buenos Aires, José Emilio Visca, for example, shared the reservations of his fellow party member Beretta. Visca recognized the legitimacy of the Kollas' demands as well as those of the Colique tribe in Buenos Aires, but he argued that "these Indians did not need to come in caravan, on foot, suffering what they have suffered; they could have advanced their demands with the help of the public powers, traveling in the Railroads of the State, so that they would be able to arrive in our Capital *like the Argentines they are*."[47] Visca's comment suggests that he resented the refusal of indigenous people to see themselves, like the rest of the Pueblo, as beneficiaries of the state.[48] As a result,

Visca questioned their "true" intentions. Nonetheless, in the end César Guillot's motion was approved, and the president of the chamber created a commission to receive the caravan.[49]

The legislative debates addressed, albeit superficially, the legal owner-ship of the lands the Kollas had occupied, but they did not touch on the rights of the indigenous to elect new authorities at the Department of Aboriginal Protection. The legislators expressed their views on the na-ture of indigenous people as well as the desires and grievances they attributed to them. They did not, however, allow for the possibility that the indigenous might have their own political opinion or vision of politi-cal citizenship; instead the legislators assumed that the protestors were merely expressing their ancient suffering.

The Peronist Guillot was careful to emphasize that it was the state's responsibility to ensure that the Indian obtained what was rightfully his, making clear that the state, rather than indigenous people themselves, must ensure that rights were guaranteed. In this way the state would grant Indians protected incorporation: "The State exercises a right of patronage over the Indian, and when it is necessary to give him some-thing, the state will do it with care—as it has been doing since this patronage began—to ensure that the protection of the Indian is not distorted and so that he obtains, *in his child-like innocence*, that to which he has a right."[50]

The marchers in the caravan, some on foot, others on horseback or in wagons, entered the capital via Liniers on 3 August 1946. They were greeted by the director of aboriginal protection—the very director whom they hoped to replace—and housed in the Immigrants Hotel. A repre-sentative delegation was granted a meeting with a group of congressional legislators. According to some versions of the story they also met with Perón himself.[51] Nonetheless, in reality the conversations with the Casa Rosada (the presidential offices) were not fruitful, and the delegation waited three weeks for an answer to their demands. Meanwhile, "colorful notes" about the activities of the visitors abounded in the Buenos Aires press. Finally, on the morning of 28 August, 174 Kolla citizens housed at the Immigrants Hotel were violently evicted by the Coast Guard and Federal Police and forced onto an express train redirected from its nor-mal route. The provincial police forces received orders to prevent the forced passengers from fleeing in cities along the way. Later the Peronist authorities explained the episode as a the result of simple negligence or a misunderstanding on the part of the officials responsible for protecting the demonstrators. Nonetheless, the coordination between different security forces and the railroad administrators makes clear that the action was planned at a high level of the national government. The participants in the Malón of Peace, with the exception of a few who were able to escape the police raid, were returned by force to their homes in the highlands of Salta and Jujuy without having achieved any of the trip's objectives and humiliated by the harsh government response. The government never offered them an explanation.

A month later an opposition deputy from the capital, Alberto M. Candioti, introduced a project demanding an explanation for the executive's actions surrounding the Malón of Peace.[52] Candioti requested that the government explain why the indigenous citizens were forcibly expelled from the Immigrants Hotel and identify who had given the orders for the expulsion. He also asked for a detailed account of how those orders were carried out. In addition, he demanded a report to Congress on the petitions and demands that the Malón of Peace had presented and how the responsible government agencies carried out their duties. A week later the project was debated on the chamber floor. Defending his point, Candioti criticized the indigenism then popular in official and literary circles, before recounting the events as he had seen them:

> A parliamentary commission was finally named to greet the Collas at the doors of this House . . . There this *carnival troupe* [*comparsa*] was met with great solemnity: the Argentine Parliament, through its representatives, gave large hugs to the one who called himself *cacique* [chief] and also to the impresario of this carnivalesque caravan . . . The *comparsa* continued until the Plaza de Mayo, kneeling down to pray in front of the Column of Liberty. In the balcony of the Casa Rosada stood the president of the Republic, with his ministers and the vice president of the Nation, and the Collas were obliged to kneel in front of the first magistrat . . . After all of these displays, which already reflected so poorly on our national honor, the citizenry awoke one day to the news that the indigenous people had been violently taken from the Immigrants Hotel, where they had been staying. Forced to ride a boxcar, the 170 indigenous people with their 60 domesticated animals and their wagons were returned to their place of origin. What had happened?[53]

Candioti was as indignant over the "exploitation of the ignorance of the Indian," who, lacking instruction in republican dignities, had knelt in front of civil authorities, as he was over the possibility that a white person (the "impresario" Bertonasco) might have attempted to take advantage of it. The unfortunate outcome seemed to validate many people's suspicions regarding the motivations of any white person who would live among Indians.[54]

As Zapiola and Frites establish, the Buenos Aires press accused Bertonasco of political ambitions, pointing particularly to a sealed envelope that the Kollas gave to Perón in which—according to rumors—they asked him to intervene in the Department of Aboriginal Protection.[55] Some concluded that Bertonasco's goal was to become the director of that department. On 30 August, the authors add, Lieutenant Bertonasco sent a telegram to Perón, denying that he was looking for any political post and reaffirming his "struggle on behalf of the indigenous to end their age-old exploitation."

In Congress the majority of Candioti's requests for explanatory reports were approved almost unanimously. The legislators approved the first five requests for information from the National Executive Power, with only a few modifications. The final request, which asked "how the Department of Aboriginal Protection fulfills its mission," was rejected. Those who opposed it argued that the efficacy of the department was not the issue at hand.[56] Some time later Deputy Candioti protested that Perón's government had not responded to the request for "information about the outcome of the *aboriginal* delegation and the list of demands presented by *these criollos of the North* who arrived in the Capital in the so-called *Malón of Peace* . . . The press makes known daily that *the aborigines, the true and authentic descamisados of the North*, find themselves again in the Capital of Republic, going door to door looking for protection, bread, land, and social justice."[57] Candioti asked his colleagues "to invoke the most adequate parliamentary procedure so as to reiterate to the executive power the request for information . . . We want to know who is responsible for the fact that the aborigines came with the dream of insisting on the fulfillment of an electoral promise. Those aborigines are, yes, authentic descamisados, not honorary ones nor props!"[58]

It was true that a small number of Kollas remained in the city. Between three and thirty participants in the "Malón," depending on the source, had managed to avoid deportation and received hospitality in "family homes" and "some Workers unions and railroad workers centers,"[59] enabling them to remain in Buenos Aires for a few months. *La Prensa*, for example, printed a telegram of solidarity with the Malón from the Leather Goods Union.[60]

The dynamics of the Peronist approach to the "pueblo" is the key to understanding the bitter conclusion of the "caravan." The homogenizing and "harmonizing" efforts of justicialism, which sought to unify the nation against the oligarchy, did not tolerate internal dissidence. More important, it refused to permit the visualization of categories or classifications along other lines, and thus rejected the raising of other problematics. The outcome of the Malón of Peace foreshadowed the construction of the nation that would be codified in the Constitution of 1949.[61] Some justicialists expressed enthusiasm regarding the Malón as it approached the city, because they could frame the participants as members of the pueblo—"authentic descamisados"—who struggled against the most antiquated oligarchy, represented by the Patrón Costas family. Within this framework every representative of the pueblo could (and perhaps should) assume the Kollas' demands as their own. "Public opinion," as portrayed in the press, seemed to endorse this understanding of the Kolla and was by extension sympathetic to the caravan.[62]

Following this logic, the government's rejection of the Kollas' demands—expressed forcefully in the protestors' expulsion—might be the result of the failure of the members of the caravan to remain within the limits of their categorization as Perón's workers. In opposing the government's assignment of non-indigenous leaders to the Department of Aboriginal Protection, they reaffirmed their indigenous identity and struck a discordant note in the justicialist project of constructing a unified nation. Their decision not to use the state railroads added another element to their refusal to subordinate themselves to the symbolism of the welfare state. Finally, the participation of a "white person," who was not a priest, separated them from the traditional symbolism of indigenous passivity, thereby locating them in a "dangerous" liminal space.

The declarations of Perón himself to the newspaper *Democracia* on

30 November 1946 signaled his refusal to see the members of the Malón as *authentic* indigenous people:[63] according to Perón, the pilgrims did not represent authentic indigenous aspirations, did not come on foot, were not born in the northern provinces, and so on. The president did not deny that indigenous complaints were real and that Congress should pass a law to address them. What he denied was that those who dared question the state were actually indigenous. In general the discourse of the press and the political class during the conflict stressed the passivity of the indigenous, even those who decided to launch a protest of such size. The "colorful notes" about the "circus-like" exploitation of the caravan seemed to suggest that even the most dedicated indigenous people, those who came to the capital to protest, could be tricked by a marginal *white man*. In these portrayals the distance between self and other is maximized along an axis that runs from the "mentality of children" to intelligent citizenship.

Unsurprisingly, a writ of habeas corpus submitted by Viviano Dionisio to block the Kollas' expulsion received much less attention. Dionisio was a Kolla member of the labor party and provincial deputy for Cochinoca, Jujuy, whose father, Dionisio Vivanco, took part in the caravan. On 30 August 1946 the Supreme Court rejected his appeal on the ground that it "did not have the right to intercede in the case in the first place." That same day, the secretary of labor and social security announced that he had initiated an investigation into what happened.[64] Months later the press and Congress continued referring to the "unfortunate Malón of Peace"[65] as an example and symbol of the limits of social justice.

Despite its immediate outcome, the Kolla mobilization of 1946 increased the visibility of the indigenous question in northwestern Argentina. Moreover, the mobilization has been directly linked to the subsequent promulgation of decrees expropriating and adjudicating lands in the province of Jujuy to be handed over to indigenous communities, as well as the creation of new oversight bodies.[66] In the words of Eulogio Frites: "The Malón of Peace afforded us the victory of recuperating for the community the lands that were expropriated in Jujuy in the year '49."[67]

In the following years many legislative initiatives sought to expand the expropriations and adjudications initiated by the executive branch, proposing in particular their extension to Salta, but these initiatives were unsuccessful. All these projects were framed according to the precepts of "justicialist thought." One legislator noted that the "program of the [current] government" can be summarized "in a few words: the free man and his own land . . . The expropriations that this project speaks of have as a goal giving land to more than 30,000 people in the province of Jujuy, because it belonged to them since antiquity, because of the right of occupation, because of their history, and because of the debt of gratitude that the Argentine Nation owes to the *race* that defended it in the times of independence."[68]

These legal texts do not make explicit reference to "aborigines" but rather to "families of native workers." Nonetheless, the rhetorical images employed in defense of these proposals do invoke indigeneity. The use of these images suggests a form of elliptical discourse that highlights ethnic differences on an informal level to make the matter at hand understandable, even as it erases these subjects, or makes them invisible, in normative, legal texts, in accord with the homogenizing ideal of Peronism.

The return of lands to Kolla communities in northwestern Argentina occurred only after a long struggle and remains incomplete. In Salta the Indigenous Community of the Pueblo Kolla of Santiago Estate (also called Negra Muerta), which includes a population of four thousand indigenous people divided in the "ayllu-communities" of Colanzuli, Volcán Higueras, Isla de Cañas, and Río Cortaderas, would have to wait until 19 March 1997 for the restitution of 125,000 hectares of their land. To achieve this the National Congress passed an expropriation law in 1994. The ceremony at which legal land titles were awarded in late 1999 became a major event for the community; participants included surviving members of the Malón of Peace, such as Buenaventura Yurquina. Elsewhere in Salta the Provincial Legislature expropriated the totality of the San Andrés Estate as early as 1949, but the transfer of lands was not completed at that time. In 1993 the Comunidad Kolla Tinkunaki finally achieved the expropriation by national law of 19,000 hectares of the total 129,000 hectares that constituted their traditional territory. This expropriation is still pending judgment after an appeal lodged by the sugar mill, now owned by the Seabord Corporation. The expropriation is further complicated by the conflict over the Nor Andino gas pipeline which crosses through communal land. In Jujuy in the late 1990s, 24,000 hectares of the Tumbaya estate were expropriated by national law and returned to the Comunidad Aborigen Kolla of Tumbaya Estate.

Beyond the transformations and ambiguities that marked the Malón of Peace as an epitomizing event,[69] the Kolla mobilization certainly did foment a national debate on the lands of indigenous people in northwestern Argentina, even if it did not enable a discussion on the right of those indigenous people to choose the public authorities who would handle their affairs.[70] For the national government the reception of the Malón of Peace was a public legitimation of the principles of justicialist social justice. For elites in the opposition, meanwhile, the Malón revealed the limitations of the government's ideology and the spuriousness of its leader. The opposition press chose to dwell on this theme, promoting a mythic portrayal of the exploitation of the protestors: as one newspaper put it, "The episode of the Coyas reveals the farce of the so-called social justice of Peronism."[71]

Nevertheless, the militants in contemporary Kolla organizations still remember the achievement of some of the caravan's goals—the expropriations in Jujuy in the years immediately following the Malón and the immediate end to mandatory rents—as important if partial victories, and the story has acquired an epic quality over time. It is clear that the Malón of Peace functions as an "origin myth" for certain contemporary indigenous militants. The caravan to Buenos Aires has become an indigenous October 17. Instead of demanding the physical return of Perón, the members of the caravan demanded that the leader live up to his own ideology and discourse. By comparing the caravan to the massive, urban demonstration of October 17, 1945, this version of the story breaks with the dominant view of indigenous agency, inserting the Kollas directly into the history of the nation and revealing their strategic capacity to confront a fluid and complex political conjuncture.

The selective indigenous tradition portrays the caravan of 1946 in epic terms. By doing so the narrative affords the Malón a privileged place in the construction of the subjectivities of native people in northwestern Argentina, while devaluing previous and subsequent mobilizations. In effect many militants of urban Kolla organizations today construct the trajectory of their struggles from a "zero point" located in the social movement of 1946, though their perception of that moment is mediated and influenced by the realignment of identities during the rise of militant political indigenous organizations in the 1970s[72] and by the pan-indigenous tendencies of the 1980s and 1990s. This affirmation of identity, which involves the active and selective use of the past, is even deployed by organizations—especially the Indigenous Association of the Argentine Republic (AIRA)—that claim to represent all native peoples living within the national territory, not just the Kolla.

The construction of the Malón of Peace as the only important moment of Kolla militancy is reinforced by a western view that ignores or negates the capacity of natives to make demands, to protest, and to mobilize autonomously.[73] The excessive attention that the press and the political world paid to the white officer who supported the protest reflects this tendency to downplay indigenous agency. This prejudice has now been reproduced in scholarly works. The indigenous people's own understanding of this moment as foundational to Kolla indigenous identity dovetails with the western understanding of the event, with both contributing to the belief that the Malón of Peace was the "first and only" large Kolla protest. This misapprehension has been particularly powerful because of the timing of the Malón, which occurred just as the inextricable bond between the Peronist phenomenon and the mass media was being formed.

NOTES

1 Diana Lenton, "De centauros a protegidos: la construcción del sujeto de la política indigenista argentina a través de los debates parlamentarios entre 1880 y 1970" (Ph.D. diss., University of Buenos Aires, 2005).

2 See Walter Delrio, "Mecanismos de tribalización en la Patagonia: desde la gran crisis al primer gobierno peronista," *Memoria Americana*, Instituto de Ciencias Antropológicas, University of Buenos Aires, 2007.

3 Translator's note: In nineteenth-century Argentina and Chile *malón* referred to the sporadic raids of Mapuche warriors against the frontier settlements. The naming of the movement Malón de la Paz (Raid for Peace; 1946) was intended to be oxymoronic—juxtaposing the word "peace" with the word "raid" and its warlike connotations.

4 The terms "Indian," "Indigene," "Aborigine," and "native" are ambiguously defined ethnonyms that are used interchangeably to describe the relationship between a national society that considers itself ethnically defined and those communities or individuals recognized as the descendents of the

groups who inhabited the territory before colonization. While each of these terms has different connotations, the choice of one or the other has more to do with the preference of the speaker and the context. During the period studied here the term "aborigine" was gradually replacing "indigenous" and "Indian" in Argentine public discourse.

5 See Andrés Serbín, "Las organizaciones indígenas en la Argentina," *América Indígena* 41, no. 3 (1981), 407–33; Tesler, *Los aborígenes durante el peronismo y los gobiernos militares*; Carrasco, "Hegemonía y políticas indigenistas argentinas en el Chaco centro-occidental"; Luis Zapiola and Eulogio Frites, "El Malón de la Paz: el pueblo Kolla de pie," *Boletín Pueblos Indigenas: Por los Derechos Indígenas* (2001).

6 See for example Martínez Sarasola, *Nuestros paisanos los indios*.

7 Acha, "Sociedad civil y sociedad política durante el primer peronismo."

8 Alexander Dawson, "From Models for the Nation to Model Citizens: Indigenismo and the 'Revindication' of the Mexican Indian, 1920–40," *Journal of Latin American Studies* 30, no. 2 (1998); Lenton, "De centauros a protegidos," 94. While Argentina did not send a representative to this Congress, it was a signatory at its precursor, the Eighth American International Congress held in Lima in 1938. The conference of 1940 was originally scheduled for 1939 in La Paz, Bolivia. Nonetheless, at the insistence of President Lázaro Cárdenas of Mexico, it was delayed for one year and ultimately held in Pátzcuaro. This conference led to the creation of the Inter-American Indigenous Institute in Mexico. It is possible that Argentina did not participate in the Pátzcuaro conference because it mistrusted Cárdenas's role.

9 The analysis of governmentality focuses not on the law but on the truth regimes in which the law arises and endures. Michel Foucault, "Governmentality," *The Foucault Effect: Studies in Governmentality*, ed. G. Burchell, C. Gordon, and P. Miller (Chicago: University of Chicago Press, 1991), 73–86. In the Foucauldian perspective the state as an institution or system of institutions is a function of government practices and not vice versa. See Briones, "Formaciones de alteridad."

10 There are a few brief references to the reconstruction of communal memory regarding the Malón of Peace in the classic films of Jorge Preloán, *Hermógenes Cayo* (1969), and Miguel Mirra, *Hombres de Barro* (1988). See also Adriana Kindgard, "Tradición y conflicto social en los Andes argentinos: Primeras Jornadas Provinciales de Educación Intercultural en San Salvador de Jujuy, 24 and 25, October 2002: en torno al Malón de la Paz de 1946," *Estudios Interdisciplinarios de America Latina y el Caribe,* 15, no. 1 (2004), 165–85; Marcelo Valko's recent book, *Los indios invisibles del Malón de la Paz*; and the documentary work initiated by Instituto Interdisciplinario Tilcara of the

Universidad de Buenos Aires through its Programa Institucional de Investigación y Transferencia, "Memorias de la opresión"; Belli, Slavutsky, and Rueda, eds., *Malón de la Paz.*

11 Briones *La alteridad del Cuarto Mundo*; Étienne Balibar, "The Nation Form: History and Ideology," *Race, Nation, Class. Ambiguous Identities*, ed. Étienne Balibar and Immanuel Wallerstein (New York: Verso, 1991), 86–106.

12 Peronist Party, *Anteproyecto de Reforma de la Constitución Nacional: aprobado por el Consejo Superior del Partido Peronista el día 6 de enero de 1949* (Buenos Aires: Edición del Partido Peronista, 1949) (emphasis mine).

13 Peronist Party, *Anteproyecto de Reforma de la Constitución Nacional.*

14 Founded in 1912 by President Roque Sáenz Peña to articulate the administration and state control over indigenous reserves, colonies, and religious missions in the National Territories and some provinces, this commission was especially recognized in the north of the country as the authorized interlocutor during the first decades of the twentieth century, although it never attained the influence it was intended to have. See Lenton, "De centauros a protegidos."

15 Lenton, "De centauros a protegidos."

16 Department of Parliamentary Information [D.I.P.], *Tratamiento de la cuestión indígena* (Buenos Aires: Honorable Cámara de Diputados de la Nación, 1991), 174.

17 Department of Parliamentary Information [D.I.P.], *Tratamiento de la cuestión indígena*, 175.

18 See for example Daily Sessions of the House of Deputies of the Congress of the Nation, 1947 Period, March 7, 1947, session; 1954 Period, September 24, 1954, session.

19 A few years earlier Alexander M. Carr-Saunders argued in *Población mundial* (México City: Fondo de Cultura Económica, 1939 [1936]) that these nations all designed ethnic policies characterized by "statism, elitism, racism, Europeanism." Carr-Saunders emphasized that "authoritarian regimes" —Germany, Italy, Spain—were not alone in their interest in ethnic policies, but rather that this interest was shared by more liberal nations. It is worth remembering Ruth Benedict's pioneering efforts in ethnography, which denounced the social effects of that paradigm. See Ruth Benedict, *Race: Science and Politics* (New York: Viking, 1945).

20 See Ramella, *Una Argentina racista.*

21 An extensive analysis of the role of this institution in the biopolitics of justicialism is discussed in Lazzari, "Antropología en el Estado." See also Senkman, "Etnicidad e inmigración durante el primer peronismo."

22 See for example Michel Foucault, *The History of Sexuality*, vol. 1 (London:

Penguin, 1998), 140. In Argentina José Ingenieros and José M. Ramos Mejía are considered precursors in the biopolitical treatment of diversity.

23 Decree of the National Executive Power 7559 of 9 April 1945.

24 See Jelin and Langland, "Introducción."

25 Claudia Briones, "Qué importa quién gane si nosotros perdemos siempre: los partidos políticos desde la minoría mapuche" (paper presented at the VI Congreso Argentino de Antropología Social, Rosario, July 1990). In the particular case of the community that Briones visited, the indigenous people's ability to obtain national documents occurred as part of the attainment of political citizenship by the inhabitants of Neuquén after the constitutional reform of 1949, which allowed the inhabitants of national territories to elect legislatures and send delegates to the National Congress. An oral tradition recorded more recently in Nam Qom, Formosa, shows a similar evaluation. See Israel Alegre and Timoteo Francia, *Historias nunca contadas* (Buenos Aires: El Tatú, 2001), 91; see also Gastón Gordillo, "The Burden of Citizenship: State Fetishism in the Argentinean Chaco" (paper presented at the Symposium on Formas indígenas de mestizaje, formas mestizas de la indianidad (América, siglos XVI–XXI), Casa de Velázquez, Madrid, 12–13 December 2003).

26 Juan Domingo Perón, *The Organized Community* (Buenos Aires: Club de Lectores, 1954 [1949]).

27 *Diario de Sesiones del Senado*, 1948 Period, 2 June 1948.

28 "Kolla," "Coya," and "Colla" are different spellings of the same popular name that includes all the various groups of native peoples, predominantly Quechua speakers, who in pre-Columbian times inhabited the southernmost province of the Inca empire, known as Kollasuyu.

29 Tesler, *Los aborígenes durante el peronismo y los gobiernos militares*; Zapiola and Frites, "El Malón de la Paz"; Martínez Sarasola, *Nuestros paisanos los indios*; Valko, *Los indios invisibles del Malón de la Paz*.

30 Kindgard, "Tradición y conflicto social en los Andes argentinos"; Lenton, "De centauros a protegidos."

31 Diana Lenton, "Debates parlamentarios y aboriginalidad: cuando la oligarquía perdió una batalla (pero no la guerra)," Papeles de Trabajo, Centro de Estudios Interdisciplinarios en Etnolingüística y Antropología, Universidad Nacional de Rosario y C.I.C.E.A., no. 9 (2001), 7–30.

32 Conti, de Lagos, and Lagos, *Mano de obra indígena en los ingenios de Jujuy a principios de siglo*.

33 Carlos A. León and Carlos A. Rossi have located an early expropriation decree for the Patrón Costas Estate in Salta, which was to be executed by the National Agrarian Council in December 1945. This decree had not been

enforced by the time of the Malón. See León and Rossi, "Aportes para la historia de las instituciones agrarias en la Argentina: el Consejo Agrario Nacional," *Realidad Económica* 198 (2003).

34 Lenton, "De centauros a protegidos."

35 Zapiola and Frites, "El Malón de la Paz."

36 *Diario de Sesiones de la Cámara de Diputados del Congreso Nacional*, 1946 period, 2–3 August 1946.

37 *Diario de Sesiones de la Cámara de Diputados del Congreso Nacional*, 1946 period, 2–3 August 1946.

38 *Diario de Sesiones de la Cámara de Diputados del Congreso Nacional*, 1946 period, 2–3 August 1946. On the folklore movement see Oscar Chamosa's chapter in this volume.

39 *Diario de Sesiones de la Cámara de Diputados del Congreso Nacional*, 1946 period, August 2–3, 1946.

40 Delrio, *Memorias de expropiación.*

41 See Prelorán, *Hermógenes Cayo.*

42 See for example *La Prensa* of Jujuy, 29 May 1946.

43 Documentary material of the Instituto Interdisciplinario Tilcara, "Memorias de la opresión."

44 *Diario de Sesiones de la Cámara de Diputados del Congreso Nacional*, 1946 Period, 2–3 August 1946.

45 *Diario de Sesiones de la Cámara de Diputados del Congreso Nacional*, 1946 Period, 2–3 August 1946.

46 The Honorary Commission of Indian Reservations had actually already been replaced by the Department of Aboriginal Protection by Decree 1594 of 17 January 1946.

47 *Diario de Sesiones de la Cámara de Diputados del Congreso Nacional*, period 1946, 2–3 August 1946.

48 What lent more force to this critique was that the railroads were about to be nationalized—or in other words that Perón was rescuing them for "the pueblo"—through agreements signed with Great Britain and France in September 1946. The "Railroads of the State" were the lines nationalized during Castillo's presidency; they would be renamed the "General Belgrano Railroad."

49 *Diario de Sesiones de la Cámara de Diputados del Congreso Nacional*, 1946 Period, 2–3 August 1946.

50 *Diario de Sesiones de la Cámara de Diputados del Congreso Nacional*, 1946 Period, 2–3 August 1946.

51 Anke F. Schwittay took oral testimony from one of the participants in the march who repeated the words that President Perón offered during this

alleged meeting. Anke F. Shwittay, "From Peasant Favors to Indigenous Rights: The Articulation of an Indigenous Identity and Land Struggle in Northwestern Argentina," *Journal of Latin American Anthropology* 8, no. 3 (2003), 127–54.

52 *Diario de Sesiones de la Cámara de Diputados del Congreso Nacional,* 1946 Period, 9 September 1946.

53 *Diario de Sesiones de la Cámara de Diputados del Congreso Nacional,* 1946 Period, 9 September 1946 (emphasis in original).

54 Briones, *La alteridad del Cuarto Mundo.*

55 Zapiola and Frites, *El Malón de la Paz.*

56 *Diario de Sesiones de la Cámara de Diputados del Congreso Nacional,* 1946 Period, 12–13 September 1946.

57 Emphasis in original.

58 *Diario de Sesiones de la Cámara de Diputados del Congreso Nacional,* 1946 Period, 31 October 1946.

59 *La Prensa,* 31 August 1946.

60 *La Prensa,* 1 September 1946.

61 "It is prohibited to establish racial or any other class of distinctions among the inhabitants of the nation." Peronist Party, *Anteproyecto de Reforma de la Constitución Nacional.*

62 For example, on 22 July 1946 the newspaper *El Laborista* editorialized: "These Indian workers, weak and suffering, come to protest against their *patrón,* against the feudal lord who owns the lives and haciendas of their province. This feudal lord is named Robustiano Patrón Costas and was about to be President of the Republic . . . he occupies the land of the Kollas and evicts the poor Indians from where they have lived for centuries, and no one can say anything about it. He hires them to work in his refinery and pays them what he wants. If they find that the conditions in the refinery are too difficult and they escape before fulfilling their contracts, the private police of Patrón Costas pursue them as if they were big game and they shoot and kill them if it is necessary." Reproduced in Zapiola and Frites, *El Malón de la Paz.*

63 Reproduced in Zapiola and Frites, *El Malón de la Paz.*

64 *La Prensa,* 1 September 1946.

65 Speech of Deputy Manuel Sarmiento, *Diario de Sesiones de la Cámara de Diputados del Congreso Nacional,* 1946 Period, 28–29 November.

66 Carrasco and Briones, *La tierra que nos quitaron.*

67 Mirra, *Hombres de Barro.*

68 *Diario de Sesiones de la Cámara de Diputados del Congreso Nacional,* 1946 Period, 4 September 1946.

69 Briones, *La alteridad del Cuarto Mundo,* 108.

70 For a brief period in 1953 the leadership of the Department of Aboriginal Protection was given—without an election—to Jerónimo Maliqueo, a Mapuche leader.

71 *La Provincia*, September 1946.

72 The choice of the Malón of Peace as a point of departure for the story of indigenous political struggle is made most frequently by indigenous organizations that were created—or that grew out of organizations created—in the 1970s, during the third Peronist government and on the eve of the military coup of 1976.

73 In recent years commemorations of the Malón of Peace have become more common, although they often fail to contextualize the movement. In 2006 the sixtieth anniversary of the Malón, another large Kolla mobilization to demand territory and resources, this time with a different normative framework and supported by other native groups, was named the "Second Malón of Peace."

Oscar Chamosa

....

CRIOLLO AND PERONIST

The Argentine Folklore Movement during the First Peronism, 1943–1955

The history of Peronism cannot be isolated from the cultural and racial divide that separated the children of nineteenth-century European immigrants from Argentine *mestizos,* more commonly called *criollos.* Rural workers, many of whom were criollos, represented a key constituency of the Peronist movement.[1] They were also purveyors of local cultures with indigenous, Spanish, and in some cases African roots that contrasted with the cosmopolitan urban culture of Argentina.[2] As thousands of rural Argentines moved to the metropolitan area of Buenos Aires and other coastal cities during the first government of Perón, upper- and middle-class Argentines resented the new arrivals, calling them *cabecitas negras* (little blackheads), a term that referred to their dark skin and hair but also, as Natalia Milanesio discusses in chapter 2, had cultural, class, and political implications.[3] It is little known, though, that the social and demographic transformations of the Peronist period coincided with a cultural phenomenon that tended to emphasize the cultural legacy of the criollos and, interestingly, received support from both the Perón government and the elites who resisted him. As more and more criollos from the interior moved to the cities, their music, dances, and poetic lore became objects of study at all three levels of education, and objects of cultural consumption through the electronic and print media.

While this criollo folklore movement began many years before 1945, the Peronist government embraced it on a scale that surpassed the previous Radical and Conservative governments (1917–43). Those governments did advance folklore research projects, but Perón's administration made folklore research and promotion a matter of state policy. The first five-year plan, issued in 1947, quotes Perón's assertion that "only with the cultivation of traditions will the nation be preserved,"[4] and folklore occupied a prominent place in the government's cultural policies.[5] The plan recommends action to preserve oral poetry, dances, and music from the countryside and the design of programs to educate all citizens about the criollo traditions through school lessons, festivals, and radio broadcasts. Similar provisions were included in the second Five-Year Plan of 1953. As a result of Peronist folklore policies, a generation of Argentines grew up learning that the culture of the rural criollo from the interior constituted the authentic manifestation of Argentine nationality. That was not a minor legacy.

Peronist folklore policy implied a challenge to the historical representation of Argentina as a white nation. In much of Latin America, from the early twentieth century elites promoted an idea of nationhood based on the alleged mixture of races and culture that characterize the Latin American mestizo.[6] Though the discourse of *mestizaje* was eminently assimilationist, it failed to recognize the individuality of indigenous cultures or foster social and economic development for traditionally underprivileged, dark-skinned citizens.[7] In Argentina a different, yet equally skewed assimilationist myth asserted that there were no ethnic or racial differences within the Argentine nation and that Argentines were homogenously white. This discourse is what the historian Mónica Quijada and others call the myth of the white nation.[8]

After the passage of the constitution in 1853, successive Argentine governments worked hard to strengthen economic, cultural, and demographic ties with Europe. Half a century later, and after almost four million European immigrants had populated the thinly settled pampas, a proud Argentine elite judged the experiment successful and rushed to declare Argentina "the only white country of Latin America," ignoring the existence of dark-skinned, non-European Argentines.[9] From the architecture of public and private buildings to the busy opera season in Teatro Colón, porteños demonstrated that their hearts lay in Europe. School curricula tied the history of the country to the "westward advance" of western civilization and taught children to look down on the indigenous and criollo legacy.[10] As a result, before Perón rose to power two generations of Argentines of immigrant descent had learned to view themselves as part of the European diaspora, an isolated white outpost on the South American continent.

All this changed during the Peronist government. In this chapter I argue that the vindication of criollo culture was consistent with other policies aimed at improving the lifestyle of the working class, criollo or otherwise, and at securing its loyalty to Peronism. While the celebration of criollo folk culture during Peronism certainly did not put an end to the myth of a white Argentina—in part because of the internal contradictions of the Peronist folklore program—it did represent an important alternative to the hegemonic representation of Argentine ethnicity.

I also argue that criollo folklore was one aspect of Peronism that transcended the sharp political and social divide of mid-twentieth-century Argentina and was embraced by sectors of the urban middle class and even national elites. Folklore may have had cross-class appeal because the attention that the Peronist government gave to it was not a complete break with the past. The folklore movement partially derived from a nineteenth-century literary movement called criollismo that celebrated, and sometimes mimicked, the culture of the legendary gauchos of the pampas.[11] It also built on the program of the so-called Generation of the Centenary, which first raised the romantic idea that the soul of the Argentine nation laid in the deep interior.[12] Finally, Peronist officials drew on the mass of folklore resources generated during the Conservative government of the 1930s. Thanks to these intellectual antecedents, Peronist folklore policy was able to address a sector of the population beyond the regime's primarily working-class constituency.

Peronist officials actively sought to expand the popularity of criollo folklore beyond the circles of nationalist intellectuals. Therefore the state promoted folk music on the radio, in schools, and at festivals. While private radio stations began broadcasting criollo music regularly in the late 1930s, in 1943 the military government's secretary of telecommunications, Colonel Aníbal Imbert (one of Perón's allies), mandated the radio programming of folk music.[13] The Peronist government continued the military regime's cultural policies and tightened official controls over broadcasting content.

Simultaneously, folk music as popular entertainment experienced an extraordinary expansion during this period. The public responded positively, as indicated by the increasing number of professional folk musicians, public interest in their art, and the explosive proliferation of peñas—social clubs and academies where members met to listen and dance to live folk music. Sales of folk music records became a profitable business for the first time in the history of the Argentine recording industry, with some musicians such as Antonio Tormo of San Juan achieving sales figures comparable to those of the most popular tango orchestras. The folklore movement gathered momentum at the end of Perón's government in the mid 1950s and remained popular until the mid-1960s.

Study of the folklore policies of Peronism affords a means of exploring how perceptions of ethnicity and culture changed in Argentina during the momentous years of the mid-twentieth century. It also offers an opportunity to evaluate the cultural policies of Peronism that transcended the construction of partisan loyalty. The Peronist propaganda machine skillfully used the mass media, school curricula, and street demonstrations to secure a loyal following and promote a cult of personality around the figures of the presidential couple. The different mechanisms of cooptation devised by the Peronist state have received ample and justified attention from recent historiography, including contributors to this volume.[14] Most works focus on practices that helped to create a longstanding cleavage between Peronists and anti-Peronists, one that characterized Argentine society for the next four decades. In this chapter I propose to discuss an aspect of Peronist cultural policy that did not pursue short-term partisan goals but rather attempted (with some success) to create a permanent place for criollo culture as the official symbol of the nation.

The novel treatment of criollo folklore by the Peronist government had its share of complexities and ambiguities. Perón seemed to adhere to a *hispanista* definition of criollo culture that overemphasized the colonial Spanish influence and understated or ignored the strong indigenous and African legacies. On the other hand, both Juan and Eva Perón mostly avoided using ethnic language when addressing members of the working class. As the historian Daniel James points out, they addressed workers as a social class and emphasized the economic gains that Peronism offered them.[15] This was a rational strategy for a new movement that tried to build a class alliance and attract a maximum of votes both from the descendants of immigrants and from criollos. However, as Milanesio shows, Peronist leaders also embraced the racialized epithet of *cabecita negra* that the urban middle class hurled against their followers. The novelty of Peronist ethnic policies was not so much that it openly defied the myth of the white Argentina as that it aimed to extend to criollos the new political and social rights gained by the working class during the Peronist administration. Yet even if Peronism did not refute the myth of white Argentina, the promotion of criollo folklore as the authentic national culture was a clear step toward dignifying dark-skinned workers from the interior.

ANTECEDENTS OF THE FOLKLORE MOVEMENT

As mentioned above, Peronist folklore policies were successful because the folklore movement drew from a well-established literary and academic discourse that celebrated criollo culture as the foundation of Argentine nationality. Both criollismo and the Generation of the Centenary contributed to generate a current of sympathy toward the criollo, but the Conservative folklore research project based in Tucumán Province during the 1930s was the immediate antecedent and most important influence on official Peronist policies. At the same time, before Perón came to power criollo folk music from the interior developed as a commercially viable genre that reached diverse audiences through live performances, radio shows, and records. I will briefly describe the rise of the folklore movement in the 1930s, both in its academic and its popular culture dimensions.

The earliest precedent of the folklore movement was the Criollista movement that began with the publication of *Martín Fierro* in 1872 and peaked at the turn of the nineteenth century with the popular criollo dramas performed in circuses and small-town theaters. Together with Martín Fierro, fictional gaucho heroes such as Santos Vega and Juan Moreira embodied a romantic view of the cattle frontier beyond Buenos Aires, where mestizo ranch hands, bandits, and bards hopelessly resisted the encroachment of progress. Literary critics have understood this movement as an intellectual search for a national identity amid rapid demographic change, a search that achieved enormous popularity across regions and class.[16] By 1910 a new group of authors—known in the history of Argentine literature as "the generation of the centenary"— further developed the nativist impulses of criollismo. Armed with more sophisticated intellectual tools, writers such as Joaquín V. González, Ricardo Rojas, and Leopoldo Lugones reinforced the discursive contradiction between the soulless and spurious Argentina of Buenos Aires and the authentic one, located in the far interior, and constituted by the beliefs and practices of the rural criollo.

The basic concepts of the generation of the centenary also influenced a group of writers whose work typifies what is referred to as "realist regionalism."[17] The gaucho of criollista literature was a classic folk hero whose life and mores belonged to the past, not an active citizen of the modern Argentine nation. While criollista authors expressed nostalgia for bygone gaucho ways—allegedly wiped out by the wave of prosaic European immigrants—they remained curiously indifferent to the fate of the contemporary rural populations of criollo descent. In the regions of the Northwest, the Northeast, Chaco, and Cuyo most criollos were small farmers rather than the horse-riding ranch hands symbolized by the gaucho type. The same farmers, together with indigenous migrants from Chaco and Bolivia, provided seasonal labor for the sugarcane, yerba mate, cotton, and grape harvests, enduring conditions altogether different from those of the legendary riders of the pampas. Similarly, other criollos and indigenous workers found employment in the mines of the Andean highlands or the logging camps of the Chaco and Misiones forests. Regionalist authors such as Juan Carlos Dávalos and Mateo Booz looked at the lives of those other criollos from beyond the fringes of the more developed *pampa húmeda* (the eastern pampas), where indigenous culture still loomed large.

In fact the criollos of Cuyo, the Northwest, and the Northeast represented a wide range of local cultures quite different from that of the pampas' gauchos. The Northwest, including the provinces of Jujuy, Salta, Tucumán, Catamarca, and Santiago del Estero, bore a strong influence from the central Andes and Chaco indigenous cultures. This region was itself very diverse. The Andean indigenous influence was more noticeable in the arid plateau of Puna and the high valleys of Humahuaca and Calchaquí. There some communities alternated between preserving their indigenous roots and adopting the criollo identity. In the lower and more fertile lands, Argentina's sugar country, Spanish colonial rule left visible marks in architecture, language, and music, but the majority of the population was criollo, with a strong Andean background. Toward the region's eastern fringes the dry forest offered refuge for the remnants of the once numerous Chaco indigenous cultures. In Cuyo, which includes the provinces of Mendoza, San Juan, La Rioja, and San Luis, criollo culture was similar to that of the northwestern lowlands, but the influence of Chile's central valley was noticeable in vocabulary and musical style. Finally, the criollo culture of the Northeast, including the provinces of Corrientes and Misiones, and to a lesser extent Chaco and Formosa, reflected the combined background of the Guaraní, the Jesuit missions, and the recent Eastern European migrations.

Though these regional criollo cultures received little attention from the gaucho eulogists based in Buenos Aires, the metropolitan press and progressive politicians often brought attention to the miserable conditions of the rural workers of the interior. Between 1910 and 1930 the sugar industry of the Northwest became known to the urban public as the bastion of archaic labor practices such as debt peonage and corporal punishment. The sugar industrialists not only denied allegations that these practices persisted but also mounted a sophisticated public relations campaign to counteract the negative press. As part of this campaign they sponsored a plan of folkloric research among rural criollos throughout the Northwest. The sugar mill owners attempted to demonstrate that their industry was not only attuned to the needs of rural criollos but also working toward preserving authentic Argentine folk culture. Corporate propagandists argued that the sugar industry was an example of true patriotism and ought to be protected against unionization and government interference.[18]

The Tucumán sugar mill owner and veteran conservative politician Ernesto Padilla steered the Asociación Azucarera (Sugar Producers Association) to pay special attention to promoting the folklore of the Northwest as an indirect way to bolster public support for the embattled business. Between the late 1920s and early 1940s, with the financial and political support of the sugar industrialists, the folklorist Juan Alfonso Carrizo assembled a collection of oral poetry from all the provinces of the Northwest, with special attention to Tucumán. The musicologists Carlos Vega and Isabel Aretz, also sponsored by the sugar industrialists, followed Carrizo's footsteps across the Northwest, recording scores of local criollo musicians. These three scholars and their students managed to construct a monumental record of criollo folklore and established the folkloric canon of Argentina for many years to come. At the same time, again because of pressure from sugar industrialists, the conservative governments of the 1930s incorporated folklore into the public school curricula, using the works of Carrizo, Vega, and Aretz as textbooks. This educational program made knowledge of criollo music and dances such as the *zamba* and *chacarera* widespread (and mandatory) among urban Argentine school children, a majority of them descendants of European immigrants, if not immigrants themselves.

Through his published work Carrizo publicized among the Argentine educated class his conviction that northwestern criollo society was the richest and most authentic Argentine folk culture. He also stressed that the main historical source of criollo folk culture was the oral tradition of "golden age" Spain (mid-sixteenth to mid-seventeenth century). Carrizo further insisted that the criollo of the Tucumán, Salta, Jujuy, Santiago del Estero, and Catamarca were direct descendants of the conquistadors and retained little of the Andean indigenous culture that preceded them. Many right-wing Argentine intellectuals, who identified themselves as Catholic and hispanistas (i.e. sympathizers with Spain, Francisco Franco's governing style, and traditional culture), may have found compelling Carrizos's theory of the Spanish roots of criollo culture. This theory offered them an alternative version of the myth of white Argentina to compete with the "cosmopolitan" white Argentina, which they viewed as bowing to Anglo-Saxon culture. Some prominent right-wing Nationalist and Axis sympathizers such as Gustavo Martínez Zuviría and Alberto Baldrich attained positions of control within the public education system under the military government of 1943 (in which Perón served as secretary of labor, and later as vice-president and minister of defense) and helped to reinforce criollo folklore education following the line of Carrizo and his colleagues.

Yet the criollo folklore movement was far from being a spinoff of the Argentine fascists' agenda. The movement attracted quite different interest groups from across a diverse ideological spectrum. The sugar mill owner Padilla was more an old-school conservative than a fascist. Members of the Padilla group distrusted the pro-Axis right-wingers on many accounts, especially on their understanding of Argentine history. Another group that played a crucial role in popularizing folklore was media businessmen, who are best classified as liberals in the North American sense. This group included the radio owners Antonio Devoto and Jaime Yankelevich, and the entertainment magazine editors Julio Korn and

Emilio Kartulovicz. Finally, there were prominent folk artists such as Héctor Chavero (better known by his stage name Atahualpa Yupanqui). Yupanqui was a left-wing activist who used his superb artistic skills to increase awareness of the plight of the criollo workers of the interior.

The radio networks together with the public schools were the main proponents of the folklore movement. Like the schools, the radio networks (Yankelevich's Radio Belgrano inaugurated its national network in 1938) played a crucial role in unifying popular culture across the different provincial and regional enclaves. The nationwide reach of stations in Buenos Aires had the effect of nationalizing the popular culture of the capital, epitomized in the music and lyrics of the tango. But at the same time the stations made an effort to "federalize" radio programming by including programs dedicated to criollo folk music. At the beginning of the 1940s stations in Buenos Aires broadcast for the entire country the live performances of a small but highly qualified group of musicians from the Northwest and Cuyo. Regular performers included Carlos Montbrun Ocampo from Mendoza, Andrés Chazarreta from Santiago del Estero, and Marta de los Ríos and Atahualpa Yupanqui from Tucumán. The variety of folk styles diversified the radio offerings previously monopolized by tango and foreign rhythms, and helped to develop a sense of shared culture.

Folklore concerts were intended to combine entertainment with education. Performers explained the meaning of themes and local context, many times interpolating personal anecdotes obtained in their own interaction with local folk musicians. Atahualpa Yupanqui excelled in recollecting the experience acquired from years of traveling across the Argentine interior. However, his storytelling transcended the colorful anecdote. His lyrics in particular spoke of the travails of the criollo in the cane fields, mines, and logging camps.[19] In ideological terms his lyrics were clearly left-leaning, but rather than being partisan or even overtly revolutionary they were essentially humanist. The revolution that Yupanqui sought was supposed to restore the dignity of the work of the rural criollo. This theme resonated with wider audiences, even among those who had no connection to the interior, in part because urban public opinion attributed the poor conditions of the countryside during and after the Depression to the interference of foreign capital.

This likely explains the popularity of Yupanqui's "El arriero" (The Cattle Driver), which includes the chorus:

Las penas son de nosotros,	We own the sorrows,
las vaquitas son ajenas.	[but] strangers own the cows.

Yupanqui later denied that this stanza was conceived as political commentary.[20]

This song, as well as many other compositions by Yupanqui and his colleagues Chazarreta and Montbrun Ocampo, competed in popularity with tango, raising awareness of the cultural traditions of Cuyo and the Northwest, and, in the case of Yupanqui, of the living and working conditions of the rural criollo.

During the 1930s and early 1940s folklore research and commercial folk music, different but related phenomena, consolidated their positions in the academy and the entertainment business. They also consolidated the symbolic ascension of the rural criollo from the interior to the position of archetypical Argentine, a move that had been prepared by the literatures of criollismo, the generation of the centenary, and realist regionalism. Academic research created a vast archival base that documented the culture of the rural criollo, while folksongs popularized that culture among varied audiences. After 1943 this process was further consolidated by the military government that gave Perón and his allies control of the central national state. In this government right-wing Catholic nationalists maintained control of key offices from which they exercised lasting influence over the education and cultural apparatus. The team of academic folklorists protected by Tucumán's sugar barons formed part of this group and seized the opportunity to institutionalize their discipline. At the same time, in the field of popular culture production, telecommunication officials intervened to curb media cosmopolitanism and nationalize broadcasting contents. Yupanqui and many other folk musicians of high quality obtained secure contracts with the radio networks. The military officers shared with other groups the belief that government sponsorship of criollo folklore could help unify the diverse population of the country. In this sense the short-lived military regime of 1943–45 represented a crucial ally for those who saw in criollo folklore a means to reformulate the Argentine nationality. As the Peronist movement emerged from this military government and continued most of its cultural policies, the folklore movement gathered momentum.

CRIOLLO FOLKLORE UNDER PERONIST RULE

After taking power in April 1946 the Peronist government followed many of the policies laid out by previous governments regarding folklore. However, these policies acquired a different meaning in the context of the labor and social reforms inaugurated by Perón. Conservative provincial elites celebrated criollo culture to counteract progressive cosmopolitanism, reinforce traditional values, and garner support for the economic activities they controlled. Peronism shared some of these tenets. Bolstering Catholicism and Hispanismo were after all important goals among the cultural authorities in the first Peronist government. The key difference between the Peronists and the Conservatives was that the celebration of criollo folklore under Perón accompanied sweeping reforms such as unionization of sugar and wine workers, as well as the regulation of rural day labor, that empowered the rural criollo, at least in the realm of public perceptions. Furthermore, I argue that the Peronist embrace of criollo folklore can be understood as a significant revision of the official discourse on Argentine ethnicity. Yet this challenge to the myth of white Argentina had several contradictions and pitfalls.

The new role inhabited by the working class during the era of Juan and Eva Perón marked a turning point in the nation-building process. This transformation, while mostly expressed in terms of class, contained an ethnic element, something that many scholars of Peronism have noted but few have studied in detail. In this volume Natalia Milanesio shows that race and class stereotypes coincided to shape urban middle-class anti-Peronist discourse. From the point of view of the Porteño elite, dark-skinned urban immigrants, industrial workers, and Peronist followers composed an undifferentiated whole that threatened the established urban way of life. As Milanesio also argues, the Peronist movement responded to this stereotyping by embracing the association between Peronist followers and the dark-skinned criollo.

This new attitude is clearly documented in the graphic propaganda produced by the government. Several photographs show Eva and to a lesser extent Juan Perón fraternizing with dark-skinned Argentines. A black-and-white photo shows Perón and Evita holding a little girl in their arms. Perón, in sport shirt and slacks, cheerfully addresses the girl while Evita, in dotted shirt and white beret, looks at the camera with a cheeky grin. The girl, aloof and uncomfortable, probably unaware of the magnitude of the event, is a wide-eyed little criolla. Another photograph shows Evita surrounded by more than a dozen miners in their heavy overalls and security helmets. Evita, in an elegant tweed jacket, stands slightly off-center while the miners crowd around her with apparent familiarity, some stretching their necks over the First Lady's shoulders, others crouching in front of her, facing the camera. The conjunction creates the appearance of a circle of helmeted heads out of which the figure of Evita emerges beaming. All of the miners look like northwestern criollos, perhaps from the copper mines of San Antonio de los Cobres in Salta or the iron mines of Abra Pampa in Jujuy.

In dozens of similar pictures a glowing Eva smiles at, hold hands with, and kisses old ladies, children, workers, and the sick, most of them dark-skinned criollos. The photogaphs are clearly staged for propaganda purposes, but that should not be equated with hypocrisy. Nicholas Frazer and Maryza Navarro, together with Eva's other biographers, argue that Eva performed with real passion her role as a "bridge between Perón and the workers."[21] Among the daily bevy of indigents who paraded before her desk, Eva did not seem to see race but rather poverty and exclusion. When she addressed the poor with affectionate terms such as "*mis grasitas*"—"my greasers"—she was not patronizing or feigning, but reaching out to those bogged down where she had been only a few years before. When Eva presided in Buenos Aires, most of the grasitas were criollos, rural immigrants like herself, but many others were poor whites. In Santiago del Estero, Salta, or Tucumán, the tens of thousands who packed the streets to see her, and later to mourn her, were overwhelmingly criollos. No one from the powerful classes had ever talked to them or treated them with respect until that blond fairy appeared, promising a workers' paradise, and they responded with unconcealed loyalty.

Peronist discourse in relation to workers subordinated ethnic specificity to class-consciousness and loyalty to Perón and Eva. This is apparent in the profuse iconography of the Peronist masses produced by government propaganda and friendly media. Renderings of el *descamisado*, the prototypical male Peronist worker, portray him sometimes as European, sometimes as criollo, and most commonly as ethnically neutral.[22] In fact, the descamisado identity signature was an unbuttoned white shirt with sleeves rolled up, a marker of material poverty inscribed in class rather than ethnic terms. In discussing the design of a proposed monument to el descamisado, which never materialized, Perón suggested that it should include images of Indians, colonial peasants (of no specific race), gauchos, and immigrants on its flanks, and "as a central figure, the descamisado of today, the one we see in the streets, the one we saw on October 17th."[23] Unfortunately Perón abstained from giving a detailed representation of the later stage of descamisado-ness, but we may assume that it was a synthesis of the early stages, indigenous, criollo, and white, constituting a Peronist version of the discourse of mestizaje (although again, Africans were left out of the Argentine melting pot).

The unprecedented acceptance of Argentine racial complexity provided a new dimension to the official endorsement of criollo folklore. In the Conservative period folklore appeared dissociated from the rural workers who produced it. In contrast, Peronism made the association explicit. As discussed below, Peronist public demonstrations and regional festivities included live performances by criollo musicians and dancers. In contrast to disembodied radio programs, these state-sponsored mass folklore performances allowed a visual connection between the working-class audiences and the criollo artists. Summoning dark-skinned criollo artists to the same stage from which Perón and Eva addressed the multitudes was a way of representing in practical and symbolic terms the incorporation of all Argentines into the body of the nation.

Yet Peronist discourse on criollo culture had its share of ambiguities, showing the lasting pull of Eurocentrism on Peronist policymakers. The Eurocentric inertia is discernable in the wording of cultural policies included in the two consecutive five-year plans. In the text of the first of these plans (1947–52), the section on culture opened with a quote from Perón vowing "to fortify the prolific patrimony of the Greco-Latin civilization bequeathed to us, of which we are the perpetuators."[24] The planners in charge of editing the section further elaborated on Perón's words, claiming that those "noble origins of the European culture" were transmitted by the Spanish conquistadors and, after receiving the influence of autochthonous elements, preserved by oral tradition until the present. Having established the origins of Argentine culture, the planners defined the core of the traditional patrimony as "language, religion, the cult of the family, popular poetry, folklore, popular dances, and the cult of the national holidays." They requested the protection of the state and further specified: "The study of popular poetry will be attended so the philosophical expression of the past can serve as a norm and inspiration for the present." Perón's definition of Argentine culture as Greco-Latin is reminiscent of Ricardo Rojas and reflects his fascination with the fascist myth of Rome's civilizing mission. More *hispanista* than Perón's formula, the planners' addendum clearly reveals the influence of Carrizo.

The planners recommended actions to protect the traditional patrimony and make it available to a larger number of Argentines, especially foreign-born residents. According to the plan these goals were as important as the economic reforms aimed to elevate workers' material standard of living. More specifically, the plan suggested creating institutions to achieve these goals and reinvigorating those that already existed. As a result, over the following few years the state increased the institutionalization of folklore research that had begun in 1943 with the creation of the Institute of Tradition.

The Eurocentric tinge of Peronist folklore policy reflected the continuity in the culture bureaucracy of officials formed under Conservative influence. That was the case with Juan Alfonso Carrizo, who despite his obvious connections to Tucumán's sugar industry managed to preserve his position as director of the institute now renamed the Institute of Tradition and Folklore. The government also maintained the National Culture Commission, the main state sponsor of art expositions, concerts, theater, academic conferences, and humanities research, staffed mostly with *Integristas* (Integralists, or right-wing Catholic Nationalists), including the notorious anti-Semitic writer Gustavo Martínez Zuviría. In 1943 the commission began funding folklore research.[25] The culture commission would eventually yield part of its functions to the Directorate of Culture, while folklore would have its own national commission on which, predictably, Carrizo served.[26] Another consequence of the five-year plans' recommendations was the creation of an archive of Argentine music, which eventually became the Institute of Ethnomusicology.[27] The directorship was conferred on Carlos Vega, and its most conspicuous researcher was Isabel Aretz. Padilla could then retire satisfied, knowing that the regime that ousted his fellow landowners from power maintained his protégés in office and continued the program of folklore protection and promotion for which he had always fought.[28] The retention of conservatives in the institutions of folklore research muffled the revolutionary impact of the Peronist embrace of rural criollo culture. But research was just one aspect of folklore policy. In the following pages I will show how public folklore performances during the first Peronist government represented a more thorough revision of the place of the criollo in the "New Argentina," one that exerted a more powerful impact on common Argentine citizens.

HARVEST QUEENS, DESCAMISADOS, AND PACHAMAMAS

Peronism was a movement of public demonstrations. On October 17, 1945, after the military government demoted Perón from his positions of secretary of labor and minister of defense, people took to the streets to demand the reappointment of their hero. From this day, the birthday of the Peronist movement, until Perón was forced out of office by a military rebellion in September 1955, the movement's mostly working-class followers did not leave Main Street. Huge public demonstrations became part of the urban landscape across the country. For events such as the national holidays and the two Peronist *jornadas* (May Day and October 17), openings, festivals, party assemblies, and electoral rallies, people packed the plazas and parks to glimpse, hear, and cheer Perón and Eva. Each of these events was a reenactment of the original October 17. As the historian Mariano Ben Plotkin explains, "The aim of the celebration was clearly to give Peronist supporters the opportunity to reaffirm their devotion for their leader and to recreate the fundamental basis of the regime's legitimacy: the charismatic leadership of Perón based on his contact with the people without intermediaries."[29]

The public ceremonies were also popular celebrations of what workers perceived as a national rebirth and deep transformation of the country's social structures. That transformation included a new status for the criollo too. Although the central act was Perón's or Eva's speech, many ceremonies were more complex and included parades, live music, contests, and even beauty pageants. Furthermore, only a few Peronist celebrations included the physical presence of Perón or Evita. During the jornadas all provincial capitals and mid-sized towns held massive demonstrations. Perón could only be there in effigy and through the ubiquitous outdoor speakers that amplified the live broadcast from the Plaza de Mayo.

There were also many events, big and small, organized by unions, local Peronist party committees, municipalities, and civic associations. In the long term the provincial and local festivals may have been even more effective in crafting a lasting Peronist loyalty across the country than the centralized displays in Buenos Aires. More important for our purposes, criollo folk music figured prominently in all these events, reinforcing the sense of locality in rituals that tended to refer to long-range identities based on working-class and party affiliation.

The most important provincial festivals were those related to local production of agricultural products such as wine, sugar, and cotton. Those festivals predated Peronism, but the new government co-opted them much as it did the May Day celebration. With the nationalization of provincial festivals, agencies such as the Institute of Tradition and the National Culture Commission were assigned to assist the provinces in organizing the festivals. Thus the academic folklore discourse (Catholic and Nationalist) trickled down to the masses and merged with both criollo folk entertainment and Peronist propaganda.

The oldest and best-organized provincial festival was the Fiesta de la Vendimia—vintage festival—of Mendoza, first celebrated in 1936. As the historians Cecilia Belej, Ana Martin, and Alina Silveira have demonstrated, the organizers carefully crafted the ceremony to conjoin the different dichotomies of provincial life—nation and province, church and state, capital and counties, gringos and criollos, employers and workers, growers and wineries—into a harmonious totality.[30] In this way the province sought to heal the wounds opened by the painful structural adjustments that resulted from the Depression and to spread an idyllic view of Argentina's wine country. Mendoza's Vintage Festival was an instant success that attracted national attention, partly because it was broadcast live by the Radio Belgrano national network. The festival comprised five elements: a parade of allegorical floats; a Catholic Mass, procession, and blessing of the fruits; speeches by provincial and national authorities; the stage performance of regional music and dances; and, at its liminal moment, the selection of the "Vintage queen." This festival soon became a template for analogous celebrations throughout the country.

One of the emulators was Tucumán, which organized the first Fiesta de la Zafra in 1942. The event was not particularly memorable and failed to bring important national authorities, but it did inspire the provincial towns in the sugar country to build their own floats and choose their own beauty queens.[31] The public patronized many of the free-access ceremonies, including the Mass, but the newspapers complained that to appreciate the coronation of the Zafra queen, the public had to buy a prohibitively priced ticket. The closing event of the ceremony thus lacked popular enthusiasm.[32] The next year, the military coup precluded organization of the event, and for a few years Tucumán did not hold another Zafra festival. The festival reemerged, however, under Perón's government.

Peronists reenergized and re-signified the provincial festivals starting with the Vintage Festival in Mendoza in 1947. The same year, the government revived Tucumán's Zafra Festival, taking it to a higher level of stagecraft. In the words of a public report by the National Culture Commission, the Zafra Festival aimed to restore the spirit of the domestic harvest ceremonies that in the Argentine northwest "amalgamated surviving pagan agrarian rituals, inherited from Medieval Europe through Spain."[33] Here again the Culture Commission decided to ignore the indigenous history of the Northwest and invent a European past for this region. (Certainly the Andean people were not aware of the existence of sugar cane, but neither was ancient Europe.)[34] The commission report continues, expressing regret that those domestic rituals of medieval lineage had lost their spontaneity because of the modernization of economic relations, implying that the social policies of the Peronist government would restore the traditional link between work and merriment. The Zafra Festival of 1947 had very little of the spontaneity that the Culture Commission yearned for, but what it lacked in spontaneity it gained in grandeur, certainly by Tucumán standards.

When the day of the festival came, the vast crowd from Tucumán and neighboring provinces encountered a grand central stage. Though designed in modernist style, the columned hemicycle was crowned with a towering cross, more reminiscent of Saint Peter's Square than of Hitler's

Zepeline Tribüne in Nuremberg. This contraption faced a giant open space in Tucumán's central park and accommodated more than 200,000 spectators. Most came principally to pay homage to the leader they idolized, although nominally the central subject of the celebration was the unionized sugar worker personified in the *zafrero*, the sugar cane cutter. One zafrero was in charge of lighting a votive torch: the representative of the sugar workers' federation reached the stage wearing the symbolic attire of the descamisado, a white shirt with rolled-up sleeves. Other zafreros and descamisados offered Perón cane stalks as fruits of their work and a machete, the basic tool of the harvester's trade. Perón took the cane and cut it with the machete, signifying his communion with the cane harvesters and, in pure pagan fashion, adopting a priestly role to secure a bountiful harvest and the workers' well-being.

The workers' descamisado attire exemplified the kinship between the criollo harvesters and the national working class beyond their region. Nation and region also blended in other ceremonial acts that emphasized the criollo heritage. For example, a dance troupe from Santiago del Estero performed vidalas and cuecas in honor of the president. One dance number was a consecration of the Zafra queen and her honor court, who arrived on top of a float representing the Andean deity Pachamama. They were escorted by mounted gauchos from Salta, Tucumán, and Jujuy. The young women took the stage while zamba music sounded in the background.[35]

Nominally a celebration of the criollo sugar worker, the festival became an occasion for Peronist leaders to rally their bases. The tucumano elite understood it in this way, and thus only gave the festival a lukewarm endorsement. In 1947 the representative of the Sugar Association resigned from the festival organizing committee two days before the festival date. During the ceremony the archbishop of Tucumán voiced the industrialists' concerns when he reminded the huge crowd that the sugar industry of Tucumán would not have existed without the capital, intellect, and effort of the mill owners. An editorial in the elite newspaper *La Gaceta* advanced the same arguments the next year. Nevertheless, at the festival of 1948, Evita used her speech to chastise the sugar elite. Addressing the "descamisados de Tucumán" directly, Evita said: "You, who had suffered from an soulless oligarchy; You, who had suffered the oppression of withered hearts . . . You know what Perón has done for you [he] brought you material, social, and moral independence. And for that reason, the humble people of Tucumán will always be present in all the demonstrations in which they can show, with their generous criollo hearts, their gratitude to Perón."[36] The celebration of the sugar worker, if we understand Evita's words correctly, was at the same time a celebration of Perón, the hero of the working classes. Evita warned the crowd to watch the movements of the "treacherous oligarchy" because they would not condone the social justice that Perón had brought to the people.

While the government attempted to make the Zafra festival the central event in the Northwest, the deterioration of labor relations in the province conspired against the survival of the festival. During the harvest of 1949 the Sugar Worker Federation struck against several mills that refused to pay the salaries negotiated through collective bargaining. The federal government, concerned with the supply of sugar to the urban centers, declared the strike illegal and interdicted the union. The symbiotic relation between the Sugar Workers Union and the Peronist party became strained during the conflict, and, not surprisingly there was no Zafra festival that year.

As the national Peronist state absorbed existing provincial festivals, the provincial Peronist state co-opted municipal and local folk festivals, infusing them with a dose of Peronist propaganda. In Tucumán and other provinces the legislatures declared several festivals, processions, and annual fairs traditionally celebrated in rural towns as being of "provincial interest." The label implied that the provincial government would support them financially and that the governor and other provincial authorities would participate in the festivities. In other words, the festivals would be turned into political pageants used to demonstrate people's loyalty to the local representatives of the Peronist government.

One of the local festivals that received considerable attention from the Tucumano Peronist government was the traditional carnival celebrated in the Calchaquí Valley, in the western, mountainous section of the province. In organizing this provincial festival the Tucumano cultural authorities, in contrast to the National Culture Commission's Eurocentric discourse, showed an interest in the indigenous origins of rural criollo culture. The carnival was in fact recast as the "Provincial *Pachamama* Festival."[37] The traditional Calchaquí rituals around carnival time included cattle-branding rodeos at which Pachamama, the Andean mother earth, received libations and sacrifices. The festival included the more carnavalesque practices of *topamientos* (lit. "the bumping"—men and women colliding on their horse mounts), *harinadas* (face washing with flour), and *bagualeadas* (singing tournaments between men and women accompanied by the *caja*, a flat, shaman-like drum). In February 1947, less than a year after Perón's electoral triumph, the government of Tucumán and representatives from Catamarca, Salta, and Santiago del Estero moved en masse to the Calchaquí community of Amaicha to celebrate the first Pachamama festival.[38]

The festival, described by a newspaper as "an evocation of the Incaic myth," was a celebration of Calchaquí folklore at which representatives from all the Calchaquí communities performed dances and music and gave equestrian demonstrations to the visiting authorities of the state. The ceremonies lasted for two days and included novelties such as the crowning of the Pachamama in the person of the village's oldest woman, an agricultural and livestock fair, the singing of the national anthem, an open-air Mass, and an official speech that paid homage to the Calchaquí people "among whom live, in pristine purity, the essential virtues of their ancestors."[39] The celebration also provided authorities with the opportunity to inaugurate roads, bridges, and irrigation dams and to promise funding for future public works.

It would be erroneous to dismiss these provincial and regional festivals as mere electoral pandering. By tapping into the local festivals, Peronism aimed to cement its legitimacy as a federal, popular movement by appropriating the symbolic capital generated by community-building rituals. The organizers modified the rituals to accommodate the presence and reflect the interests of the Peronist authorities. Most importantly, the ritual acquired national transcendence: the pact with Pachamama would benefit not just the valleys but the nation as a whole, while in exchange the nation would bring roads and irrigation. In this way Peronism ritually linked the mythical past of the Argentine Andes, personified in the Pachamama, with the golden future promised by President Perón.

Festivals such as the Vintage and Zafra at the provincial level and the Pachamama at the local level constituted part of an annual cycle that culminated in the Día del Trabajo, the international labor day celebrated on 1 May and resignified as one of the two highest Peronist holidays. Like the regional festivals, the Labor Day festival conceived by the Catholic

nationalist ministers of education, Oscar Ivanissevich and José Casti-
ñeira de Dios, was a combination of artistic spectacle, parade, and political demonstration.[40] On the main stage musicians and dancers alternated with politicians and labor leaders, while in the streets delegations
from different provinces and unions paraded with their floats. The artistic slate for the Labor Day celebration in the Plaza de Mayo in 1948
included the folk musicians the Abalos Brothers, Juan Carlos Mareco,
and Carlos Montbrun Ocampo, and a comparable number of tango
performers. The equal time devoted to porteño tango and provinciano
folklore symbolized the idea that Peronism's working-class nationalism
could overcome the historical rift between the port capital and the
interior, in this case through the mediating influence of popular culture.

A central part of the festival was the "queen of labor" pageant, in
which the provincial queens competed, including those elected at the
Vintage, Zafra, Wheat, Yerba Mate, Petrol, and a host of similar festivals.
Lobato, Damilakou, and Tornay argue that the ideal of female beauty and
virtue espoused in this official, labor-oriented pageant was not different
from the contemporary bourgeois models as expressed in the popular
feminine magazines of the time. The press and official statements described the participants as delicate, feminine, and patriotic and emphasized that they were preparing themselves to be good mothers and
housewives.[41] Although the pictures of the participants published in
newspapers show young women of European descent, some of them
with blonde or dyed hair, officials and journalists called them "criollo
beauties." The apparent contradiction again shows the ambiguous sense
of the term, here used to identify criollo ethnicity with the entire Argentine working class. The election in 1948 as National Queen of Labor of
the Queen of the Flowers and Fragrance, from the flower-growing northern suburbs of Buenos Aires, followed by the election as National Princess of Labor of the tucumano Zafra Queen shows the importance
placed by the organizers on balancing Buenos Aires and the interior as
proof that the working class under Peronist leadership was unified.

At local, provincial, and national celebrations the Peronist government programmed live folklore performances in an attempt to identify
the government with a revisionist view of national identity. The airing of
different regional rhythms during the celebrations, like the presence of
provincial beauty queens, was evidence of the intention of respecting the

federal constitution of the country. Conservatives, especially those from provincial elites, also conceived folklore as the embodiment of their regions and provinces. But while for conservatives the criollo music and dance evoked nostalgia for the colonial past, for Peronists the same dances represented the criollo who created them. These criollos were also the citizens who voted for Perón, the party supporters who marched in the streets during official demonstrations and the internal migrants who poured into Buenos Aires to fill the new jobs created by industrialization. The incorporation of folk music in the official Peronist celebrations as well as the Peronization of provincial and local folk festivities confirmed the symbiotic relationship between the criollo working class and the Peronist political project. Interestingly, during the Perón years criollo folklore as a form of entertainment experienced steady growth, expanding from its rural, working-class origins to the urban middle class, a group not known for its fondness for Perón and his followers.

THE HOUR OF THE *PEÑAS*

Government efforts in favor of folklore were in fact accompanied by the increasing popularity of folklore music and dance among urban audiences. During the 1940s Buenos Aires and other eastern cities saw the sustained growth of *peñas folklóricas*. This label encompassed commercial venues such as live music clubs and restaurants as well as nonprofit civic associations. The nonprofit peñas sought to educate their members on music interpretation and especially dance, but they would hire professional folklore musicians for their galas. Itinerant musicians from the interior would find in these engagements an alternative and sometimes more reliable source of income to supplement their radio contracts. Some folk musicians, such as the Abalos Brothers and Margarita Palacios, would open their own for-profit peñas, where they hosted other professional musicians. The peñas phenomenon suggests that folklore had a place in civic society beyond government sponsorship and the media entertainment industry.

The profile of the peñas' members and customers cut across social classes and regional backgrounds. Some peñas operated in fashionable downtown *confiterías* (teahouses) while others met at the more homely *sociedades de fomento*, or neighborhood associations. There were nonprofit peñas such as El Cardón that attracted rich porteños to dance gato, zamba, and chacarera. Provincial college students in Buenos Aires, La Plata, and Cordoba created support organizations and amused each other with traditional music and dance from their province. Labor unions sponsored fundraising or celebration balls where tango and folklore orchestras provided music for their regionally diverse audiences. Peñas also included dance schools where volunteers or paid instructors would teach the dance steps to children and adults. The peñas were not limited to the cities of the pampas. In Tucumán there was also an explosion of folklore centers of different kinds during the Peronist period, both in the capital and in the small rural towns. The rapid expansion of peñas shows that criollo folklore was rising in popularity among different social classes and different geographical settings. Arguably the popularization of folklore in cities and towns attests to the success of the government's sponsorship of folklore in radio, schools, and festivals.

In an article published in *Sintonía* a photograph appears of Ernesto Padilla and his wife participating in a soiree at the exclusive peña El Cardón, of which Padilla was the honorary president. The photographer captured unequivocal expressions of satisfaction in the faces of the husband and wife as they watched a couple dancing a gato. Their gratification was justified. The rich porteño youngster dancing to criollo rhythms with panache was the fulfillment of Padilla's lifelong ambition. And judging from the pictures, the room was full of these young people, including the daughter of the owner of the Splendid Broadcasting Network. I have already noted that the provincial elite youth were socialized to master criollo dances, but the activities of El Cardón during the Peronist period represented a further step. The youngsters dancing there were porteños from the social classes vilified by Peronism. It is true that during the 1920s many members of the porteño golden youth shunned the liberal traditions of their families to embrace Catholic nationalism. But that was then. In 1946 the rich were the *oligarquía vendepatria*, the treacherous oligarchy who demonstrated while singing the *Marseillaise*, led by the United States ambassador, and who voted against Perón. They were those whom Evita would denounce as scoundrels lurking in their lairs, waiting for the moment to stamp out the economic justice that Perón gave to his people. What then were these oligarchs doing in plain sight at El Cardón? Simply put, they were reclaiming bodily the nationality denied them by government rhetoric and the popular imagination.

In the context of Argentine history, it is striking that porteño elite men and women learned to reproduce in dance the body language of the Calchaquí villagers, the Humahuaca herders, or the Santiago itinerant workers. The folklore movement at the peñas aimed to bridge a vast and deep cultural gap that separated the two extremes of the Argentine social ladder: on the one hand, the only beneficiaries of a (still) prosperous but skewed economy; on the other, the folk from the geographic and economic margins whose possession of value was the cultural capital of their traditions. The communion of rich and poor happened in a ritualized setting where the latter were present only in the person of the musicians, sometimes the dancers, and symbolically in their music and dances. From this ritual the rich emerged more Argentine, after a total immersion in the baptismal waters of criollo culture. In exchange, the poor obtained symbolic recognition of their cultural precedence.

The popularity of the peñas mirrored the development of folklore as commercial music. The Buenos Aires branches of RCA Victor and Odeon had been recording folk music since the 1920s, but their folklore titles constituted a minuscule part of a market dominated by tango. This situation began to change in the late 1940s with the success of San Juan's singer and composer Antonio Tormo. His single for RCA Victor, "El rancho 'e la Cambicha" (1950), sold an astounding five million copies (the Argentine population at the time was sixteen million), breaking all sales records of the Argentine recording industry.[42] Almost instantly Tormo signed a contract with Radio Belgrano to play live on a popular segment that was broadcast Sundays at noon. The key to Tormo's success was his eclectic interpretation of criollo folklore. He included rhythms from the Andean region as well as from the Northeast. He also incorporated melodic harmonies and upbeat rhythms that departed from more purist renderings of criollo folklore and put him closer to popular commercial music. "El rancho 'e la Cambicha" was based on a polka rhythm from the Northeast popularly known as *chamamé*. This style appeared to satisfy the growing market of internal migrants in search of entertainment and a cultural connection with their provinces of origin. However, the record's high sales figures suggest that Tormo's music reached well beyond the criollo market, possibly to include working-class Argentines of European descent.

The popularity of Tormo continued until the fall of Perón in 1955.

After that year Tormo found it difficult to obtain contracts with recording companies and radio stations, a victim of the military regime's blacklisting of artists associated with the Peronist government.[43] It is not clear whether Tormo was a Peronist militant, but his popularity among Peronist followers made him a symbol of the ousted government.[44] The system imposed by the anti-Peronist regime was in retaliation for blacklists that had been applied during the Peronist period. It is well known that the Peronists tightly controlled who could appear in radio and films.

One of the most notorious victims of these authoritarian methods was Atahualpa Yupanqui. Although Yupanqui's known communist sympathies did not prevent him from playing on the radio during the military regime of 1943–45, after the inauguration of Perón in 1946 he had fewer opportunities to obtain radio contracts. This exclusion forced him to seek his living on the peñas circuit, even though he had to endure the harassment of the federal police, who jailed Yupanqui several times. Seeking relief from persecution, Yupanqui embarked on a European tour, sponsored by the Communist Party, in 1949. As part of that tour Yupanqui played for the first time in Paris, where he subsequently resided for half of every year. After his return to Buenos Aires in 1950, however, the federal police imprisoned Yupanqui for nine months without trial, during which time he may have suffered torture. After his release in 1951 the harassment of the Peronist authorities suddenly ended, and Yupanqui was able to play in public.

That Yupanqui continued to enjoy popularity and was still embraced by Peronist cultural authorities despite his persecution by the government's repressive apparatus reveals the strength of the folkloric movement. In May 1951, fresh from jail, Yupanqui wrote to his wife, Nennete Pepin, that he attended the Labor Day celebration in Plaza de Mayo and was surprised that one of the dance numbers was his "zamba del grillo." No less surprising was the mere fact of Yupanqui's attendance at a Peronist gathering. Furthermore, he found the celebrations very compelling and commented favorably on the election of the queen. Two years later Yupanqui made a triumphal comeback to Tucumán for a series of concerts. For the occasion the Peronist governor organized a fete in homage to the artist and officially named him the province's "favorite son and pride of its working class." The normally restrained Yupanqui admitted in private that this gesture made him very emotional. This puzzling interaction between persecuting state and persecuted artist can be understood as a manifestation of the common aesthetic understanding that existed among different agents in the folklore movement, despite their bitter ideological differences.

The well-funded Peronist propaganda machine called the period that began with the election of Juan Domingo Perón to the presidency *La Nueva Argentina*—"New Argentina." The cliché may seem uninspired and pompous—most governments want to be seen as representing the dawn of a new era—but in this case the cliché makers deserve some credit. During the Peronist period Argentina experienced sweeping reforms of its political, economic, and social structures, reforms designed to improve the living conditions of the working class. But the new Argentina also had an ethnic dimension. The Peronist movement established a lasting alliance with the criollo workers, both rural and urban. The government reinforced this special relation by embracing a rising folklore movement that celebrated the culture of the criollos from the interior as the only authentic Argentine culture.

In the sphere of academic work, the Peronist government supported cultural institutions whose goal was the research and study of folklore. In this regard the Peronist government co-opted a cadre of academic folklorists that had been working closely with the previous conservative governments, in particular with sugar industrialists from Tucumán Province. These folklorists emphasized the aspects of criollo folklore derived from Hispanic roots while neglecting those derived from indigenous and African roots. This bias made the academic folklore of the Peronist period less radical in approach than one might have expected. It also made academic folklore palatable to Peronist education authorities, known for their enthusiasm for Catholic Spain. In the view of these authorities the teaching in public schools of criollo folklore curtailed the influence of cosmopolitan trends and instilled the traditions of a homeland that they imagined to be hierarchical and pious. Peronist support of folklore was not limited to research and education. Criollo art became the predominant aesthetic of the Peronist party's public performances. This is most noticeable in the regional festivals associated with local production.

The folklore movement was not the exclusive province of government policies. The vibrant media of the time, especially radio networks, participated in the movement for their own motives. While it is true that the Peronist government exerted legal pressure to expand the programming of criollo music, it was merely continuing and expanding a policy that had been initiated by the networks themselves long before government intervention. The general enthusiasm for criollo music and dance transcended Peronist plans. During years of bitter resentment between supporters and foes of Juan and Eva Perón, people from different social and ideological backgrounds participated together in peñas, as both musicians and patrons, joining forces to celebrate the zamba.

In the public performances of the Peronist movement, in the cultural policies of the regime, and even in the personal gestures of the presidential couple one can observe a distinct change of attitude toward the criollo. In these performances we can see at work the construction of an alternative Argentine nation, and in them criollo folk culture found an important place in this new stage of the nation-building process. Although the class-based political identity of Peronism transcended ethnic divisions, the Peronist appropriation of folk culture represented an important shift in the way Argentines represented themselves. The adoption of folklore aesthetics from those strongly opposed to the government reveals that the folklore movement was a point of contact beyond ideology. For this reason, perhaps, the folklore movement did not die after the fall of Perón in 1955. If anything it became stronger; more musicians entered the market, and the public appetite for criollo music grew. The folklore movement boomed in the early 1960s, during the window of opportunity after the fall of tango and before the rise of rock *nacional*. Criollo folklore remained a hegemonic aesthetic representation of Argentina even during the years of violent confrontation between the right and the left. This may explain why I learned to sing and play Yupanqui's hymns "El arriero va" and "Lunita tucumana" in the public schools under the military dictatorship of 1976, at the exact same time the death squads established the epicenter of the state terror campaign in the countryside of Tucumán.

NOTES

1 During this period the term "criollo" was used to distinguish the descendants of the pre-immigration population from European immigrants and

their descendants. That is the sense in which I am using the term in this chapter. According to the national censuses of 1895 and 1914, native-born Argentines, presumably criollos, constituted a majority in the rural regions of the Northwest, the Northeast, and Cuyo. In provinces that received significant immigration like Entre Ríos and Santa Fe, immigrants appear disproportionately among business and farm owners and renters, while the Argentine-born appear disproportionately among rural wage earners. República Argentina, *Segundo censo de la República Argentina, Mayo 10, 1895*, vol. 2 (Buenos Aires: Penitenciaría Nacional, 1898), cliii, cxc; República Argentina, *Tercer censo nacional, levantado el 1 de junio de 1914*, vol. 5 (Buenos Aires: Rosso, 1919), 354, 367, 477, 575.

2 Isabel Aretz, *El folklore musical argentino* (Buenos Aires: Ricordi Americana, 1952), 7–14.

3 Statistics about the origin of the internal immigrants are imprecise. The census of 1947 shows that among the 698,284 provincial migrants to Buenos Aires city and province, 47 percent were born in Entre Ríos, Santa Fe, and Córdoba, 21 percent in the Northwest, 11 percent in the Northeast, 10.1 percent in Cuyo, and 0.93 percent in the national territories of La Pampa and Patagonia. While most immigrants from the Northwest and Northeast were probably criollo, the proportion of criollos among migrants from the other regions is impossible to determine. In any case the larger provincial migration took place after 1947, when more than a million people moved from the provinces to the metropolitan area. Unfortunately the census of 1960 does not provide information on the origins of those internal immigrants. República Argentina, *Anuario estadístico 1978* (Buenos Aires: INDEC, 1979), 66–76. See also Margulis, *Migración y marginalidad en la sociedad argentina*, 54; Mafud, *Sociología del Peronismo*, 31; Alfredo Lattes, "Esplendor y ocaso de las migraciones internas," *Población y bienestar en la Argentina del primer al segundo centenario*, ed. Susana Torrado (Buenos Aires: Edhasa, 2007), 29.

4 "El Arte Nativo y el Plan Quinquenal," *Sintonía* 479 (January 1947), 12.

5 Argentine Republic, Presidencia, *El Plan Quinquenal del Gobierno del Presidente Perón* (Buenos Aires, 1947), 28; Argentine Republic, Presidencia, *Manual Práctico del 2° Plan Quinquenal* (Buenos Aires: Subsecretaria de Informaciones, 1953), 81–86.

6 De la Cadena, *Indigenous Mestizos*; Jeffrey Gould, *To Die in This Way: Nicaraguan Indians and the Myth of Mestizaje* (Durham: Duke University Press, 1998), 40–50; Jean Muteba Rahier, "Introduction: *Mestizaje, Muletaje, Mestiçagem* in Latin American Ideologies of National Identities," *Journal of Latin American Anthropology* 8, no. 1 (2003), 40–50.

7 Carol Smith, "Myths, Intellectuals, and Race/Class/Gender Distinctions in

the Formation of Latin American Nations," *Journal of Latin American Anthropology* 2, no. 1 (1996), 149.

8 Quijada, "Indígenas," 28.

9 An official expression of this discourse can be found in Comisión Nacional de Censos Argentina, *Segundo censo nacional, levantado el 10 de Mayo de 1895* (Buenos Aires: Taller Tipográfico de la Penitenciaría, 1898), vol. 2, xlvi–xlviii.

10 A good example of the Eurocentric contents is Ernestina Lopez de Nelson's third-grade reader *La Señorita Raquel* (Buenos Aires: Coni, 1920).

11 Delaney, "Making Sense of Modernity.".

12 Ricardo Rojas, *La restauración nacionalista: crítica de la educación argentina y bases para una reforma en el estudio de las humanidades modernas* (Buenos Aires: La Facultad, 1922).

13 "Estatuto radial de las orquestas," *Radiolandia* 17, no. 804 (14 August 1943), 5; "El 1° de septiembre entran en vigor las modificaciones reglamentarias, *Radiolandia* 17, no. 806 (28 August 1943), 5.

14 Plotkin, *Mañana es San Perón*; Lobato "La Política como espectáculo." See also Gené, *Un mundo feliz*.

15 James, *Resistance and Integration*, 22.

16 Pellettieri, "Cambios en el sistema teatral de la gauchesca rioplatense"; Prieto, *El discurso criollista en la formación de la Argentina moderna*; Delaney, "Making Sense of Modernity."

17 Delgado, "Realismo y región."

18 For more on this topic see my "Indigenous or Criollos? The Myth of White Argentina in Tucumán's Calchaquí Valley, 1900–1945," *Hispanic American Historical Review* 88, no. 1 (2008), 71–106.

19 Orquera, "Marxismo, peronismo, indocriollismo."

20 Atahualpa Yupanqui, Introduction to "El Arriero," *Viajes por el mundo* (Epsa Music, 2003) [sound recording].

21 Fraser and Navarro, *Eva Perón*, 134–47.

22 For more on "descamisado" iconography see the contributions to this volume by Natalia Milanesio and Anahi Ballent, as well as Gené, *Un mundo feliz*.

23 "Sobre el monumento al descamisado habló el presidente de la Nación," *Guía Quincenal de la Actividad Intelectual y Artística Argentina* 8 (1947), 59.

24 Presidencia de la Nación, "Plan Quinquenal de gobierno del presidente Perón" (Buenos Aires, 1947), 28.

25 *Comisión Nacional de Cultura: su labor en 1944* (Buenos Aires, 1945), 25–26.

26 "Comisión Nacional de Tradición y Folklore," *Guía Quincenal de la Actividad Intelectual y Artística Argentina* 8 (1947), 98.

27 "Biblioteca, Archivo, y Discoteca Nacional de la Música Argentina," *Guía Quincenal de la Actividad Intelectual y Artística Argentina* 2 (1947), 71.

28 Interview with Miguel Antonio Espeche, Buenos Aires, 21 June 2000.

29 Plotkin, *Mañana es San Perón*, 75.

30 Belej, Martín, and Silveira, "La más bella de los viñedos."

31 *La Union* (San Miguel de Tucumán), 13 June 1942, 6, and 14 July 1942, 1–5.

32 *La Union* (San Miguel de Tucumán), 16 July 1942, 7.

33 "Consagración y alegría del trabajo en la Argentina: la fiesta de la zafra," *Revista Quincenal de Actividad Intelectual y Artistica en Argentina* 6 (July 1947), 69.

34 See Sidney Mintz, *Sweetness and Power: The Place of Sugar in Modern History* (New York: Viking Penguin, 1985).

35 *La Gaceta* (San Miguel de Tucumán), 9 July 1947, 1.

36 *La Gaceta* (San Miguel de Tucumán), 6 November 1948, 1.

37 *La Gaceta* (San Miguel de Tucumán), 5 February 1947, 5.

38 *La Gaceta* (San Miguel de Tucumán), 18 February 1947, 2.

39 *La Gaceta* (San Miguel de Tucumán), 18 February 1947, 3.

40 See Lobato, Damilakou, and Tornay, "Working-Class Beauty Queens under Peronism," in this volume.

41 Lobato, Damilakou, and Tornay, "Working-Class Beauty Queens under Peronism."

42 Pedro Portorico, *Diccionario de música argentina de raíz folklórica* (Buenos Aires, self-published, 1997), 370–71.

43 "Los que no actuan," *Radiolandia*, 28 April 1956, 6.

44 Luis Alberto Romero singles outs Tormo as one of the popular artists who enjoyed the support of the Peronist government. See his *A History of Argentina in the Twentieth Century*, 117.

Anahi Ballent

....

Translated by Beatrice D. Gurwitz

UNFORGETTABLE KITSCH

Images around Eva Perón

> We wanted to make a true home and if one day we were to live in [this house],
> I confess that we would feel at home . . . It has been possible to convert it into
> a joyful and comfortable paradise, so that everyone finds a happiness in this
> home that they have not found in others.[1]

EVA PERÓN, 3 APRIL 1948

> My "homes" are generously rich . . . I even want to surpass myself. I want them
> to be luxurious. Precisely because a century of miserable asylums cannot be
> wiped out except by another century of "excessively luxurious" homes. Yes,
> excessively luxurious. . . . No, I am not afraid (that the poor will get ac-
> customed to living like the rich). On the contrary, I wish them to accustom
> themselves to live like the rich . . . to feel worthy to live among the greatest
> riches. For when all is said and done, everyone has the right to be rich on this
> Argentine soil . . . and in any part of the world. The world has sufficient
> available riches for all men to be rich. When justice is done, no one will
> be poor, at least no one who does not want to be. That is why I am a
> justicialist . . . What makes my works my own is that they set a seal of
> indignation against the injustices of a bitter century for the poor.[2]

EVA PERÓN, *MY MISSION IN LIFE*

The Peronist government placed a significant emphasis on public works
projects, including homes, schools, hospitals, and administrative and
government buildings. At the same time, the government made extensive, propagandistic use of the architectural images it created, displaying

them at exhibitions and publicizing them through books and pamphlets published by the state and the party. The endurance and political force of these images within the Peronist imaginary leads us to consider the relationship between politics and architecture: in what way might an architectural work constitute an "aesthetic of the political," to borrow loosely an expression coined by Walter Benjamin?[3]

Any analysis along these lines must confront a plural universe of forms, since the architectural works of the Peronist period were not confined to one particular style. Instead there were at least four prominent aesthetics within state and party production: the California style, used in works of the Fundación Eva Perón, the Ministerio de Obras Públicas, and the Plan de vivienda Eva Perón for the Banco Hipotecario Nacional; the neoclassical style, used in the central headquarters of the foundation and the Eva Perón Memorial; muted modernism, in various public buildings like the Ezeiza airport; and radical modernism, in the buildings of the Comisión de la Vivienda, the municipal government's Estudio para el Plan de Buenos Aires, and the buildings of the Secretaría de Comunicaciones, among others.

The California style in Argentina, as well as in other countries in the Americas, is essentially the mission style, which had been popular in California since the end of the nineteenth century. Rustic and picturesque, it is known for its white walls and sloping tiled roofs, which evoked images of Spanish colonial architecture. The neoclassical style, popular from the eighteenth century until the 1930s and 1940s, drew on the architectural vocabulary of classical antiquity. Modernist styles, which eschewed ornamentation in favor of simplified geometric forms and modern materials such as iron, reinforced concrete, and glass, ranged from muted to radical. All these styles except for the most radical modernism emerged in the 1930s and came to fruition in the public works of the 1940s and 1950s in proposals that did not live beyond the Peronist period. Radical modernism also appeared in Argentina in the 1930s, but it was employed most fully in state projects after 1955.

It is thus necessary to forgo a search for a single "Peronist architecture," understood as a unique group of forms that expressed the values of Peronist politics. The stylistic heterogeneity that characterized official architecture in this period is indicative of the diversity within Peronism itself, which was a conglomeration of different political groups and ideologies. Consequently we should analyze the relationship between architectural aesthetics and politics with a refined lens, and a recognition that aesthetic proposals were the result of a complex relationship between the sponsoring institutions of state and party, the functional and symbolic aspects of architectural styles, and the positions and profiles of the architects.

Along these lines, the following analysis will focus on the architectural production surrounding Eva Perón, a body of work that exemplifies the promotion of particular images during the period. Because of the strong connection between Eva Perón and certain architectural images and the intense media diffusion of those images, the creations associated with her are among the most relevant symbols of the period. These works include the buildings created for the social programs run by the Fundación Eva Perón (1946/8–55), the architecture of the central headquarters of the foundation (1950), and the large-scale evocation of the figure of Eva in her monument and mausoleum (1952–55). This was essentially the only body of architectural work during the Peronist period that was so closely tied to a particular public figure, generating a strong identification between a political personality and her work. Aesthetic elaboration was instrumental in constructing the political myth of Eva: she herself became the most important icon created by Peronism. The aestheticization of Eva continued even after her death: her body was obliged to remain eternally beautiful and immutable, becoming a total work of art, in which the subject and its representation were fused completely and definitively.

The architecture that has remained linked to Eva Perón is characterized by rustic images (California chalets) and neoclassical forms (the foundation building and her monument). Within twentieth-century aesthetics rusticity and neoclassicism are architectural languages that belong to the realm of kitsch, which can be defined as that which contemporary "high culture" considers conventional, saccharine, and predictable. Matei Calinescu has offered a description (rather than a normative assessment) that emphasizes the connection between kitsch and modernity and the notion that the search for beauty leads to the creation and consumption of kitsch. He avoids making an overdetermined connection between kitsch, conspicuous consumption, and the quest for social prestige, arguing instead that while consumption and prestige are connected to kitsch, other things are as well. In the architectural production tied to Eva Perón there are two recognizable variants of kitsch: employing Calinescu's distinctions, we can call these "market kitsch," which involves rustic or excessively Frenchified images, and the "kitsch of political propaganda," which is characterized by a hackneyed version of the sublime.[4] Still, these two forms of kitsch do not define the complete work of the Fundación Eva Perón, which as early as 1952 was fostering modernist works like the dining hall of the University of La Plata, the Ramos Mejia Thoracic Clinical Surgery Hospital in Greater Buenos Aires, and the General Regional Hospital of Santa Fe. Nonetheless, these modernist images have not endured in the social imaginary as symbols of the institution because they became prominent only after the death of Eva Perón, the critical turning point in the life of the institution. By the time of her death the representations and images of the foundation had already been forged by other pieces of work. In other words, these later varieties of modernist architecture ultimately became part of the institution's material production but were never part of its symbolic program.

The aesthetics of the foundation were not innovative. Instead they built on an existing and time-honored repertory, using the California style architecture that was prominent in the 1920s and 1930s for both middle-class homes and state architectural production. The choice of these recognized forms had various consequences. First, in the symbolic realm it supported the redistributive program of the foundation by offering to the popular sectors a group of forms and images that had until then been exclusively available to the middle and upper classes. Second, from a political perspective it showed a unity between the foundation's work and the state's work, since beginning in the 1930s the California style had been introduced in some state developments. Finally, from the point of view of execution, it must be remembered that the foundation completed a great deal of work in a short time. Like any institution working on a tight schedule, it was not well suited to experimentation or technical innovation.

Architectural aesthetic choices thus reflected the needs of social and technical communication, but these choices also had political meanings. The political character of aesthetic choices became apparent when the works were presented publicly. Those who had done the technical work were ignored because, according to the political propaganda, Eva Perón was responsible for the output, as she herself suggests in the quote from

La razón de mi vida (My Mission in Life) cited in the second epigraph to this chapter.

Both epigraphs imply that Eva herself controlled the projects, or at least that she imbued them with her personal touch or her spirit. But this was not so in practice: the architect Mario Colli, the foundation's senior project designer between 1947 and 1952, only saw her on a few occasions, always at public affairs, and received no comments from her on his work.[5] Moreover, there is no evidence that she ever approached a drawing board; instructions on the projects (for example, the rustic images that Colli called the "Foundation style") were given by the engineer Carlos Bonnani, chief of construction, who was in contact with Armando Méndez San Martín, a central figure in running the foundation. After 1950 the architect Jorge Sabaté became the institution's consulting architect and designed many works for it. In other words, the hierarchy of the institution and its technical arm mediated between Eva Perón and the output of the foundation. Thus in reality Eva Perón was not the "author" but rather the "usufructuary" of a collective architectural endeavor with which she was undoubtedly in agreement. Still, the extensive and intense connection between architecture and politics that is visible in the work of the foundation was not undermined by Eva Perón's lack of involvement in design; the technical bureaucracy, with no interest in autonomy, accepted its mission of constructing an architectural face for Peronist political goals. In this sense we can imagine that the choice to use recognized and established aesthetics was not intended to appeal only to the foundation's beneficiaries but also to Eva Perón herself, principal and privileged consumer of the building plans.

The following analysis examines the work of the foundation on three intersecting levels. First, I analyze its architectural production in light of institutional changes and the institution's goals at different moments. Second, I inquire about the political motivation behind the stylistic and visual choices that went into the production of architectural kitsch. Finally, I explore the role of these choices in constructing the image of Eva Perón as a political leader.

LOVE: SOCIAL ACTION AND WELFARE PROGRAMS

Around 1947, even before the foundation was formally established in 1948, Eva Perón began putting into effect various social action programs.[6]

Eva Perón Foundation, *Hogar de Tránsito no. 1* (Women and Children Shelter no. 1), Buenos Aires, n.d. COURTESY OF ARCHIVO GENERAL DE LA NACIÓN (ARGENTINA).

Children's City "Amanda Allen," Buenos Aires, n.d. COURTESY OF ARCHIVO GENERAL DE LA NACIÓN (ARGENTINA).

Model of the monument to the "descamisado," n.d. COURTESY OF ARCHIVO GENERAL DE LA NACIÓN (ARGENTINA).

Model of Eva Perón Foundation Headquarters, n.d. COURTESY OF ARCHIVO GENERAL DE LA NACIÓN (ARGENTINA).

Constructing a physical infrastructure was essential to realizing these programs. The buildings had precise functions that went beyond just the typological or programmatic aspects of the architecture; they included symbolic, stylistic, and aesthetic elements intended to shape a political imaginary. The metaphor of the machine is particularly appropriate in characterizing the architectural efforts of the foundation, because its buildings constituted organisms whose complex functioning was rigorously and rationally planned, all with the intention of solidifying a social action program and the political meanings associated with it. On the other side of this architectural production process were the recipients of social programs: the "dispossessed" or the "humble," those who had remained outside the protection of the state, which now reached workers and employees.

Although not all the foundation's buildings were directly related to its social program—notable exceptions included the headquarters of the Confederación General del Trabajo (CGT) in Buenos Aires and the University of Córdoba's new campus—that program did inspire most of the foundation's efforts and decisions. Eva Perón began her work in the field of social action with the support of Armando Méndez San Martín, then the government-appointed director of the Sociedad de Beneficencia, formerly Argentina's most prestigious private charity. In effect her "crusade" began before she had her own institution. She worked at first in conjunction with the Dirección Nacional de Asistencia Social, a subsection of the Secretaría de Trabajo y Previsión that was created in 1944 and led by Méndez San Martín. Upon leaving this institution Eva Perón began to organize her own technical team, whose construction efforts were initially led by the engineer Carlos Bonanni. This was not her only attempt to develop an institutional framework for her future social action work: she also approached the Ministerio de Obras Públicas and the municipal government of Buenos Aires. Nonetheless, her strongest connection was with the Dirección Nacional de Asistencia Social, which shared her vision and supplied technical support. Thus the foundation was rooted in state action, and particularly in the reforms that Méndez San Martín had brought to the Sociedad de Beneficencia. In addition to restructuring the management of the institution, he had abolished the use of uniforms in the establishments under his jurisdiction and initiated the construction of hogares de tránsito, transitory shelters for single mothers and their children, inaugurating the first of these on 1 June 1947. Later the construction of hogares continued under the auspices of the Fundación Eva Perón.[7]

As is well known, the discourse of the foundation was built on a critique of existing methods of charity, social action, and traditional education, critiques in which architecture was used metaphorically to characterize the old and new philosophies. The foundation described architectural proposals of the past as courtly, cold, and practically prison-like, while the educational programs they housed were anachronistic and the social programs humiliated the most helpless members of society. This was a stereotypical image that the foundation used to construct its own identity. In fact, many of the programs that the foundation pursued—such as its vacation developments for workers and its housing for weak children—had already been initiated by the National Board of Education, by municipal and provincial governments, and by private charities. Likewise, the architectural proposals of the foundation had antecedents in earlier social action projects, which over a decade earlier had abandoned courtly and cloistral typologies in favor of picturesque styles and freer forms. Examples include the summer camps of the Consejo Nacional de Educación, the colonia hogar Ricardo Gutiérrez of the Patronato Nacional de Menores, the shelters of the San Vicente de Paul Society, and the plans for public schools dating from the 1920s and 1930s, which had abandoned classicism in favor of neocolonial elements. Another example was the Casa de la Empleada (House of the Working Woman), founded by Monsignor Miguel de Andrea in 1923 for the Unión de Empleadas Católicas. With respect to hospitals, the "monoblock" type adopted as an innovation by the foundation had many similarities with hospitals built in the 1930s, such as the Federal Police Hospital. Pre-Peronist efforts to revamp the system of juvenile incarceration, through reformatories for example, were even disseminated in film. Carlos Borcosque's film *Y mañana serán hombres* (Tomorrow They Will Be Men, 1939), showed the transformed Colonia de Marcos Paz in Córdoba as a model of the genre.[8] As an examination of the foundation's architectural proposals reveals, the institution often completed projects that had been conceived and sometimes partially executed in the previous period. The first instance of this was the government of Mendoza's Ciudad Infantil (Children's City), created in 1938 within a broader system of homes for mothers and children.[9] The second was the Consejo Nacional de Educación's proposal in 1932 for the construction of "educational villages," a group of farms and boarding schools in rural areas.[10] The boarding schools that the foundation developed fifteen years later followed a similar plan to tackle similar problems. Both were based on the recognition that in vast parts of the Argentine interior, the school-age population did not go to school because of social and economic problems and lack of transport.

The work of the foundation was thus in line with previous efforts to renovate social welfare and educational buildings. Still, given the substantial differences in origins, historical moment, and management style, the foundation's efforts were hardly identical to those that came before. The differences allowed the foundation to craft a discourse that completely dismissed previous developments in social action, education, and health. Furthermore, even given the continuity that existed between the old and new projects, there were undoubtedly differences between the cores of these proposals. The foundation opted for more personalized treatment of residents and tended to avoid stigmatizing them (through required clothing, for example). It also implemented more liberal guidelines for the relationship between people inside and outside the institutions. Therefore, though the projects of the foundation did not depart radically from the renovation of social service establishments already under way, they did offer a major change in the symbolic aspects of these establishments.

THE CHILDREN'S CITY

La Ciudad Infantil (the Children's City), founded in the neighborhood of Belgrano in Buenos Aires in 1949, combined many of the elements and meanings typical of the architecture created for the foundation's social programs.[11] The Children's City was part of a series of interconnected boarding and education facilities, each designated a "city" (the Children's City, the Student City, and the University City). The inhabitants of these cities were separated based on age and education level. The space in between the Children's City and the Student City was occupied by "home schools" in a single building dedicated to primary education.

The Children's City served children of preschool age, of whom some boarded and others attended for the day; it was meant particularly for "poor children," and preference was given to "orphans" and neglected children. They received schooling, food, and medical attention and enjoyed leisure activities. Political propaganda linked the city to the ideas of Froebel and Montessori, describing it as a new effort to expand preschool education, which despite having been initiated in Argentina at the end of the nineteenth century, had not been highly developed. The main building, done in the California style, housed the administration, bedrooms, a cafeteria, and offices, and alongside it stood a miniature rustic city. In this way the Children's City combined three functions: boarding school, nursery school, and Lilliputian city. I have already mentioned several precursors for the first two functions; the Lilliputian city also had antecedents, although these were more often related to entertainment than pedagogy. This type of installation tended to appear in fairs, amusement parks, and expositions. In the foundation's proposal, however, childhood entertainment had an educational purpose: "[It is] something like a small capital of a make-believe nation . . . where at every twist you expect to see a circle of dwarves or a princess in a crystal carriage. A chimerical but real city that constitutes the vigorous expression of a new sense of children's education. . . . Mrs. Perón longed to create a strict and at the same time kind institution that would unerringly guide children's first steps. A special, enchanting atmosphere was, thus, indispensable. It was also necessary to offer a safe place for the children of workers. So this exquisite work was conceived, composed of solid materials, but graceful and beautiful forms."[12] This "world of illusion" was therefore not an end in itself but rather a pedagogical tool. In contrast to the República de los Niños (Republic of Children) built by the Peronist government of Buenos Aires near the provincial capital of La Plata, the Children's City did not draw on the exotic images of children's stories.[13] Such a project might have found an architectural model in nineteenth-century zoos, which balanced parody and romance. But since the ultimate goal of the Children's City was education rather than leisure, it did not draw on romantic imagery. Instead it attempted to be a "real" city in miniature, and included the elements and institutions that make up a real city. There was a bank and a municipal government building—on Worker's Rights Square—and a service station, police station, school, church, and homes, as well as the "Rights of the Elderly" bridge. In an environment built to their scale, the children "learned" how to use a city, becoming citizens; there they were given an education "so that one day they would feel lucky to 'live in a large, powerful, and just Fatherland' as Eva Perón has put it."[14] The Children's City aspired to be a scale model rather than an imaginary construction; in effect the atmosphere that it created was "magical," but the components of the city were completely realistic.

Given the way it pursued its pedagogical goals, the Children's City is an emphatic example of the notion that buildings can be "educational machines." The idea that buildings themselves could play a privileged role in transforming individuals characterizes all educational and welfare architecture since the late eighteenth century. With its origins in the Enlightenment, this idea reflected an extreme confidence in the power of architectural spaces, articulated with social programs, to shape behavior and ideas. *My Mission in Life* embraced these concepts, although it inverted the values embedded in previous thought about social action programs: "All 'social service' of the century which preceded us was like that: cold, sordid, mean and selfish. Every asylum built by the oligarchy perfectly expresses the exploitative soul of a breed which, happily, will die out in this century, a victim of its own pride, its own selfishness. The children 'they' tried to save will never forget that 'they' were their tormentors. 'They' made them *'communists'* by putting them in a gray uniform, giving them insufficient meals, shutting all doors to human happiness, to the simple happiness of having a home, or at least an imitation of a home. . . . The honor of destroying some of those old ideas has fallen to me through my work."[15] "They" made them communists. The text proposes a direct relationship between political ideology and material conditions that persists, even if its results are valued in different ways. Beyond inheriting these ideas, the foundation expanded on them, bringing them to fruition in a literal way, without mediations: just as the Children's City built a miniature replica in order to teach children how to live in a city, the Student City—built nearby—reproduced parts of the Presidential Palace, as a "pedagogical tool that [would contribute] to the students' civic formation," developing "a broad and strict sense of the responsibilities of citizenship."[16]

What was the "real city" upon which the Children's City was based? The picturesque paths and rustic chalets were not reminiscent of traditional Argentine cities, but rather of the new urban planning endeavors of Peronism, such as Ciudad Evita or Barrio General Perón in Buenos Aires (now known as Barrio Saavedra), which although linked to the foundation were designed by the Ministerio de Obras Públicas. In other words, children were to learn to live in the new type of city that Peronism was creating. The Children's City was a scale model in a double sense, since the new Peronist neighborhoods were themselves intended to be alternatives to the "real city." The Children's City was a "space of illusion" built on another "space of illusion."[17]

These Peronist urban planning decisions, though not necessarily co-ordinated with each other, constructed a political imaginary, since the connections between the different projects were apparent. The magazine *Mundo Peronista*, for example, published in 1953 a Peronist worker's "in-vention": the "Peronist watch," whose face contained "a multi-colored miniature city" with every hour marked by a "Peronist building" repre-sented by a rustic architectural miniature ("hospitals, workers neigh-borhoods, technical schools, children's parks, old-age homes, summer camps").[18] Was the "Peronist watch" based on Evita City or the Chil-dren's City? It could have been either. One referred to the other: both were "spaces of illusion" separated from the "real city," new constructions that promised perpetual happiness. Shortly after the death of Eva Perón, an initiative of Mayor Jorge Sabaté inverted the relationship between the real city and the works of the foundation: it modified the zoning regula-tions in the area around the Children's and Student's Cities, providing them with an "adequate urban setting" by following the forms and oc-cupations that the two cities had created. This also offered "an urban planning solution for the area 'Bajo Belgrano' . . . [converting] this zone into a garden city."[19] Slightly before, in 1951, as an advisor to the founda-tion Sabaté had attempted to push the model of the Children's City further with a proposed project that was never actualized: el Mundo de Infancia (the Children's World) in Ezeiza, a municipality in Greater Buenos Aires.[20] Much larger and more ambitious than the original, the project was to cover a hundred hectares and contain a much more complex city, with core areas dedicated to particular themes—civics, welfare, and commerce, but also rural life and the military—and includ-ing one area dedicated to "instruction and fantasy" as well as a separate "recreation" zone, containing a large park of mechanical games. This project would have extended the didactic message of the Children's City to dimensions originally unimagined.

THE POLITICAL MEANING OF KITSCH

The "cities" of the Fundación Eva Perón were not its only projects with an obviously didactic intent: all of the foundation's architecture attempted to communicate clear political messages. The architecture associated with social programs displayed a combination of three elements common to a kitsch aesthetic: "luxury," conventionalism, and direct references to images of domesticity.

Luxury constituted a sort of brand that the institution introduced in its architecture to differentiate its designs from those that came before. As a political operation, luxury had a redistributive and compensatory character and was the foundation's hallmark, as can be seen in the quote from *My Mission in Life* in the second epigraph to this chapter. Luxury was understood as a demand, and in an indirect way it politicized the social action programs: luxurious and exuberant social action programs were synonymous with the actions of Eva Perón. According to *Mundo Peronista*, the young inhabitants of the Student City affirmed: "we live like kings."[21] This meant that they inhabited forms reserved in previous decades for the recreational spaces of the middle class—this was the foundation's idea of luxury. A good example of the way the California style could be used to fulfill these intentions was the façade of the main building in the Student City. A rectangular ground plan was covered with seven roof lines. The verticality of the tower broke the horizontal monotony of the whole. The semi-exterior spaces (covered porches and balconies) offered an array of formal and material solutions: half-arches, lowered arches, straight-lined wooden doorways. No form became repetitive because there was always a break, a detail, or a change to reinforce the idea of variety. These were dense and visually busy complexes, with contrasts in textures, colors, and materials accentuated by the familiar tendency of rustic architecture to increase the number of sections and the size of details. This was an architecture of excess, because like the warehouses of the foundation—packed with toys, clothing, and household items—these physical spaces were to be a "cornucopia" at the disposal of the underprivileged. The California style, owing to its compositional flexibility and tendency toward contrast and variety, was impeccably suited to this purpose.

Still another aspect of the California style served the political objectives of the institution well: its markedly conventional character, as an established and time-honored group of forms. In effect the redistributive work of the foundation tended not to create new forms, but to reappropriate and give new meaning to what already existed. In other words, the more conventional and less innovative the architecture, the better it could achieve its political objective. As Harold Rosenberg has written, kitsch is a predictable aesthetic in all its aspects: rules, effects, and rewards.[22]

After luxuriousness and conventionalism, the third characteristic of this architecture was its appeal to images of "homes," since rustic styles were groups of forms fundamentally associated with the domestic world. It is important to remember that Eva Perón first had contact with these styles before the foundation's program took shape. Applying the California style to these programs allowed the foundation to recast the image of the social service organization: the metaphor of the home came to replace the courtly and institutional styles that the foundation associated with the social assistance programs of the past, and that derived in many cases from hospital architecture. In this transition between metaphors—from hospital to home—the figure of the mother replaced that of the state.[23]

Luxury, conventionalism, and domesticity were thus three characteristics that expressed the politics of this architecture. Nonetheless, the relationship between these characteristics and their political meanings was indirect, in the sense that the Peronist political messages present in the architecture were mediated by elements that did not belong to the political field but rather referred to social values. Of course there were some direct references to politics, from the names of the buildings (Eva Perón Pavilion, 17th of October Building, and so on) to the innumerable photos of the Peróns and political slogans painted on the walls. But these explicit references were rarely incorporated in substantial ways into the architecture designed for social programs; they functioned instead as added elements that were superfluous to the architecture. In contrast, the emphasis on the formal and aesthetic aspects of the buildings and the redistributive character assigned to them does suggest that one goal of the buildings was to offer *beauty* (which is to say socially accepted forms of beauty) or, more precisely, aesthetic pleasure to a public that had been previously excluded from enjoying it. The idea of a "right to beauty" was never formulated explicitly, but it does offer an important key for reading this group of works, which differed from the architecture generally produced by the Peronist state.

During the Peronist period some of Eva Perón's detractors were particularly critical of her aesthetic of luxury and excess. Because of its oddity as a miniature city, the Children's City was seen as a symptom of the arbitrariness and impulsiveness typical of the leaders of Peronism. One foreign observer described the city as Eva's "dream come true . . . the fancy of a little girl who never had her own doll house."[24] Other observers seemed to agree with this assessment. As the newspapers of the period reveal, Eva Perón invited most of the foreign visitors who merited an official welcome to visit the city. She was perhaps more proud of it than of any other work; she considered it a clear illustration of her social action efforts, and showing it off seemed to give her sincere pleasure. Nonetheless, beyond its personal aspects this pleasure was clearly subordinate to its political meaning. In effect Eva Perón's pride was of a public nature: the pride that public figures cannot repress when exhibiting the work they have promoted.[25]

This sort of slippage between public and private in analyses of Eva Perón's works is encouraged by Eva's public image, which mixed these different planes. Such was the case with the public presentation of her personal image and the role played by the aesthetics of her wardrobe, her jewels, and her hairstyles. In particular, and in relation to the topic at hand, we can see a relationship between the transformation of her personal image and the aesthetics of the architecture promoted by the foundation. This relationship should not be understood simply as a banal display of private life in the public world but rather as the use of private aspects in constructing a political image.

The foundation's strategies began to take shape during the first years of Eva's political career. The moment of architectural imagining—the foundational moment that defined forms and meanings and shaped future developments—can thus be situated between 1947 and 1948. This was also the moment when Eva Perón began to present herself insistently as Evita: "I have preferred to be Evita rather than the wife of the President if this Evita is said to ease a pain somewhere in my fatherland. I prefer to be the *compañera* of all the humble workers than to be the formal wife of the President; I have wanted to be a beacon of light and of hope for them and it is for them that I work, struggle and fight."[26] Evita presented herself as "a woman of the people, [who] alongside a patriot, has known how to hear the popular heartbeat." This image of the young and smiling lady, comrade to the humble, adopted a physical appearance that remained much closer to the affinities and tastes of the radio actress she had once been than to those of the wife of the president she now was: her hair still worn long and falling on her forehead, the furs, the big hats, the extremely high heels, the complex combinations of colors and textures, the profusion of accessories and jewels.[27] As with the architecture of the foundation, luxury manifested itself in Evita's clothing through contrast and abundance. We see her dressed up this way in photographs from the inaugurations of her first projects: at one inauguration of a hogar de tránsito in 1948, for example, she is pictured in furs and a large hat with feathers and a veil.

At this initial moment there was a coherence between Eva Perón's personal image and her architecture, and while it is impossible to know if this was intentional, together the two served to create the political persona of Evita. As is known, Eva Perón's personal image gradually changed as her political power increased. A more elegant and sober image emerged, moving away from Paco Jamandreu and toward Christian Dior, with tailored suits and hair pulled back: Evita transformed herself into "La Señora." More than a transformation, understood as the substitution of one image for another, this was a separation of roles: as Fraser and Navarro have argued, Evita began to "distinguish between her ceremonial Eva Perón role of receiving honors and attending state functions and her role as Evita, doing her social and political work."[28] Her physical appearance, however, began to be guided by the first role more than by the second.

As is demonstrated by the design for a new headquarters in 1950, the architecture of the Fundación Eva Perón also changed in that sector of its production which aimed to display the institutional power accrued on the basis of Eva Perón's earlier work. Nevertheless, the architecture of the social action programs, in which familiar images counted for a great deal, did not change. The Eva Perón who inaugurated works until 1949 was different from the later one who visited them and showed them off in operation. It was the very prestige and power afforded her by those earlier works that facilitated her transformation. The new and sober image of Eva, "La Señora," now offered a counterpoint to the rustic architecture of the foundation: the coherence of 1947 or 1948 was gone.

A NEOCLASSICAL TEMPLE OUT OF PLACE:
THE HEADQUARTERS OF THE FUNDACIÓN EVA PERÓN

The building to house the foundation's new headquarters was proposed in 1950, and it was about to be inaugurated when Perón was overthrown five years later. The undertaking began at a turning point within the trajectory of the institution—it was at this moment that it became known as the Fundación Eva Perón (instead of the Fundación María Eva Duarte de Perón) and that its charter was modified. As Bianchi and Sanchís have noted, it was also then that the activities of the institution were broadened and that Eva Perón strengthened her control over them; in this way the foundation was transformed into "a privileged instrument for the exercise of a personalized power."[29] At the same time, in 1950 Congress began to increase the resources destined for the institution, allowing a blurring of the line between the foundation and the state. In October 1950 Law 13.992 ordered the University of Buenos Aires to donate the land where the new headquarters would be built.[30] This law also enabled the state to contribute to the support of the foundation's welfare establishments and authorized the foundation to administer public welfare programs. Although the foundation was a private entity, its functions were considered "in the public realm and of national interest." Even as this law was being passed, the Subsecretaría de Informaciones was putting on the exhibition "Eva Perón and her Social Work" to publicize the foundation's efforts. In the exhibition two models surprised visitors with their size and location within the display: the Children's City (inaugurated in 1949) and the future headquarters. The buildings can be interpreted as images that synthesize two moments in the institution's development: the efforts to serve the underprivileged through the welfare programs' rustic style; and the affirmation of institutional power, expressed in the neoclassical language of the headquarters. The latter was thus related to a new moment in the foundation's development. Its architecture did not represent the state, since the neoclassical style was not used frequently in public buildings during the period; instead it referred to the power of a political leader over the state, without seeking to imitate that leader.

In fact the headquarters of the foundation was directly related, in formal terms, to one building that did represent the state: the Facultad de Derecho (University of Buenos Aires Law School). Perón's administration constructed the building and inaugurated it in 1949, though it was first envisioned in the government-sponsored design competition of 1940.[31] At that point neoclassicism was still used in some state programs that for different reasons eschewed modernist images and appealed to values of the past. Neoclassicism made sense given the building's function, since references to the classical period were common in buildings associated with the law. In the 1930s this style had a strong presence in the public architecture of many countries, not only those dominated by authoritarian regimes; the United States is a prime example. Even within the production of authoritarian states the link with politics did not completely rule out other possible uses of neoclassical languages, given that classicism had not completely lost its historical prestige.[32] In other words, at the end of the 1930s the neoclassicism of the Law School was not completely out of date. In contrast, it is more difficult to explain the neoclassicism of the foundation headquarters, given that this style had disappeared from the international architectural repertory after the Second World War. Clearly the search for a strong institutional image overpowered contemporary trends in architecture. As has been stressed with respect to the foundation's social programs, the foundation did not create new images but rather appropriated existing ones. Furthermore, the headquarters brought together several design elements that did not appear in the Law School: sculptures on the cornice, for example. In these sculptures, from San Martín to the *descamisado*, passing through an allegory of justice, the message of the architecture was reinforced by a figurative program: the building represented the foundation's integration into national history. Architecture no longer sought to make emblematic the work of a "*compañera* of the poor" but rather the work of a nation builder.

THE MONUMENT, 1952–1955: MARBLE OR BRONZE

The monument to Eva Perón was ordered built after her death by Law 14.124, and it deepened the architectural rhetoric that had been rehearsed in the foundation's headquarters. The sculptor León Tomassi, who had crafted the sculptures at the headquarters, designed the project with architectural advice from Carlos F. Krag, the vice-dean of the Architecture School at the University of Buenos Aires and an advisor to the foundation. The Comisión Pro-Monumento a Eva Perón, founded in 1952 and led by Senator Juana Larrauri, managed the project.

The monument, to be located in front of the presidential residence, was to consist of a column, the base of which would contain the mausoleum, and upon which would rest a gigantic sculpture of a descamisado. It was intended to be "the largest monument in the world" and to become "the eighth wonder." The total height of the monument was to be 450 feet (by comparison, the Statue of Liberty measures only 150 feet); the statue alone was to be 197 feet tall, and the main staircase some 328 feet wide. The design included fourteen elevators and a silver sarcophagus. Verticality was the most striking element of the composition. Visitors would be able to climb to the head of the figure, 433 feet high, and there were to be various observation points along the way, including a terrace above the descamisado's anvil. Viewed from the river, the monument would dominate the city's skyline. It was intended to be an urban symbol like the Statue of Liberty or the mythical Colossus of Rhodes, the most noteworthy sight when approaching the city.[33] Manuel A. Domínguez, dean of the School of Architecture and Urban Design at the University of Buenos Aires, proposed the following reading of the monument: "Future travelers leaning over the prow of ships as they file into our port, will spy in the distance a bare-chested, bronze colossus with an air of gravity and security, beside the anvil where injustice was smashed and where the happiness of the Argentine people and the greatness of the nation was forged. And they will wonder . . . what nation is this that raises a monument of this magnitude, stripped of trophies and bellicose allegories, where all is a song to dignity and human solidarity?"[34] The location was also a central aspect of the work, not only because the monument was to dominate the view of the city from the river but also because it was to be contiguous with the presidential residence. The model indicates that Libertador Avenue was to be rerouted so that the residence and the monument could occupy the same property. This layout made it impossible to imagine anyone other than Perón living in the presidential residence; a statue meant primarily to immortalize a dead leader ultimately reaffirmed the power of one who was still alive.

According to *Mundo Peronista*, the raising of a monument "in which she hoped to rest when she died" had been one of Eva Perón's last wishes; the commission would only later decide to replace the figure of Eva Perón with the descamisado. She had been pleased with the original model, asserting, "This is marvelous because it is large and simple. This is what I wanted."[35] According to the Peronist daily *El Líder*, Eva Perón had commissioned Tomassi to build the Descamisado Monument in 1951; in December of that year she saw the model, and exclaimed: "This is where I hope to rest when I die." Upon her death the commission proposed replacing the descamisado with a statue of Eva Perón, but Tomassi disagreed. According to the sculptor, a statue of Eva demanded marble and therefore would need to be in "normal dimensions," while the giant figure would be done in oxidized copper plating.[36] Given the press accounts of the activities of the commission and that a whole year passed between the death of Eva Perón and presentation of the model, it seems unlikely that Eva Perón ever approved the project as her own resting place. The story, impossible to verify, appears to have been invented after her death to legitimize the project.

Beyond these different versions about the promotion of the monument, an analysis of the work itself is instructive. It is important to note that the monument fused two programs: the mausoleum, conceived after the death of Eva Perón, and the Monument to the Descamisado. The building of the latter had been an early Peronist initiative, launched in 1946, for which the government organized collections and mandated wage deductions; designed by Jorge Sabaté, this monument was to be built at the intersection of the Avenida de Mayo and 9 de Julio, but construction never began.[37] The fusion between the two monuments could have been the realization of this unfulfilled promise.

The figure of the descamisado was the Argentine form of the "new man," a myth that recurred in various national contexts between 1930 and 1945. While this myth was common to the political culture of different European countries and of the United States, it took on a different concrete form in each case.[38] In 1947, when the National Honorary Commission for the Monument to the Descamisado met Perón, he set out an aesthetic and figurative program for the monument. "I think that what would be interesting is to make a monument that will be profoundly evocative, for the simple reason that it will be an eminently popular monument, whose form and intention must be easily interpreted. It should not be complicated, but rather something the people can understand, . . . and the people understand what moves their senses and feelings. The monument should be simple, and the people as they see themselves, through the different eras of our history, should be represented in it. Its central figure should be the descamisado who we all know and see in the street, the one that we saw on the 17th of October."[39] Perón suggested a particular work as a point of reference: the Monumento al Ejército de los Andes (the Monument to the Army of the Andes) in the Cerro de la Gloria (Hill of Glory) in Mendoza. He had inaugurated it shortly before and believed that "no one could contemplate it without emotion." He added that the descamisado monument "should be a monument in movement, rejecting the immobility that dominates sculpture these days."[40] This initial program, except for its appeal to realism, bore little relationship with the ultimate monument to Eva Perón. The transformation can be directly related to the change in the monument's central theme, from the construction of the descamisado to the cult of Eva Perón. Likewise, the change in meaning imprinted on the political imaginary of Peronism between 1946 and 1952 also demanded artistic modification.

There remains one feature to emphasize in the fact that the cult to Eva Perón was to take the form of the descamisado. As with the social action programs and the headquarters of the foundation, the references to Eva Perón were indirect, mediated by other figures. To understand this choice we can compare the monument with a similar artistic endeavor drawn from a different national context: Boris M. Iofan's design for the Palace of Soviets in Moscow (1933–34), which also was never finished. The structure was to be a statue of Lenin (curiously, another embalmed leader), 328 feet tall and resting on a column. Nonetheless, in Argentina it was not the figure of Eva Perón that assumed immense dimensions: she was to be represented indirectly. The need for colossal and blunt representations was linked, paradoxically, with a need to displace the meaning of the represented.

From this point of view it is possible to reinterpret the discussions regarding the characteristics of the monument. The commission sought a "bronzed Eva Perón"—which is how the project is titled in the adorned published volume of parliamentary speeches in support of the commission's formation. The sculptor, meanwhile, proposed a marble Eva Perón built on a human scale. This proposal won out, and the bronze was discarded. This choice of representation was reaffirmed by the expression that was to be engraved on the crown of the crypt's rotunda: "At Perón's side was a woman who dedicated herself to bringing to the President the hopes of the pueblo, which Perón later converted into reality. All we know of that woman is that the pueblo lovingly called her Evita."[41] "Evita," the image of humility, stood in opposition to the "bronzed Eva Perón," the colossal image of power; the "human" image that she built for herself at first contrasted with the image she later consolidated through the exercise of political power. The discussion signaled a confrontation between different representations of the same figure, although it was not put in these terms. Which image was to be adopted now that Eva Perón was not there to decide? How would her political legacy be managed? Perhaps the construction of the monument reflects the perplexity and doubts of the Peronist leadership in the moments after her death. The solution chosen can be interpreted as a compromise between the two representations: the colossal is present, but only to speak in an indirect way about the "human" figure. Eva would only come to "bronze" by accepting the "humility" of marble.

"SYMBOLIC JUSTICIALIST ARCHITECTURE"

As we have seen, the death of Eva Perón did not halt the production of images surrounding her figure but rather seemed to stimulate their production, deepening the already fantastic associations of her visual image. Many representations drew on Catholic iconography, portraying her with a halo and saintly attributes, much as Tomassi had done in his sculptures for the monument.[42] In support of this proliferation of images, Ramón Asís, civil engineer, former vice-governor and secretary of public works in Córdoba, published a curious pamphlet in 1953, entitled "Toward a Symbolic Justicialist Architecture." In it he proposed building public buildings with utilitarian ends (hospitals, for example) in the shape of colossal sculptures of the Peronist leaders. He based his proposal on the idea that "any profound change in the psychic structure of a people requires a change in the means of expressing aesthetic values." Therefore the New Argentina had to "elaborate its own architectural style, abandoning the imitation of foreign schools that do not move us and say nothing to our national soul." The new style would celebrate "elevated forms of conduct, using the sculptural figure of great Argentines as symbols of virtues." According to Asís this new architectural style had been elaborated "in its general form by Mrs. Eva Perón, who wanted to bring the spirit of the revolution into all art forms."[43]

Asís's imaginative proposal was never taken up in the architecture of the state. Nevertheless, leaving aside the practical and economic difficulties implicit in the type of buildings he suggested, his proposal was not merely one man's feverish fantasy. Although he did not mention it, his idea did have strong similarities with the Eva Perón Monument project. One might argue that he expanded on the monument proposal in two ways: he proposed to extend it to the functional buildings of the state, and he replaced the descamisado with images of political leaders. Asís clearly based his vision on Peronist dreams, but he traversed the limits that Peronism had accepted. Asís's assertion that his proposals were related to those of Eva herself is revealing. In effect, surrounding her image was a proliferation of creations that could be called, without exaggeration, architectural *bizarreries*, a genre not uncommon in art closely linked to power: a miniature city, an anachronistic neoclassical temple, a colossus. Asís was simply continuing down a course of architectural representations that had already been charted around the figure and work of Eva Perón. His advance toward state architecture and toward the direct and colossal representation of the leaders was a step that official architecture would never take under Peronism. This nucleus of bizarreries remained the unique and exclusive property of Eva Perón.

This chapter has analyzed a group of forms and images that were tightly linked to politics. As noted at the outset, there were several other trends in the architecture at the time, and the images around Eva Perón represent only one part of a broad and diverse field of architectural production. There were significant state projects that promoted radical and sophisticated modernist architecture, while others appealed to a more muted modernism that was less innovative but equally committed to high-quality construction. This state architecture was much more plentiful than that promoted by the Fundación Eva Perón, which produced only a limited number of works. Nonetheless, it is the foundation's works that have remained fixed with the greatest intensity in the imaginary of Peronism.

1 Eva Perón, "Palabras prononciadas el 3 de abril de 1948 al inaugurarse el primer hogar de tránsito que llevó el nombre de Evita," *Discursos completos* (Buenos Aires: Megafón, 1985–86), vol. 1, 204–5.

2 Eva Perón, *My Mission in Life*, trans. Ethel Cherry (New York, Vintage, 1952), 144–45.

3 The expression "aestheticization of the political" was first employed by Walter Benjamin in reference to fascism in his *Theorien des deutschen Faschismus*. Nonetheless, studies such as Maurizio Vaudagna and Gianpiero Brunetta, *L'estetica della politica: Europa e America negli anni Trenta* (Bari: Laterza, 1989), have shown that the emphasis on the aestheticization of politics is not limited to totalitarian governments, as evidenced by the United States in the 1930s. See Sandro Scarrocchia, "Mefisto o la arquitectura del totalitarismo," *Bloc: revista de cultura arquitectónica* 5 (2000), 54–63.

4 See Calinescu, *Five Faces of Modernity*, 225–56.

5 Interview with the architect Mario Colli, Buenos Aires, 16 July 1993.

6 Eva Perón's activities in this field began in 1946, first out of the presidential residence and later from her office at the Secretariat of Labor and Social Security. The Cruzada de Acción Social María Eva Duarte de Perón began at the end of that year with a food distribution program. On the origins and works of the foundation see Bianchi and Sanchís, *El Partido Peronista Femenino*; Fraser and Navarro, *Eva Perón*; Ferioli, *La Fundación Eva Perón*; Plotkin, *Mañana es San Perón*, 137–64. An overview of the foundation's architectural work can be found in the *Revista de Arquitectura* (Buenos Aires) 370 (1953).

7 The first Hogar de Tránsito in Buenos Aires was located on Salta Street; later the foundation built others on Carlos Calvo Street (April 1948), Lafinur Street (June 1948), and Austria Street (August 1948).

8 *Antena*, August 1939, 25.

9 Provincia de Mendoza, *Mensaje elevado a la Honorable Legislatura por el Gobernador de la Provincia Dr. Guillermo G. Cano, período de mandato 18 de febrero de 1935 al 18 de febrero de 1938* (Mendoza: Gildo D'Arcurzio, 1938), 21.

10 Ramón J. Cárcano. See Ramón J. Cárcano, *800.000 analfabetos: aldeas escolares* (Buenos Aires: Roldán, 1933).

11 It is located at Echeverría Street, between Húsares Street and Dragones Street. The Student City was built close by and inaugurated in 1951.

12 Argentine Republic, Subsecretaría de Informaciones de la Presidencia de la Nación, *Ciudad Infantil "Amanda Allen"* (Buenos Aires, 1950).

13 The "Republic of Children" in Gonnet (near La Plata, Buenos Aires Prov-

ince) was developed by the government of the Province of Buenos Aires and then transferred successively to the foundation and the Unión de Estudiantes Secundarios for its use.

14 Argentine Republic, Subsecretaria de Informaciones, *Ciudad Infantil.*

15 Perón, *My Mission in Life*, 144.

16 Argentine Republic, Subsecretaria de Informaciones, *Ciudad Estudiantil* (Buenos Aires, 1951).

17 It should be clarified that this was not a conscious decision: the designer of the Children's City—Mario Colli—said that he had not taken the neighborhoods proposed by the ministry as a reference point. The ministry's project, meanwhile, was built at the same time as the Children's City. Regardless, the similarity may have been due to similar choices in architectural forms (rustic and Californian) and to the purpose of the program (the Children's City as a model for the city of adults).

18 *Mundo Peronista* 45 (July 1953), 25–26.

19 Municipal Decree 6080/952, 29 August 1952, *Boletín Municipal de la Ciudad de Buenos Aires* 9442 (5 September 1952), 1526.

20 It was to be on the corner of Avenida General Paz and Autopista Ricchieri, close to Villa Madero Station. Jorge Sabaté Archive, Museo Evita of Buenos Aires.

21 *Mundo Peronista* 24 (1 July 1952), 28–30.

22 Harold Rosenberg, *The Tradition of the New* (New York: Da Capo, 1994), 266.

23 The desire to imbue different spaces with domestic elements can be seen in the political *unidades básicas* of the Partido Peronista Femenino, as Bianchi and Sanchís have noted. This was an attempt to present these environments to women as "houses," making them "an agreeable and warm environment." The goal was "differentiating the basic unit from the 'party committee,' which women perceived to be distasteful and foreign, and giving the basic unit its own identity." Bianchi and Sanchís, *El Partido Peronista Femenino*, vol. 1, 80.

24 Barnes, *Eva Perón*, 213.

25 To analyze the political actions of a public figure as completely attributable to his or her personality or biography leads to a simplified and incorrect understanding. Two works that tackle this problem are Sarlo, "Eva Perón"; and Navarro, ed., *Evita*. More on those arguments in my "All about Eve."

26 Eva Perón, "Discurso pronunciado el 6 de mayo de 1949 ante una manifestación popular, en la Plaza San Martín de la ciudad de Rosario," *Discursos completos*, vol. 2, 36–40.

27 This is a theme that was observed at the time and also in different biographies of Eva Perón. See for example Fraser and Navarro, *Eva Perón*, 136–37.

28 Fraser and Navarro, *Eva Perón*, 101.

29 Bianchi and Sanchís, *El Partido Peronista Femenino*, vol. 1, 88.

30 The site was bounded by Paseo Colón Boulevard, Estados Unidos Street, Azopardo Street, and Independencia Street, currently the site of the Facultad de Ingeniería (Engineering School) of the University of Buenos Aires.

31 For this reason it cannot be understood as an example of state strategies under Peronism. There were similar cases, such as the Banco Nación, the Casa de la Moneda (National Mint), and the Facultad de Medicina of the University of Buenos Aires, projects that were brought to fruition under Peronism but were based on architectural visions and plans from the 1930s.

32 An example of this same style, undertaken a few years before the University of Buenos Aires Law School, is the Kunsthaus (Munich, 1933–37) of Paul L. Troost, one of Hitler's favorite buildings and a symbol of Nazism. Political associations did not overshadow the other qualities of the Kunsthaus, which recreated the nineteenth-century neoclassical elegance of the Altes Museum of Karl F. Schinkel (Berlín, 1823). For an important discussion see Ciucci, "Linguaggi classicisti negli anni Trenta in Europa e in America"; and Winfried Nerdinger, "A Hierarchy of Styles: National Socialist Architecture between Neoclassicism and Regionalism," *Art and Power: Europe under the Dictators, 1930–1945*, ed. Dawn Ades et al. (London: Hayward Gallery, 1996), 322–25.

33 *Boletín de la Facultad de Arquitectura y Urbanismo* 4 (November 1953), 7. On the colossus in architecture see Martin Warnke, *Political Landscape: The Art History of Nature* (Cambridge: Harvard University Press, 1995), 89–114; and Simon Schama, *Landscape and Memory* (London: Harper Collins, 1996), 385–516.

34 *Boletín de la Facultad de Arquitectura y Urbanismo* 4 (November 1953), 7.

35 *Mundo Peronista* 47 (August 1953), 21–23.

36 *El Líder*, 26 July 1953, 1–2. Fraser and Navarro maintain that Eva Perón commissioned Tomassi in 1951 to build the monument to the descamisado. Impressed by Napoleon's tomb in Les Invalides, she would have added a crypt to the monument in which a few descamisados would rest. Fraser and Navarro, *Eva Perón*, 169.

37 The first blueprint for a monument to the descamisado had more modest dimensions than Eva Perón's memorial: forty-five meters high and twelve meters long. In 1950 a model was constructed, according to the press, "of normal size" in the chosen location. *Democracia*, 10 January 1950, 4; *Clarín*, 10 January 1950, 24.

38 Giorgio Ciucci suggests that the "new man" was represented in sculptures at the following sites: on the patio of the Chancellor's Building of Berlin (1938); at the "World of Tomorrow" pavilion at the New York World's Fair (1939); around the Palazzo della Civilitá Italiana, designed for Italy's exposition of 1942, or "E42" (1939); and over the Soviet pavilion at the International Exposition of Paris (1937). According to Ciucci, differences are often overlooked in these representations: in Italy and Germany the "new man" is shown in his "timeless, athletic nudity" to express the myth of racial regeneration, while in the Soviet Union and the United States he is represented as a worker (as in Argentina). Other sculptures sharing features that cross national lines include several representing the founders of new "empires": the four presidential heads at Mount Rushmore (1927–41), the colossal statue of fascism in Monte Mario, and the profile of Mussolini in Monte Soratte. Ciucci, "Linguaggi classicisti negli anni Trenta in Europa e in America," 48–49.

39 *El Líder*, 25 July 1947, 12.

40 *El Líder*, 25 July 1947, 12.

41 *El Líder*, 25 July 1947, 12.

42 Other examples include "Evita, Madona de América" (lacquer on display in the Van Riel Gallery) and the monument to Eva Perón proposed to be erected in Lebanon by the Confederación de entidades libanesas en Argentina. Archivo General de la Nación, Sección Documentos Gráficos.

43 Ramón Asís, *Hacia una arquitectura simbólica justicialista* (Buenos Aires, 1953), 6–8. I thank Mariano Plotkin for introducing me to this pamphlet.

Mirta Zaida Lobato, María Damilakou, and Lizel Tornay

....

Translated by Beatrice D. Gurwitz

WORKING-CLASS BEAUTY QUEENS UNDER PERONISM

"It was not a beauty pageant; it was more to pay tribute to the working-class person," Edna Constantini told us when we interviewed her in the city of Santa Rosa in the province of La Pampa. It was June 2003, and a radiant Edna had welcomed us into her spacious home. On her mantelpiece she displayed some photographs of her family alongside others which showed her posing with General Juan Domingo Perón, as Evita placed a crown on her head.

Edna was one of eight "Queens of Labor"[1] chosen during the first period of Perón's rule (1946–55). The selection of queens was among the changes introduced by Peronism to the annual labor celebration on the first of May. In the Peronist reformulation of May Day, a ritual initiated in 1890 by the most militant workers, women held a privileged place. The workers' celebration culminated in the coronation of their new queen: a "criolla beauty," the representative of a union or a regional industry, who would be crowned before the multitude by Evita, while she was alive, and later by Perón. The military coup of 1955 ended the worker celebrations and the election of queens. By the time the selection of the working-class beauty queen reappeared on the political scene in 1974 and 1975, the ritual did not have the same resonance in Argentina's thoroughly transformed political, social, and cultural life.

This chapter analyzes the fanfare surrounding the selection of the Queen of Labor on May Day, her coronation, the parade through the city streets, the stage, the set design, and also, although only partially, the lived experience of the women who participated in the events. These ritualized celebrations raise a series of questions about the relationship between ritual, political action, and feminine beauty during the period between 1948 and 1955; about the failure to fully recreate the ritual in the political context of the 1970s; and about gender relations during the first Peronism and the political radicalization that characterized Perón's final presidency. We find possible answers to these questions in the traces and clues preserved in photographs housed at the National Archive (AGN), in photographs published in the newspapers of the period and the Peronist press, in the many newsreels (from Noticiero Argentino and Noticiero Panamericano) of the first Peronist governments, and in the testimonies of the participants and their personal photo albums and newspaper clippings.

The "queens" of the first Peronism have been mentioned in several works, either in discussions of the propaganda that the regime used to build political consensus or as an example of the invention of a new political tradition.[2] The selection of queens in the 1970s has attracted less attention: a partial evacuation of the Plaza de Mayo on 1 May 1974 in response to the demonstrations of the radicalized Peronist Youth has overshadowed the pageant held on the same day, while the competition of 1975 is barely remembered.[3] Nevertheless, the existence of these contests speaks of the public exhibition of the female body, of plebeian royalty, of monarchical representations, and of limited democracies. The choice of a working-class beauty queen during the first Peronism was part of a mass cult articulated through both words and images in a liturgy that mixed diverse rites and symbols. It was a political spectacle that was imbricated with a particular formulation of "feminine beauty" and with an aesthetic of ostentatious monumentality that could not be recuperated twenty years later.

NEW MEANINGS FOR MAY DAY

May Day was established as an international workers' ritual in 1890. Its creation was the result of a deliberate political act aimed at creating the working class through the pedagogy of celebration. Largely created from above by the most organized workers, the May Day celebration became a tradition, with symbols and slogans that made the multitude visible to suggest the consensus purportedly existing among workers.[4] From 1890 on, anarchist, socialist, and communist workers would demonstrate on the streets of Buenos Aires with posters, flags, and musical bands and then meet in the Plaza Lorea or the Plaza Miserere, where they would sing revolutionary hymns.[5] The goal was to make the strength and demands of organized workers known both nationally and internationally. May Day demonstrations, at times well ordered and at times tumultuous, were occasionally the object of state repression, resulting in injuries and deaths.

Between 1890 and the advent of the Perón regime in 1946 there were hundreds of May Day events in the city of Buenos Aires and in the interior of the country. The workers' day had become a ritual that commemorated the many workers who had been repressed, killed, wounded, and arrested in protests for better salaries, for an eight-hour work day, against capitalist exploitation, or in solidarity with other workers. Faced with these traditions, Peronism produced both a rupture and a change in the meaning of the ritual. May Day became a battle for control of symbolic space. In 1950 it acquired a highly celebratory tone, which it maintained until 1955, even if it lost some of its brilliance after the death of Eva Perón in 1952.

At the festivities of 1 May 1946, held less than three months after the election that brought Perón to power, the meanings that Peronism would later assign to the ritual were not yet clearly defined. In some places leaders held competing events. The national celebration was organized by the Confederación General del Trabajo (CGT) with the support of the Labor Party, which had organized the political mobilization that culminated in Juan Perón's electoral victory in February 1946. Juan Domingo Perón, María Eva Duarte, and Domingo Mercante, governor-elect of the province of Buenos Aires, led the parade. For the first time in the fifty-five-year history of May Day, national authorities led the march together with the workers, and Perón associated the day with the emerging Peronist movement. This was the beginning of the movement's appropriation of the symbols and meanings previously associated with May Day and with the various movements that had struggled to represent the working class. Peronists also began to associate May Day with October 17, 1945, the movement's symbolic birthday.

"Yesterday and today," a phrase that the government would later use profusely in its propaganda, marked the rupture. Yesterday was associated with the excesses and abuses that fostered hate among the humble; yesterday signified the divisions in the popular masses and the presence of "imported agitators"; yesterday marked the indifference of the government and parliament. "Today," on the other hand, happiness, jubilation, and celebration reigned for all those willing to build the nation.[6] May Day became a day of celebration because the triumph of Peronism embodied the national sentiment and a clear rupture from the past, when oligarchic governments repressed workers, provoking violent confrontations.

The pamphlet "1° de mayo ayer y hoy" ("May 1st, Yesterday and Today") used words and photographs to portray contemporary Argentina as a "redeemed nation." May Day was no longer "the date for pain and misfortune, but rather for happiness. The Festival of Labor is celebrated jubilantly by those who work to build the fatherland." The accompanying photographs served as witnesses to this message. The pictures chosen to represent "yesterday" were taken by reporters from the magazine *Caras y Caretas* during the anarchist protest of May Day 1909, when the police repressed protestors, and violent clashes between the workers and the police ensued.

The "yesterday" images selected for the pamphlet highlight red anarchist flags ("synonym of death and anarchy"), a dead protestor, and some injured ones. In contrast, the "today" section begins with a transcription of the Rights of Workers and the Elderly, a photograph of Perón talking to the masses that fills a whole page, and another two-page picture of the crowds in the Plaza de Mayo under the title "The jubilation of a million workers, owners of their rights and conquests." The Queens of Labor appear on the following pages. In the working-class ritual resignified as part of the new liturgy for the Peronist regime, women occupied a privileged space: the May Day event now culminated in the coronation of the working-class beauty queen.

The popular mobilization for the May Day ceremonies was significant; both male and female workers responded to the calls of the CGT, the trades, and the union leaders to join the festivities. The reporters of the Peronist press celebrated the creativity, ingenuity, and virility of the workers. These accounts invariably described as "happy" and "festive" the "immense human ocean" and the "rivers of crowds" who gathered to march toward the Plaza de Mayo. The celebratory and popular character of the event persisted even on 1 May 1953, when the crowds responded to anti-Peronist violence by singing new lyrics to popular songs:

For four crazy days
that we will live,
let them throw another bomb,
we are going to have fun . . .

or:

The Bomb! The Bomb!
What a calamity!
the assassins of the People
are infesting the city.[7]

In discussing the threats to his government during his speech that day,
President Perón borrowed, in slightly modified form, the celebrated
phrase from the *Communist Manifesto*: "Workers of the world unite." The
queen of that year, described as "constitutional and democratic," was
Nélida María Ferreira, the representative of the province of Córdoba and
member of the Argentine Union of Theater Artists.

THE "PRETTIEST LADY WORKER"

Every year a criolla beauty who represented a union or a regional industry was crowned before the crowds at the official May Day celebrations.
This practice represented an important change in the representation of
women workers. Peronist iconography certainly included the proliferation of images of domestic women in harmonious homes, and the female
nurse willing to give her life for the sake of others became a Peronist
symbol. Nevertheless, photographs of the Queens of Labor replicated a
certain ideal type of beauty: "Argentine beauties." The key, however, is
that it was a female "worker" who was presented as the queen. In 1948,
when the first official queen was chosen, Perón spoke to the crowds,
stressing the importance of the celebration for the workers and the
government. He claimed that the presence of beautiful women workers
signaled a new era of happiness.

The public exhibition of the beauty of female workers entailed an
ideological operation that made feminine beauty a requisite component
of the broader Peronist dignification of labor. The working-class beauty
queens were the image of dignified labor. They stood in stark contrast to
the old notion, popularized in literature and the labor press, of labor as

A woman carrying a flag escapes from police repression at a Labor Day demonstration in Buenos Aires, 1 May 1909. COURTESY OF ARCHIVO GENERAL DE LA NACIÓN (ARGENTINA).

Peronist Labor Day parade, Buenos Aires, 1 May 1949. COURTESY OF ARCHIVO GENERAL DE LA NACIÓN (ARGENTINA).

humiliating and deforming to women (and their offspring). The figure of the Queen of Labor affirmed that women could be both good workers and beautiful, thereby combining two attributes long thought incompatible. For decades following the initial incorporation of women into the workforce, the woman worker was considered above all a mother who worked and as such "a shred of an abandoned home." In this view poor working women suffered the deterioration of their bodies, turning them into human remains, incapable of inciting male desire, and, to make matters worse, poisoning the health of future generations. Industrial work suppressed beauty, and if by some chance women workers did maintain their beauty, they risked harassment from bosses and foremen and might even be pushed into prostitution.[8] An important change occurred when beauty became a labor requirement for models and actresses, but the tension between beauty and competence persists today.

The newspaper *El Laborista* organized the first contest for a Queen of Labor in March 1947, in the hope that the working class would attend a big ceremony in her honor. In its words: "The *Laborista* will organize the selection of the most beautiful lady workers [*las más hermosas obreritas*] . . . with the goal of exalting their devotion to work and awakening in the nation a truer consciousness of the forces that improve themselves daily by the impulse of blood and thought, in order to forge the greatness of the Fatherland."[9] The rules were clear: any female worker affiliated with a workers' organization was eligible. The only condition was that each contestant had to be a union member; contestants had one month to affiliate or be eliminated from the contest automatically. According to the newspaper the worker who received the most votes in each union would be chosen as the union's delegate to the larger competition. Female workers and employees throughout the country participated, while the newspaper's readers served as judges (the newspaper published a ballot to send in) and commercial firms provided prizes. The headlines were eloquent: "Our Contest Enjoys Total Popular Support"; "The Elected Will Be a Faithful Expression of the New Argentina on the Move"; "And Now, to Vote!"; "Our Election of a Working-Class Beauty Queen is on the Road to Being a Huge Success. New Support from Commercial Firms"; "The Duty to Vote."[10] These headlines sought to increase participation, whether as part of the duties of citizenship or simply to make the contest a success.

Although *El Laborista* spoke of "our pretty lady workers [*nuestras lindas obreritas*]," the group of candidates was quite heterogeneous. There were pretty girls and others less so, brunette and blonde, young and old, blue-eyed and brown-eyed. The organizers sought to dignify the working woman (" 'The Working-Class Beauty Queen Will Revitalize the Working Women of Our Country"), but they emphasized beauty ("She Will Be Argentine and Beautiful Like the Fatherland," "Our Pretty Lady Workers Emulate the Most Famous Figures in All of the Arts") in a way that did not seem contradictory.[11]

The appeal to working women was also a response to their new presence in the workforce outside the home, their involvement in numerous labor and social protests, and their political demands. Since the end of the nineteenth century women held a wide range of jobs in factories and workshops in big cities like Buenos Aires and Rosario, as well as in smaller ones throughout the country. By the middle of the 1940s female labor had achieved a certain level of skill, and domestic and workplace roles were clearly differentiated. The greater visibility of women in different aspects of economic, social, and political life, as well as their participation in social conflicts, worried the government, which responded by promoting participatory structures and recognizing certain rights for women, including the right to vote.

The proposal by *El Laborista* to carry out a beauty competition was not a novelty. In the United States the *Chicago Tribune* had inaugurated this sort of contest, while various Argentine publications had organized competitions for Miss Friendliness, Miss Smile, the Spring Queens, and the queens of different ethnic communities. The magazines *Radiolandia*, *Antena*, and *Sintonía* organized competitions in search of new radio and film stars.[12] What set apart the contest organized by *El Laborista* was that it was a political proposal for a popular mobilization that would end by honoring a working woman as Queen of Work. The message in this sense was clear, and in response to numerous votes for Evita the newspaper clarified that "General Perón's wife values this distinction in all its meanings but since she herself desires that the 'Queen of Work' arise from among the workers and employees who give their services in factories, workshops, offices, shops, etc., she has resolved, in a gesture worthy of her position as Argentine first lady, to exclude herself from the competition. As a result, voters should limit themselves to ladies whose photographs appear in our paper."[13]

The outcome of the election for national Queen of Labor in 1947 reflected the votes cast by readers of *El Laborista*, but this was the first and last time that this method was used. In the following year the competition would take place within the context of the labor mobilization organized by the CGT and the government, and the jury would include union leaders, Perón, and even Monsignor Santiago Copello, the archbishop of Buenos Aires.

THE STAGE AND THE SPECTACLE

Politics, spectacle, leisure, and culture merged in the annual May Day celebration. Politics materialized in Peronism's appropriation of the labor ritual and the mobilization of workers (both men and women). The spectacle involved a parade of floats and staged events in front of the presidential offices and the CGT building. Leisure activities were visible in the festivities that the workers and their families participated in. The cultural aspects included musical performances and dances as well as the presence of various artists in the official box. The May Day ceremonies featured classical and folk music, and the national symphony orchestra or Colón Theater ballet company might perform. Peronist politics tied political propaganda to the theater and to the mass mobilizations that assertively occupied public space.[14]

Turning May Day into a performance involved creating new meanings and uses for existing spaces. For example, the stage erected in front of the presidential palace in 1950 placed the CGT on the same level as Perón and Evita as a co-organizer of the event, but the poster on stage showed a worker with his body and face turned toward the president in a position of subordination. The stairs to the stage, where the provincial working-class beauty queens stood, rose toward the images of Perón and Eva, the *"conductores del pueblo* [leaders of the people]," and toward the signs of the most important workers' organization.

The presidential offices and the Plaza de Mayo became the privileged public spaces for Peronist ceremonies, but the May Day celebrations incorporated a new locale as well: the CGT building. In addition, the parade of the queen and her court took place along the city's main

Main Stage, Labor Day celebrations, Plaza de Mayo, Buenos Aires, 1 May 1950.
COURTESY OF ARCHIVO GENERAL DE LA NACIÓN (ARGENTINA).

avenues (Avenida Corrientes, 9 de Julio, Callao, and de Mayo) and often stopped at the National Congress.

The stage was large and the scenography imposing: the flags spread their magic, forming a wall behind the throne; lights shielded the space of representation, while pages greeted the candidates and escorted them to their place on the set. It was all intended to create an image of grandeur. The parade of floats extended the scenography to the streets of the city. The impressive float that transported the queen and her princesses included a throne resting on a mechanical gear (see illustration on page 176).

The visual effects of May Day 1948 were particularly effective, with parade floats that were allegorical representations of the rights of the workers and of social justice.[15] The parade displayed the "Workers' Decalogue" of Peronism, in order: (1) the right to work, (2) the right to fair compensation, (3) the right to vocational training, (4) the right to dignified working conditions, (5) the right to health care, (6) the right to welfare, (7) the right to social security, (8) the right to protection of the family, (9) the right to economic improvement, and (10) the right to the defense of professional interests.[16] The forms of these representations varied: masculine figures, hands that pointed to the future, large and strong fists holding hammers as a symbol of creation, a scale that held money and the fruit of labor in balance. Many of the floats included hands, which could suggest various meanings. They are associated with work and action, they symbolize the authority of the father within the family, and they might be associated with the authority, protection, and power of the state.[17] Feminine images represented vocational training and health care. One female figure, reminiscent of classical statuary, held a light (a symbol of indestructibility) and a book (a symbol of a certain kind of power), representing the wisdom necessary to build a strong and powerful Argentina. In the "right to welfare" float a muscular mother holding a child embodied protection of the health of the nation and of the family.

The scenography of the floats, like that of the stage, included various spaces, levels, and representations. Spectators would see different scenes, depending on where they stood. From one angle the float representing the right to social security revealed figures tied to a wheel, a clear allusion to the exploitation of workers in the past. At the same time, observers might see the figure of an angel announcing the Peronist liberation of the present. From a Christian point of view the angel might also symbolize protection. In addition, the float included a male figure, free of danger and the bonds of exploitation. The hammer that he held is the classic tool of the blacksmith and is powerfully related to the creation story.[18]

As for the representation of women in this group of allegorical floats, the figures did not constitute a clear break with the roles of the past: the protective mother, responsible for the home and family, and companion for the man. These images were compatible with the formal ideology of Peronism but also with gender roles disseminated in iconographic and discursive traditions that date to the late nineteenth century and that were shared by such divergent ideological currents as socialism, anarchism, and Catholicism.[19] The iconography of the woman during Peronism involved a profusion of domestic images: women sitting in front of a sewing machine, women greeting their husbands when they returned from work or saying goodbye to the children as they headed to school. The peaceful, tidy, harmonious home was the woman's "place," and she was willing to dedicate herself to the needs of others. The figure of the nurse embodied this self-abnegation and altruism. But in accord with the industrializing discourse of Peronism, the image par excellence in propaganda posters, pamphlets, and film shorts was the man in overalls who represented the urban industrial worker. This image competed for prominence with that of the descamisado (a man with his shirt open), the symbol of the disruptive process initiated by the pueblo on October 17, 1945.[20]

The iconography of women in the allegorical floats and propaganda posters revealed little of this disruptiveness. In contrast, the photographs of working-class beauty queens riding on parade floats or visiting factories and tourist centers, the portraits that emphasized their beautiful faces, and the descriptions of their gentle gait constitute an image of the modern woman, much closer to the images in contemporary women's magazines. In fact, some of the queens were featured in newspaper and magazine advertisements for Manuelita soap, manufactured by the Federal soap company. These advertisements focused on the beauty queen's face to demonstrate the naturalness of the soap, in contrast to the artificial look of cosmetic powders.[21]

The mobilization of workers would begin early on the morning of 1 May, when they would gather under the flag of their union to sing and chant slogans. The newspapers, especially those strongly aligned with the government, described the contingents of workers moving through the streets toward the parade route and the Plaza de Mayo. In 1949 crowds of workers arrived in trains and on special convoys. The parade, the rally, and the performances were part of every year's events, as was one other ritual. Union members in various places throughout the country would elect local working-class beauty queens, who would arrive in the capital for the celebration and the selection of the national queen of the workers. As the newsreels and the photographs in the press demonstrate, the spectacle attracted massive crowds. They surrounded the floats, blocking their path; everyone wanted to see the "Argentine beauties." The police were forced to intervene to keep the program on schedule.

This labor festival was above all a public spectacle, part of the "optical unconscious of Peronism," the audiovisual and cinematic conditions that enabled its emerging political culture. As Walter Benjamin suggests, photography and cinema, through such devices as foreground, slow motion, and enlargement, make visible what previously could not be seen clearly, permitting the emergence of new structural forms. "The nature that speaks to the camera is different from that which speaks to the naked eye," Benjamin says. A space shaped by the consciousness of man—"man" here not as a representation of humanity but as part of the construction of an image of gender—gives way to a space not informed by any such consciousness.[22] In this space the body of the working-class beauty queens takes on density, forming part of the cultural fabric of the Peronist experience.

THE WORKING-CLASS BEAUTY QUEENS

The selection of the queens was a long process, at the end of which the most beautiful woman was elected regional or provincial representative and finally, on May Day, national queen. Who were these queens? How were they chosen? What were their aspirations?

The selection process seems to have been modified over time. At the beginning the contestants were young women who generally worked as employees in the service sector, a government agency, or a union office. The factory and workshop workers were fewer in number, although a few unions did elect their queens every May Day.[23] Nevertheless, one of the national queens was, according to the press, the representative of the Union of Various Trades of Eva Perón Province (now La Pampa). The queens were young women, between sixteen and twenty years old. For the national celebration they arrived in Buenos Aires from towns and cities in the interior. There they visited factories and were feted by various unions such as that of the rail workers; the Peronist newspapers and magazines lavished them with attention.

The beautiful women were situated in an important part of the set built for the occasion. The candidates, dressed in gala attire, with a cape, crown, and scepter, occupied steps ascending toward the stage. The scepter might have represented a magic wand, a bolt of lightning, or a phallus, but its symbolism was augmented by an industrial gear at its tip, similar to the gear symbol used by the CGT. The event was filled with bombastic gestures. In 1948, shortly after the parade of allegorical floats, a few calls of a bugle silenced the crowd for the arrival of the float that carried the regional queens of labor. When the float arrived at the great stairs that led to the "proscenium," various "pages" approached the contestants and escorted them to their place on the stairs. At the end of the coronation the Colón Theater dance company performed a symbolic parade of women workers. Later, when Perón spoke to the crowd, he described the May Day event as "livened up and adorned by the representation of the Argentine woman, whose synthesis we see in the queens of the different trades of the Republic." He proclaimed their beauty a "happy omen" that foretold years of national unity.[24] The young women, who were praised for the intensity of their gazes, their fresh smiles, or their (black) hair, represented a feminine ideal.

A poem published in the newspaper *El Laborista* celebrated the queen as a "criolla beauty." And in fact photographs reveal that despite some variation in hair color, all the queens could be described as fair-skinned criollas, with no other obvious ethnic markers. Even the representatives from provinces with a large indigenous population conformed to this standard of beauty. The poem describes the queen as an "eternal symbol of grace and harmony" who represents "the glories of the New Argentina."[25] As the poem suggests, feminine beauty fit into Peronist ideology under the rubric of harmony, a particularly central element in official discourse. Press accounts stressed that harmony characterized the "regal" group: the queens, like the floats that paraded on the city's central streets, made "a harmonious, colorful, and beautiful group."[26]

The queens could work in any industry. According to the press, Ruth Romero, the Queen of Labor in 1949, helped her parents with farm work while studying home economics and music. Práxedes Mesconi, selected as queen in 1950, was a public employee while her successor, Aída Beaumé, was a domestic employee. The queen in 1952, Edna Alicia Constantini, was a fashion designer, having studied dressmaking. The queens in 1953 and 1954, Nélida María Ferreyra and Susana (Susy) Leiva, belonged to the Argentine Union of Theater Workers, while Elsa Landaburu, queen in 1955, represented the telephone workers' union. Every job was honorable and deserved public respect, but the indispensable prerequisite for the Queen of Labor was physical beauty. The queens embodied both beauty and the spirit of the Argentine people, and they represented all women who work for "the greatness of the Nation."[27] In this way the queen's two qualities, industriousness and beauty, intertwined and extended to the entire female population of country.

To understand the meaning of this extension of qualities we need first to understand the criteria for feminine beauty during the Peronist years and to determine who was in a position to legitimize these criteria. The contest judges, with the exception of Eva Perón, were all male. The members of the secretariat of the CGT, union leaders, and President Juan Domingo Perón were the authorized voices.

That the CGT organized the contest and that it was a key component of the May Day celebrations likely shaped the discourse surrounding the candidates. They were to be workers from modest families, although not all the contestants fit these requirements. In her May Day address in 1950 Eva Perón referred to "the humble girls with big hearts who come to the capital to add a touch of spirituality, love, happiness and hope to this first of May."[28] Besides being a good Peronist, humility, beauty, and kindness were the oft-repeated requirements for the honor.

If participants in the early stages of the contest had to be women workers of relatively humble origins, according to the discourse of the organizers and the press, physical beauty was the deciding factor in the final phase. In general the judges did not vote as union leaders but as men. The female representative of the Argentine work force did not have to be the most hard-working but rather the prettiest. What does this tell us about gender relations during the first Peronism? In part, as suggested earlier, the display of feminine beauty was part of the process of dignifying labor. The public image of the beautiful woman worker was certainly something new, but it was not exceptional. Other countries, like Chile, also chose working-class beauty queens; in fact the Chilean queen sat in the official box in Argentina in 1951.[29]

The photographs of the candidates and the winners reveal the importance of certain characteristics. The photographers' eyes gravitated to the women's gaze, eyes, smile, and hair. Likewise, reporters' accounts drew readers' attention to the queen's face, dark hair, clean smile, and repeatedly her eyes, which were normally dark but always deep and bright. References to the women's bodies or clothing were not common, although some reporters did emphasize the smoothness of their gait.[30] These descriptions drew on a mass-produced and stereotypical image: these are the girls from mass-circulation magazines and serial fiction. As Beatriz Sarlo describes it in her analysis of the immensely popular weekly novels of the 1920s: "This social image of the body has privileged, hyper-meaningful zones, zones that disappear in the *chiaroscuro* of their relative importance, and others that are completely annulled in the collective erotic imaginary. These semiotic networks lay down the lines of possibility of a relationship between the sexes."[31] The photographs of working-class beauty queens operate within a semiotic in which the eyes become the foundation of a solid, feminine beauty; they are the messengers of what sometimes cannot be said in words. Other traits were also highly valued: the lips, the smile, a beauty mark, all of which carried a powerful erotic charge.

In these photographs the queens' status as "universally beautiful women" obscured their working-class character. Youth and nature, in the sense of natural beauty, blended in the representation of the ideal woman. Hers was a "classic" beauty, far from the "aesthetic democratization" of our times, when frequently "style" of dress, a particular "type," or harmonious physical proportions are more important than the natural beauty of facial features. The prizes offered to the winning contestants only accentuated further the femininity of the lucky ones: in addition to a brooch donated by the CGT, the regalia, the scepter with the mechanical gear as a symbol of industrial work, and a certain amount of money (a large part of which they returned to the Eva Perón Foundation as a donation), they also received sparkling jewels to make their beauty shine even more.

Each year the press highlighted the winner's personality and morality, stressing that she was simple, modest, diligent, and affable. These descriptions, together with the interviews of the queens published in the newspapers, allowed women workers to identify with their queens. It was not only their natural beauty but also their personality that made them "accessible" to the broader female public. The beauty queens were prettier than other women workers, but the differences were not so great in other respects. They dreamed of being wives and mothers rather than movie stars, they cried when they heard their name announced on the loudspeaker, their hearts raced during the contest, and they were not used to the lights of flash photography. They were working-class beauty queens who knew that they represented the forces building a new Argentina, but above all they wanted to be "queens of their home."

The queens were the center of everyone's attention: the judges, the spectators (men, women, and children), and the reporters. They were glorified and admired for their simplicity, their beauty, and their desire to become wives and mothers. Each queen's aspirations were reiterated in the press to the point of exhaustion: to marry, have children, build a

Ms. Dora Hermosa, Corrientes
province's candidate for Working-
Class Beauty Queen, 1948.
COURTESY OF ARCHIVO
GENERAL DE LA NACIÓN
(ARGENTINA).

María Zulema Farinazzo, San
Luis province's candidate for
Working-Class Beauty Queen,
1948. COURTESY OF ARCHIVO
GENERAL DE LA NACIÓN
(ARGENTINA).

home, and be an efficient housewife. The queens studied home economics and crafts like embroidery and needlework. They knew how to sew, cook, and clean.

Yet within this repetitive discourse, there were a few signs of a tension between what was said and what women secretly desired. When a journalist insisted that Aída Beaumé, one of the queens, confess her true desire to be a theater or movie star, Aída responded: "I cannot change my mind in two days. I am engaged to be married. My highest aspiration is to have a home and children," but she added, *"if I had had the opportunity to decide the course of my life I would have been a lawyer . . .* but since I have not been able to channel my aspirations towards this dream, I am learning to embroider, sew and cook. I am preparing myself to be an efficient housewife."[32] It seems there were limits to the fulfillment of dreams. Escaping the feminine role associated with the house and home was difficult, at least for the women of the popular classes.

The captions of the photographs offer sentimental narration; they are texts meant to produce happiness, destined for a female public that would identify with the queens. The queens' natural, accessible beauty and moral characteristics enabled other women workers to dream of a similar fate: to be chosen, crowned by Eva and Perón, hugged by Perón, and cheered on by the masses. This recognition included giving interviews and visiting the presidential palace, the newspapers, and the "temples" where Peronist welfare programs came to fruition: the unions, boarding houses for women workers, and shelters run by the Eva Perón Foundation. In the context of the unsatisfying life of privation associated with a working-class standard of living, achieving "royalty" turned the dream of traveling and visiting new places into reality. Photographs featured the queens as they arrived in Buenos Aries, as they traveled through the city, and at the Ezeiza airport. The images invariably showed smiling faces that were beautiful, natural, and modern.

The photographs helped to build a consensus on the importance of natural beauty. For the Peronist regime the exhibition of natural beauty facilitated the process of valorizing and dignifying female work, which no longer humiliated women but rather assured them public recognition. For the male population, whether judges or spectators, the natural beauty of the winners identified the men as the owners of a valued commodity. For women, the queens' "accessible" beauty, which was

Eva Perón with candidates for Working-Class Beauty Queen, Buenos Aires, 1 May 1949.
COURTESY OF ARCHIVO GENERAL DE LA NACIÓN (ARGENTINA).

Juan Domingo Perón crowns the Working-Class Beauty Queen of 1955. COURTESY OF ARCHIVO GENERAL DE LA NACIÓN (ARGENTINA).

neither overly delicate nor modeled on that of the femme fatale, allowed them to identify easily not only with the winners but also with a fantasy world drawn from literature. On another level these women were like Eva Perón, in that they reproduced the story of the humble young woman who became the queen of her people. Like Evita they loved the home, Perón, and the poor. During her reign Ruth Sesma Romero, the queen in 1949, hoped to bring to fruition Eva Perón's dream of "an effectively fair Fatherland," in which "the rich are not too rich and the poor not too poor." Práxedes Mesconi, named Queen of Labor in 1950, declared that her dream was "to have a home and many children in order to make Perón's Fatherland greater." For her part, Edna Constantini, the queen in 1952, claimed that her reign was "an homage that the CGT paid to all the women workers of the nation. I am just the vehicle of this homage . . . and I receive it in the name of all of my Peronist, Argentine sisters."[33] The photographs, along with the mass media, reinforced a "culture of beauty" as an important part of "mass culture," even as they served the political purposes of the Peronist regime.

In 1951 official discourse was marked by the language of labor efficiency. With the encouragement of the national government, men and women struggled to break production records. Two photographs are particularly meaningful. In one, President Perón and Evita are shown at the presidential offices receiving women workers who had set extraordinary production records. The photograph demonstrates that working-class beauty queens were not the only ones received by the leaders of Peronism. Also acknowledged were women who had joined the conflict-ridden world of work, even if they remained discursively confined to the home. The second photograph, taken on 29 April 1951, shows the regional Queens of Labor visiting a dressmaking workshop to "cheer on" the young women who worked there. In the foreground, beneath the smiling faces of the queens, is a young woman sitting before a sewing machine. She represents both a traditional woman (sewing is for women) and a modern one: she is fashionably dressed, and the ribbon in her hair matches the fabric of her skirt. The image reinforces the uniformity of female demeanor around models disseminated by women's magazines over a decade earlier.

The visual culture of Peronism was ambivalent: on the one hand it rigidly fixed traditional images of gender, and on the other it democratized them by producing them on a grand scale and making them visible to the masses. It promoted the confinement of women in the "agreeable" world of the home even as it pushed them to occupy public spaces. It could be argued that the self-affirmation of women, particularly those of the popular sectors, remained in constant tension with the reformulation of their subordinate status. Women, including Eva Perón herself, were glorified, but that glory did not actually democratize power.

Two photographs offer the clearest image of the construction of this ambiguous language. The first shows the Queen of Labor of 1949 sitting on a throne that in turn rested on two clear elements of the iconography of Peronism and the CGT: the closed fist, a symbol of effort, dedication, and work, and the mechanical gear, a representation of industrial work (see illustration on page 176). In the second photograph a huge crowd— itself a key sign of the period and one that appears in the first photograph as well—surrounds the queen and her court during the "magnificent" parade of 1951. The queen's float that year was once again adorned with a gigantic gear. "Beautiful and smiling," the queen and her court (made up of "authentic criolla beauties") paraded through the city. In 1951 the parade also included a float carrying "valiant workers who broke labor and production records."[34] Dressed in their work clothes, these men were the real representatives of labor and power.

"NO QUEREMOS CARNAVAL, ASAMBLEA POPULAR"

The military coup of 1955 put an end to the May Day celebrations and the selection of working-class beauty queens. The new military government persecuted the Peronist Party and its militants. In many ways Argentine culture was transformed in the years after Perón's fall, a change visible in artistic expressions, musical tastes, fashion, and fundamentally in daily life. The changes affected young men and women, particularly in the area of sexual morality. Extramarital relationships, the acceptance of enjoyment and the search for sexual pleasure, liberation from the fear of motherhood thanks to the contraceptive pill, independence, a taste for reading, politics, and film—all became part of women's lives, although to different extents and at different rates. These cultural shifts would affect the beauty competitions that reemerged when Perón returned to power in the 1970s.

The image of the modern woman in magazines like *Claudia* and

Femirama was quite different from the one disseminated by *El Hogar* and *Para Ti* in the interwar years. Although motherhood and home life continued to be the privileged realm for women, people began to question gender relations. Men could, for example, "help" their wives with chores and not compromise their virility. Modern advertising promoted new products and new values, transforming consumption patterns and transforming representations of women. Young people were the principal agents of these political and cultural changes.[35]

In 1973, after nearly two decades of cultural transformations and political instability, of proscription and frustrated hopes, Peronism returned to power. But the nation had changed significantly and witnessed the development of a culture of rebellion that in its most extreme versions took the form of armed organizations, both Marxist and Peronist. When Perón returned to Argentina, when the Peronist Héctor J. Cámpora was elected president under the banner "Cámpora to the government, Perón to power," and finally when an overwhelming majority elected Juan Domingo Perón himself to his third presidency, it was young men and women, more than workers, who had won the streets.

Even though Perón was the indisputable leader of his political movement and had an enormous influence on young people, he found that time had not stood still since the moment he had been forced to leave the government and the country. The tension between his intent to reestablish the Peronist past and the efforts of revolutionary Peronist youth to use those same traditions to build a new, leftist block threatened to explode at each step.

The attempt to restore the past became evident at the May Day celebrations of 1974 and in the effort to reestablish the Queen of Labor competition. The political culture associated with a mass spectacle linked to work could not be restored easily. Moreover, in 1974 conflict within the Peronist movement had reached the level of absurdity, as right-wing Peronist organizations waged an assassination campaign against militants of the Peronist Youth (JP), communists, members of the Revolutionary Party of the Workers (PRT), the Socialist Party of Workers (PST), and other leftist forces.[36]

Efforts of both sectors of the Peronist movement to end the stalemate made preparations for the events of May Day 1974 particularly tense. The Peronist right had issued a clear threat months before in *El Caudillo*, an organ of the Peronist Youth of the Argentine Republic (JPRA): "O los vivos se van al mazo o la cosa termina de la peor manera" (roughly, "Hey, smart-alecks, you'd better back off or things will end badly!")[37] Meanwhile, the JP and the armed Peronist revolutionaries known as the Montoneros sought to "break" the clique that purportedly surrounded Perón, preparing to mobilize with the support of the radicalized factions of the labor unions.

Early on the morning of 1 May 1974 the JP militants approached the Plaza de Mayo but had difficulties entering.[38] That same morning in the National Congress, Perón had spoken of the need for a homogeneous national project to which all sectors of society—workers, business people, intellectuals, the armed forces, and the church—could contribute.[39]

The ceremony held that afternoon at the Plaza de Mayo revealed a clear effort to recreate the spectacle of the past. The well-known radio announcer Antonio Carrizo introduced the actress and singer Susana Rinaldi, who recited a poem. Other film stars watched from the official box. The tension mounted as the columns of the JP-Montoneros entered the Plaza displaying signs, and a war of slogans ensued. One side chanted, "Mon-to-ne-ros" or "What is happening, General, that the popular government is packed with gorillas (or anti-Peronists)?"; the other side responded, "Ar-gen-ti-na." Faced with the spectacle that continued on stage, the slogan "No queremos carnaval, asamblea popular" ("We don't want carnival, we want Popular Assembly") expressed leftist opposition to the ceremony. To one side, meanwhile, young women waited for the working-class beauty queen to be announced. When Perón arrived at the plaza by helicopter, the young radicals spent ten minutes screaming for "the heads" of Alberto Villar and Luis Margaride, two officers of the Federal Police who were notorious for their violent, extralegal persecution of the left. Just before five o'clock Vice President Isabel Perón crowned María Cristina Fernández, the representative of the Health Workers union, Queen of Labor for 1974. Among other prizes she received two tickets to Europe, plus lodging and spending money. In the plaza around fifty thousand people chanted, "There is only one Evita," a clear rejection of Perón's third wife and vice president, Isabel.[40]

The rupture was inevitable; the slogans expressed contradiction and often confusion; only contemporary press reports and photographs reveal the magnitude of the conflict, showing the figure of Perón standing

Isabel Martínez de Perón crowns Graciela Lage as the Working-Class Beauty Queen of
1974. GRACIELA LAGE'S PERSONAL COLLECTION.

on the balcony in front of a half-empty plaza.[41] In the General Archive of
the Nation, the repository of the memory of the state, there are no
photographs of the plaza (perhaps they were not catalogued properly or
were irremediably lost, as has happened with other cultural artifacts).
The only two photographs that show Isabel Martínez de Perón with the
queens are from 1974 and 1975. That year the competition was held in the
television studios of Channel 7, and the television network transmitted it
to the whole nation. It was not only the setting that had changed radically from the previous years: the judges had as well. The judges in 1975
were María Fernanda, fashion specialist; María Amelia Ramírez, former
Miss Argentina and Miss Universe; the singer Alberto Marcó; the designer Vittorio; and the cosmetologist Norma Palkowsky. During the
first Peronism hard work and beauty had been mutually dignified in
the image of the Queen of Labor. Twenty years later beauty was the
top priority and mass mobilization and union participation had lost
relevance.[42]

Teresa Reale, Working-Class Beauty Queen of 1975. TERESA REALE'S PERSONAL
COLLECTION.

Speaking with the participants in these events offered us a more
complete understanding than the photographic remnants at the AGN
could offer alone. The participants had saved other traces of an event
that was politically charged at the time but had been nearly erased by the
passage of time. The face of "the queen of labor and national unity of
1974," as the newspaper *Clarín* described her, only became real when we
found other photographs. María Cristina Fernández's beauty and that
of the other contestants in 1974 was typical of those years: makeup
emphasized her eyes; she had long, loose hair; she wore psychedelic
clothing. As Isabel Perón crowned her inside the presidential palace, the
demonstrators were embroiled in their own confrontations on the Plaza
de Mayo.

The queen in 1975, Teresa Reale, a representative of the Argentine
Union of Theater Artists, was a twenty-three-year-old "beauty" from
Santa Fe Province. According to press accounts of the contest, however,
the judges evaluated more than just the physical appearance of the

candidates; they also took into account their status as working women and how cultured they were. This last factor was not considered important in the contests of the 1940s and 1950s, although some of the candidates did show off their knowledge. Some mentioned that they liked to read and cited books that were part of the school curricula in language and literature: Jorge Issac's *María* and José Mármol's *Amalia*. The queen in 1975 went much further; beyond traditional classes in piano and dance she had also studied theater and sports, and one reporter commented on her fluency in French. She also loved to read drama and included Henrik Ibsen among her favorite playwrights. To demonstrate that she was cultured enough to meet the judges' demands she mentioned her taste for "modern literature and expressionist music."[43] The year 1975 was the last time a national Queen of Labor was selected; it was the end of a tradition that had been powerfully associated with the political project of the first Peronism.

"THIS WAS NOT A BEAUTY CONTEST"

In the political culture of Peronism, the visual definition of femininity that we have traced through photographs and press coverage depicted beauty, grace, and harmony as the result of a natural gift. Peronism displayed beauty publicly to honor labor and challenge images of the past, in which female labor humiliated women and, even worse, deformed them, turning them into objects incapable of producing visual pleasure. The "queens," in contrast, stood out for their dark, deep, bright eyes, their dark hair, their smiles, their gazes. The working-class beauty queen competition can thus be interpreted as a form of glorifying women. Yet Peronist political culture was full of ambiguities: the pictorial domination through photographs of a passive, humble, and at times trivial feminine subject was a way of asserting masculine power.

The spectacle adorned with feminine beauties can be understood as an expression of mass culture, which as Andreas Huyssen suggests is identified with women in opposition to "an authentic and real culture" that remains the prerogative of men.[44] There is a risk of analyzing the Peronist May Day rituals as culture imposed from above. The analysis of photographs can lead us in that direction, but Huyssen, citing Stuart Hall, asserts that the hidden subject in the debate on mass culture is the masses themselves, their struggles, their political and cultural aspirations, and also their silencing though cultural institutions. Women were part of those masses; they "knocked on the door of a culture dominated by men," only to have their voices obscured. The words that we take from the press ("temptation," "impossibility," "limits") offer a glimpse of the possible contradictions between the ways women saw themselves and how others saw them.

But in June 2003 we interviewed Edna Constantini, one of those women who at least temporarily became one of the queens of the nation of workers. Edna, who was chosen as a candidate in the tiny town of Quemú-Quemú, recounted emotionally the moment of her arrival in Buenos Aires: "We stayed in a hotel, the Royal, I believe . . . very pretty. We were all there, it was a beautiful group, from all the provinces. . . . It was not what we would call a beauty contest, it was more a way to pay tribute to the working person."[45] The expression "it was not a beauty contest" suggests that the event did not impose a hegemonic, totalizing discourse on the participants and that various interpretations were possible depending on one's position in the event. The press and official Peronist publications reported on the views of the organizers, some spectators, and, through the mediation of reporters, some of the participants. The queens form part of the "optical unconscious" of Peronism. They are part of the visual narrative that shaped the festivities and the larger political culture of Peronism, in which women played an important yet subordinate role.

The testimony of Edna Constantini is an indication of one of the points of view held by those who participated in the overlapping of the rituals of labor and feminine beauty implicit in the May Day ceremonies. In Edna's reiteration that "it was not a beauty contest" she emphasized the word "beauty," which stresses physical characteristics more than moral values. A beautiful woman worker generated a certain tension with the stereotypes created in previous decades, when women began working in factories and workshops: beautiful women could quickly slip into a "dangerous" world. Beauty could just as easily help a woman advance in the workplace as drive her to the brothel.

On another level, a beautiful woman could undermine the traditional notion that working women were consumed by the daily efforts of labor and incapable of eliciting any desire. In this sense beauty was a tribute to the woman worker and to Eva Perón herself, the "champion of the humble." In the interview Edna reported that the speakers at the May Day ceremony kept mentioning Eva Perón Province, the name recently assigned by Congress to the former territory of La Pampa, and incidentally Edna's home. As Edna put it: "I believe that they chose me because I was the representative of the Province of Eva Perón and she was sick . . . it was an homage to Evita."[46]

Furthermore, while young participants likely viewed the contests for working-class beauty queen as a game, much like all the local competitions (for spring queens, friendliness queens, friendship queens, or carnival queens), this game extended to the whole nation. To ensure that beauty was not dangerous, it needed to be tied to moral values, particularly the dignification of workers in general and of women in particular.

In Edna's interview a few key comments suggest that for women who participated, the competition was part of a game:

E.C.: I very much liked to go to dances, I was very happy and my father very much liked to take us to dances . . . because, you see, you had to go with a chaperon . . . and my father took all of us, with my sisters, my cousins, [it was] very nice.

P.: And your sisters were queens?

E.C.: All of them.

P.: All of them?

E.C.: Everyone but the one living in Necochea had her crown. Norma was the provincial queen of wheat, [others were] queen of springtime, queen of the class, queen of I don't know what, they were all queens . . . the only queen of labor was me.[47]

Going to a dance was a normal event for young people, and if a young woman was pretty and nice, she might be chosen queen or princess. Newspapers and local business sometimes sponsored these dances and competitions. Not until the first Miss Argentina pageant, which coincided with the overthrow of Perón in 1955, did the competitions take on more or less the characteristics they have now: cosmetic and fashion companies began to sponsor the events, the young women paraded in formal wear and in bathing suits, and television, which had just come to Argentina, broadcast the program. These transformations were controversial; perhaps Edna's repeated assertions that hers was not a beauty contest, that she did not wear makeup, and that she never had to wear a bathing suit were efforts to disassociate herself from the controversial aspects of subsequent beauty pageants.

Still, an account that emerges from an interview is open to alternative interpretations. The working-class beauty queen contest, which placed a beautiful female representative of the working world atop the pyramid of power (even if only in performance), acquired a different meaning for Edna when a group of researchers "from the university" approached her to conduct an interview. When Edna spoke to us, when she looked for photographs, when she showed us her photo album, and when she told us that she had been on the cover of the magazine *Así* and had destroyed it during the last military dictatorship, the history of her "reign" acquired a new meaning for her. The interview gave her the narrator's self-consciousness, enabling her to raise issues she had not considered before. "This was not a beauty contest" could be read in light of what she said next: "It was a way to pay tribute to the working woman" and to Eva Perón, whose death it seemed to announce.

But the participants' points of view are diverse. When she was interviewed during her long reign, Malber Bertaina acknowledged feeling happy about having been selected by her workmates, but she remarked on the conflicts that participation in such competitions could entail for some young women. "I never presented myself as nor was I ever where the contests took place. For example in Rafaela there was a girl who I do not know how many times she was chosen, and she was always chosen because she was at the dances. She was open to it, she liked it, but I preferred to remain anonymous. So, I participated in the union committee. One morning I arrived to a meeting and my male and female coworkers told me: 'You know, Malber, we voted, because we had to choose a representative from the State Workers Union? And we thought of you, not only thought of you, we came to an agreement, you know that it seemed to us that you were the one who was going to represent us best.' . . . I felt overcome with so many requests that I accepted."[48] This idea of participation in the contest almost as an imposition of others also appeared in the interview with one of the princesses who competed in 1974. Dialogue with her was not easy, both because of the pressure of the political context of the 1970s and because of the tension created by the social conflicts of the present. She described her election as Queen of the Textile Workers' Union as follows: "[It] was for me a very accidental thing, very dramatic because I did not want to have anything to do with what they proposed to me. The textile union people came to my house and [said to me] that the people at my workplace wanted me to represent them . . . well, practically at the point of a gun, my family said to me: 'Go, don't be silly . . .' Well, I went. This was in the textile headquarters in Solís and they had an election with all of the representatives of the factories, and also some that were not textile workers at the moment. Well, I had the luck to become textile queen that day."[49]

Although these last two accounts share an emphasis on pressure from friends, fellow workers, and families, it is important to stress that by 1974 and 1975 there was much less political and union mobilization surrounding the selection of candidates than there had been under the first Peronism. The last dialogue also revealed important changes in the position of women. Despite her emphasis on her timidity and the drama of the election, our interviewee recounted that her selection as a candidate and then as a princess opened doors to professions in which beauty was a requirement, but that she rejected them. Her refusal to accept the offers suggests that although she succumbed to the pressure to participate in the royalty game, she maintained her independence to choose her future career. In her words: "For me, let's say, it did not change my life, there was no change because I did not risk following another course like the things that were proposed to me, through the achievement of beauty, in quotation marks, because I don't know if it is like that. But fine, a beauty competition, you are pretty, you can do this or that, like what happens today, an offer for a job here, a job there. This is not what I wanted, I did not like to work in this environment because I did not think it was going to work. I don't regret it, I won't change the life I had for anything, I could have moved on to other fields, television and because of the offers that I was made, but I don't regret it."[50]

Edna's retrospective view, like that of the princess from 1974, is contaminated by the notions of manipulation, more ethical than economic, that are today linked to beauty contests throughout the world and by the fabrication of stars through publicity, promotion, and the investment of large sums of money, time, and energy. This analysis is outside the limits of the present study, but what we would like to emphasize is that the queens—like today's film and television stars and the radio stars of the past—acted in their own sphere. Their charisma never threatened to gain enough force to become more important politically or to threaten the established powers.[51]

This chapter has been an inferential journey through photographs, newspapers, official documents, memories, and personal objects. It is also an attempt to show that cultural material objects, in particular photographic images, do not exist in tension with traditional sources used by historians, nor in tension with oral testimonies. Images, words, and objects can be analyzed and interpreted in conjunction with one another: all carry meanings forged by public authorities, by the popular classes, and by the memories constructed in the process of taking oral histories.

Every text holds various analytical and interpretive contradictions, and each contradiction is like a palimpsest that bears the marks of earlier writers. In the texts used here, the marks that remain reflect a historiography that has paid too much attention to the political and institutional factors of Peronism and not enough to the cultural aspects. The historiography has too frequently focused only on Juan Domingo Perón's first and second presidencies, and has consistently portrayed Perón alone as responsible for crafting the movement he led for decades. It has studied the image of Evita to a tiresome extent. It has emphasized again and again the relationship between the state and the unions, and the democratization of the welfare state. Meanwhile, the historiography has left too many themes obscured and many questions unanswered.

The people we have followed belong to a mass culture that brought together "liberation" and traditional currents. It was a mass culture within which behavior and ways of thinking and acting were reformulated. The press, advertisements, mass-circulations magazines, radio, and film all crafted this mass culture, disseminating images of women to Buenos Aires and to the rest of the country that offered new possibilities for women as potential subjects and as objects. The chapter has considered the politico-cultural formation of Peronism and the experiences of some of the women who were chosen as working-class beauty queens for their "natural" qualities. The women's reigns strengthened a particular notion of beauty that required care for physical appearance and was in many ways in line with the images in women's magazines and the efforts of the cosmetics industry.

The working-class beauty queens between 1948 and 1955, like the queens of certain industries (wine, sugar, petroleum, and others), shaped the construction of local, gender, and political identities. Images together with written and spoken words amplified their impact on these solidifying identities. The working-class beauty queens were the clearest example of the importance of feminine beauty in politics. The relationship between ritual, feminine beauty, and politics was certainly not simple: it was a dense, conflictual, and competitive relationship but one that shaped workers' culture and gender relations during the first Peronism. In the process of appropriating the workers' traditions, Peronism converted their May Day ritual into a performance with an artistic program actualized on a set built in front of the presidential offices. The resignified ritual, part of the broader Peronist liturgy, displayed women's privileged place in the movement with a finale that crowned a criolla beauty as the working-class beauty queen. The festivities were thus embellished by the beauty of the Argentine woman, who according to Perón and the union organizers was a harbinger of Argentine happiness.[52]

But as mentioned above, the ritual glorification of feminine beauty carried other meanings as well. The queens were part of the optical unconscious of Peronism, and Peronist political culture publicly displayed their beauty to validate women's labor. This overtly contradicted the efforts of the radical working-class movement to disseminate images of deformed female workers. In these images the degradation of work and exploitation meant anguished faces, ungainly bodies, and flaccid breasts.

But the selection of beauty queens was not an invention of Peronism. It had a long trajectory, with roots in ancient Greece and medieval Europe, where May festivals often involved representations of royalty and where innumerable other festivals were associated with peasant work. Such contests have also long been linked to politics. In the United States beauty contests were tied to important moments in the construction of the nation: when Lafayette returned triumphantly to the United States in 1826, every state elected a beautiful young woman to welcome him. French revolutionaries also used the female figure as an allegorical representation of the egalitarian principles of the republic.

A showman in the mid-nineteenth-century United States recognized the potential of beauty contests and tried to organize the first ones, but the attempts failed because the American public did not consider such displays respectable. Toward the end of the nineteenth century the newspapers adopted the idea and hosted photography competitions; most famous was the one organized by the *Chicago Tribune*. In Argentina, although we have not investigated it thoroughly, the local newspaper in the meat-packing town of Berisso, *La Voz de Berisso*, organized a competition for a queen of kindness and reported on the competitions that the town's various ethnic groups hosted.[53] The newspaper *El Laborista* played a similar role when it organized the first competition for a national working-class beauty queen in 1947 and encouraged readers to vote.

The study of beauty contests remains incomplete, and this examination certainly does not exhaust its potential. The election of queens for different trades and industries during Peronism may have created strong identities that survived in local celebrations. The Flower Festival in the town of Escobar originated in the 1960s, the Sea and Beach Festival in Mar del Plata in the 1970s. Still, these competitions were connected to the national contests discussed here: some of the representatives of the province of Buenos Aires at the national Queen of Labor contest had once been chosen "flower queens" in Escobar. In Mar del Plata the choice of a "queen of the sea" dated back to the first decade of the twentieth century, when the city began to characterize itself as a tourist center. In that year the beauty queen was chosen in the fancy and aristocratic banquet room of the Hotel Bristol. Mar del Plata's contest reflects an international trend: when swimming and spending time at the beach became fashionable vacation activities, beauty competitions stopped being the purview of the newspapers, as municipalities began organizing them to attract tourists. Miss America, for example, was organized in Atlantic City.[54]

For almost a decade Peronism as a political movement made beauty competitions an integral part of a mass culture that served the purposes of the regime. The competitions "validated" the workforce and the female worker. They also helped to rigidly fix traditional gender roles and at the same time democratize them, using a monarchical framework to display gender roles on a grand scale and make them visible to the masses. Despite the regal ritual, the apotheosis of feminine beauty in this historical period was a natural beauty. It was a beauty centered in the face and not the body, perhaps because the body had a more destabilizing potential. That said, the women who participated in the working-class beauty queen competitions do not see them today as beauty contests, perhaps because of the controversial aspects of such contests. Instead their memories are framed around respect for the female worker.

The coup of 1955 that ended the first Peronism temporarily ended the regal ritual, but not the larger transformations in feminine image, gender relations, and the nature of the public and private spheres. That Peronism could not reestablish similar political performances and could not glorify women's beauty in the same way in the 1970s as it had in 1948–55 was partly the result of the tensions within Peronism between radicalized youth, union leaders, right-wing Peronism, and Perón himself. It was also, however, the result of cultural transformations that had created new challenges and opportunities for women. Ultimately there was no way to recreate the past.

NOTES

1 I have used two expressions for the Spanish phrase "Reinas del Trabajo": "working-class beauty queens" and "Queens of Labor." The title "Queen of X" is not common for pageant-winners in the United States, where they are more often called "Miss X." However, it is important to emphasize that the title in Spanish did not include the word "beauty." — *Trans.*

2 Plotkin, *Mañana es San Perón*; and Ballent, *Las huellas de la política*. See also Ballent's chapter in this volume.

3 Godio, *Perón*; Sigal and Verón, *Perón o muerte.*

4 Lobato, ed., *El progreso, la modernización y sus límites.*

5 Viguera, "El primero de mayo en Buenos Aires"; and Suriano, *Anarquistas.*

6 "1 de mayo ayer y hoy" (government pamphlet, 1949). The press also emphasized the image of rupture. For example, the newspaper *Democracia* noted: "The celebration of the Day of the Workers, which not many years ago was limited to resentful expressions of rebellion and to tumultuous street protests under the red flag, is now an event that brings together the whole nation in a unified impulse of joy and gratitude," *Democracia*, 2 May 1949.

7 *Mundo Peronista*, January 1953.

8 Lobato, "Lenguaje laboral y de género en el trabajo industrial."

9 *El Laborista*, 4 March 1947.

10 *El Laborista*, 2, 6, and 30 April 1947.

11 *El Laborista*, 8, 13, and 19 April 1947.

12 For an analysis of the queens of wine, wheat, and petroleum and the cere-

mony for awarding prizes of virtue see Mirta Zaída Lobato, ed., *Cuando las mujeres reinaban. Belleza: virtud y poder en la Argentina del siglo XX* (Buenos Aires: Biblos, 2005). For references see *La Voz de Berisso*, 20 May 1937, 12 May 1938, and 12 August 1938; *Sintonía*, February 1938; *Radiolandia*, November and December 1942. Beatriz Sarlo also mentions beauty contests in *La pasión y la excepción*.

13 *El Laborista*, 21 March 1947.

14 Ballent, *Las huellas de la política.*

15 For an analysis of the iconography and images of Peronism see Gené, *Un mundo feliz.*

16 This "decalogue," a reference to the Ten Commandments, would be incorporated into the Constitution of 1949.

17 The references to symbolism borrow from Juan Eduardo Cirlot, *Diccionario de símbolos* (Barcelona: Labor, 1994); Gené, *Un mundo feliz*, 99, 100.

18 Gené, *Un mundo feliz*, 97.

19 Lobato, "Entre la protección y la exclusión."

20 For examinations of the representations of women under Peronism see Navarro, ed., *Evita* (Buenos Aires: Corregidor, 1981); Bianchi and Sanchís, *El Partido Peronista femenino*. The figure of the descamisado appears in Juan Carlos Torre's *17 de octubre de 1945*. With respect to iconography see Gené, *Un mundo feliz*, 129–39.

21 This advertisement also makes references to history—it evokes the period of Rosas's rule by referring to his daughter Manuelita. For an analysis of visual advertisement see Traversa, *Cuerpo de papel*.

22 Benjamín, *The Work of Art in the Age of Its Technological Reproducibility and Other Writings on Media*, 37. The relevance of the concept of the optical unconscious to Peronism has been pointed out by Kraniauskas, "Eva-Peronismo, literatura, Estado," 46.

23 The union newspaper *El trabajador de la carne* published the photograph of a beautiful woman with a note that read: "La señorita Alba E. Pazos who represents our union in the National Beauty Contest organized by the CGT," vol. 2, nos. 44–45 (May–June 1954).

24 *La Razón*, 2 May 1948 (emphasis ours).

25 Pancho Netria's poem, dedicated to the first working-class beauty queen, previously elected queen of the flower and perfume of the Province of Buenos Aires, *El Laborista*, 2 May 1948.

26 *El Laborista*, 3 May 1948.

27 Eva Perón's speech, *La Razón*, 2 May 1950.

28 Eva Perón's speech, *La Razón*, 2 May 1950.

29 Eva Perón invited Chile's queen, Olga Molina. *Democracia*, 2 May 1951.

30 "Ruth is fifteen happy years old. Fifteen years that play and jump when she smiles revealing dimples on her cheeks, as if the dimples are surprised by such attention and such happiness. Ruth looks like this: dark eyes, deep, with a naïve look. Her hair is long and dark brown, tied back with a small barrette. Her face is sizable, with a small nose that points up and an earnest mouth. A small mole, almost imperceptible but present, sits on her upper lip towards the left, completing this criollo beauty. Ruth Soccorro is not tall or short. She is the ideal height. Her body, when walking, has the grace and charm that she offers with a careful distraction that draws her from here to there, attending to this and that, to everyone," *La Razón*, 2 May 1949. Accounts like these repeat in other publications in other years.

31 Sarlo, *El imperio de los sentimientos*, 122.

32 *La Razón*, 2 May 1951 (emphasis ours).

33 *Democracia*, 3 May 1949, 4 May 1950, 3 May 1952.

34 *El Laborista* published both photographs, 3 May 1951.

35 For a complete and concise description of the period see James, ed., *Violencia, proscripción y autoritarismo*.

36 See Godio, *Perón*.

37 *El Caudillo*, 8 February 1974.

38 "The Federal police erected an impassable security blockade on access roads to the capital," *Clarín*, 2 May 1974.

39 "A Presidential Call to Dialogue and National Unity," *Clarín*, 2 May 1974.

40 For a description of the gathering see *La Razón*, *Noticias*, and *Clarín*, 2 May 1974.

41 Sigal and Verón, *Perón o muerte*.

42 Teresa Reale, interview by Mirta Zaida Lobato and Lizel Tornay, filmed by Fernando Alvarez and Alejo Araujo, San Miguel, Province of Buenos Aires, 15 July 2004.

43 *La Razón*, 2 May 1975; *Así*, 9 May 1975.

44 Huyssen, *Después de la gran división*, 94.

45 Edna Constantini, interview by Lizel Tornay, filmed by Fernando Alvarez, Santa Rosa, La Pampa, 17 June 2003.

46 Edna Constantini, interview by Mirta Zaida Lobato and Lizel Tornay, filmed by Fernando Alvarez, Buenos Aires, 16 October 2003.

47 Billorou and Rodríguez, "Reinas y campesinas."

48 Malber Bertaina, interviewed by Lizel Tornay, filmed by Fernando Alvarez, Rafaela.

49 Interview by Mirta Zaida Lobato, Lizel Tornay, and María Damilakou, Buenos Aires, 1 August 2004.

50 Interview by Mirta Zaida Lobato, Lizel Tornay, and María Damilakou, Buenos Aires, 1 August 2004.

51 For a more general analysis see Dyer, *Las estrellas cinematográficas*; and Bravo, *Il fotoromanzo*.

52 "Reflexiones sobre el 1° de Mayo: alos ferroviarios y trabajadores peronistas" (pamphlet of the railroad workers' union, Remedios de Escalada, May 1949).

53 Mirta Zaida Lobato, *La vida en las fábricas*.

54 For some aspects of the historical development of beauty contests in the United States see Cohen, Wilk, and Stoelje, eds., *Beauty Queens on the Global Stage*.

Eduardo Elena
....

PERONISM IN "GOOD TASTE"

Culture and Consumption in the Magazine *Argentina*

Recent cultural histories of Peronism have focused on the dissemination of political symbols, images, and discourses through state channels and the media, on the creation of what one leading historian has called a Peronist "subculture."[1] Thanks to this body of research we have a much better appreciation for how a constellation of state, party, and allied institutions pursued cultural policies to mobilize support and create consensus. This chapter too examines Peronist interventions in the public sphere. It shifts the focus, however, to another dimension of this era's cultural history: namely, to consumption and taste. It offers a case study of one unusual Peronist publication, a commercial magazine called *Argentina*. Rather than analyze this source for partisan imagery or doctrine, the chapter employs *Argentina* to probe the connections between populist politics and the world of mass consumption. Through this magazine state authorities and their collaborators sought to define fashionable, moral, and patriotic consumer practices in keeping with political priorities—in short, to project a vision of Peronism in "good taste."

As part of a larger study on populist politics and consumption, this chapter sheds light on the regime's pursuit of cultural orthodoxy, an understudied facet of Peronism's history. "Orthodoxy" in this context means the acceptance of established hierarchies of taste and "respectable" norms of social behavior. Under Peronist rule the official pursuit of orthodoxy included adapting stylistic distinctions associated with the preceding order, including the taste judgments of the very same elites condemned politically by Perón and other leaders. Yet *Argentina* was more than an example of continuity, as its creators adopted innovative media and propaganda tactics. That is, "conservative" tastes did not mean a rejection of new methods. Historians have commented only in passing on the problem of cultural orthodoxy in this period. Some aspects have received attention—such as propaganda makers' fondness for so-called bourgeois representations of the working-class family, with the well-dressed male laborer, wife, and children enjoying the comforts of home.[2] But on the whole the topic has eluded sustained scrutiny. One obvious reason is that the appeal of Peronism to working-class Argentines is explained by its challenge to existing class hierarchies and cultural norms, what the historian Daniel James has usefully described as the movement's "heretical" character. Anti-Peronism is often presented in the exact inverse manner, as a negative response to perceived transgression, of social deference and standards of decorum (among many other factors).[3] In light of these views, the attempts of some state officials to embrace cultural orthodoxy may appear counterintuitive, or at worst irrelevant. The purpose of this chapter is not to deny the defiant elements of Peronism or to suggest that the model of tasteful consumption put forth in *Argentina* was adopted by a majority of the regime's supporters. Instead it seeks to illuminate an apparent paradox: why the authorities of a self-consciously popular, often heretical movement embraced repeatedly orthodox norms of taste.

At first glance *Argentina* hardly seems a promising choice to address this complex subject. Published from January 1949 to July 1950, the magazine was produced with state funds and written by a team of high-ranking bureaucrats and intellectual sympathizers. It was a short-lived project that reached a smaller audience than Peronist-controlled newspapers, and consequently it is seen as a footnote to the period's intellectual history.[4] Yet *Argentina* can also be read from another vantage, one that reveals the extension of Peronist propaganda making into the field of mass consumption. Viewed in this light, *Argentina* also suggests broader tendencies in Peronist cultural policies, aesthetic choices, and official paradigms of social aspiration. At a basic level, in content and format *Argentina* closely resembled popular commercial magazines such as *Mundo Argentino* and *Qué Sucedio en 7 Dias* (or its closest North American counterpart, *Life* magazine). Like its peers, *Argentina* emphasized variety, and its pages featured articles on current events, fictional stories and poems, advice columns, and how-to sidebars on cooking and crafts.

By working within this familiar genre *Argentina* represented part of a larger Peronist drive to intervene in commercial culture.[5] Some of these measures were banal, the types of tactics adopted by politicians elsewhere at the time (such as photographing the presidential couple with sport and film celebrities); other initiatives involved sophisticated campaigns to control the media and organize leisure time. *Argentina* was not designed primarily to spread partisan symbols or document the regime's accomplishments. It aimed at a more subtle level of influence, courting an audience of mainly working- and middle-class readers on the familiar terrain of commercial culture. At the same time, its editors used this platform to reshape social behavior. Their publication advocated practices that complemented the priorities of the Peronist government and more specifically matched their own predominately Catholic, conservative, and nationalist leanings. As befitted a magazine of this sort, *Argentina* was filled with advice on how to eat, dress, shop, and consume in a "proper" manner, often in keeping with class and gender norms associated with being *culto* ("cultured" or "educated"). Its creators thus pursued a dual role, that of propaganda makers and tastemakers, adopted by other political authorities as well.

This magazine can help us better understand the difficulties faced by Peronists who adopted positions as cultural interlocutors and sought to harness the power of the commercial media for political ends. Naturally the magazine's assessments of "good taste" were subjective, and one must not assume that its overtures were greeted with uniform responses by partisan sympathizers, anti-Peronists, or others. Given the dearth of sources on social reception of the media in Perón's Argentina, this chapter concentrates on questions of production and dissemination (although as we shall see, the editors themselves acknowledged reception as a key concern and took pains to present their publication as having popular appeal). It focuses on three sets of issues: the characteristics of the magazine itself as a consumer good; the publication's paradigm of "cultured" behavior; and the contradictions of pursuing fashionable but nationalist forms of consumption. The magazine's significance lies partly in its having fallen short of these goals, a failure that can illustrate how state authorities did (and did not) concern themselves with mass consumption.

The creators of *Argentina* never disguised their loyalty to the government, and they used the publication to sing the praises of Peronism. Yet they saw themselves as more than mouthpieces of the regime. The magazine blurred the distinction between official propaganda and commercial media, an impulse common under Peronist rule: pro-regime newspapers and radio stations hid behind the façade of private ownership, many as part of the Alea media conglomerate.[6] The producers of *Argentina* went a step further, by patterning their publication around the general interest magazine. Their choice of genre reflected the aspirations of their taste-making project; rather than limit their campaign to the sphere of high culture, they employed a print medium situated in the commercial terrain between the rarefied milieu of intellectual journals and the world of lowbrow entertainments. But as they entered the sphere of the mass media, they faced the challenges of playing by a commercial logic, including an emphasis on sales and advertisements as a measure of popularity. To reinforce their credibility as cultural authorities, the creators of *Argentina* devoted considerable attention to offering evidence of their massive, voluntary readership—in essence "marketing" their propagandistic publication as a consumer good.

In most outward respects *Argentina* resembled the commercial magazines of the day. It began with a series of editorials, followed by nonfiction features and light entertainment. Numerous photographs, color illustrations, and commercial advertisements complemented the written text. Many features dealt explicitly with subjects assumed to be of special interest to women, such as cooking and fashion. The prominence of these topics may explain the large number of female writers who contributed to *Argentina*, apparently more so than in other Peronist publications. Most differences with commercial counterparts were minor. The opening editorial section was a bit longer in *Argentina*, with three or four essays on political and nationalist subjects. Less space was devoted to advertisements, and the magazine was published monthly rather than weekly.

The obvious contrast was that *Argentina* was published under the auspices of the Peronist government—indeed by one of its ministers,

Oscar Ivanissevich. An accomplished medical doctor who served as minister of education from 1948 to 1950, Ivanissevich had been an early supporter of Perón, who after the elections of 1946 rewarded him with positions as administrator of the University of Buenos Aires and ambassador to the United States. Upon his return Ivanissevich embarked on a sweeping program to reform the public schools, stressing the role of state education in creating patriotic, Catholic citizens loyal to the Peronist cause. These ambitions also informed his role as the lead editor of *Argentina*, through which he hoped to channel the didactic spirit of state policies toward an adult audience. In a speech in 1949, Ivanissevich proclaimed that the magazine's goal was to "improve and perfect the education of adults," specifically by "substituting that toxic venom of foreign literature." When combined with child schooling, he argued that this initiative would help rid the nation of *cabecitas negras*. This generally derogatory term, used in reference to dark-skinned workers from the rural interior, was loaded with racial and class connotations. Rather than convert this slur into a badge of honor, as Evita and other Peronist authorities often did, the minister argued that the goal should be to eliminate the cabecita with cultural interventions, uplifting the downtrodden and developing a "social conscience, an awareness of social responsibility" among all Argentines.[7]

The editorial board and contributing writers shared this ideological position. With Ivanissevich as the figurehead, Gustavo Martínez Zuviría served as the editor in chief and appears to have managed the magazine's production. Martínez Zuviría was one of Argentina's best-selling fiction authors (he published under the pseudonym Hugo Wast) and a celebrated member of right-wing nationalist circles. His longtime position as the director of the National Library (1931–55) gave him a degree of influence within the broader intellectual community and eventually a platform within the Peronist government.[8] Other contributors to *Argentina*, such as Carlos Ibarguren and Delfina Bunge de Gálvez, came from nationalist and Catholic backgrounds. Among the most famous of these figures was Manuel Gálvez (best known for novels that looked back nostalgically at rural life), who lent *Argentina* a degree of intellectual weight by producing occasional pieces.[9] Ivanissevich hoped to widen the relatively small number of contributors by reaching out to sympathetic bureaucrats and educators, and he used his position to invite public employees to submit their written work (noting that *Argentina* paid handsomely for such intellectual labor).[10]

Despite the pro-Peronist views of the editorial page, most articles lacked an overwhelmingly partisan tone (there were exceptions: Perón himself made it onto the cover, dressed in full army uniform, in May 1949). In the first issue of *Argentina* Ivanissevich addressed head-on the question of his magazine's relationship with the Peronist regime. His lead editorial asserted somewhat paradoxically that while *Argentina* was published by the government, it was "in no way an official magazine." Ivanissevich went on to explain that the magazine was a modern update of the nation's first publication, the *Gaceta de Buenos Ayres* of 1810. Like its famed predecessor, it sought to "disseminate and defend the cultural seeds that are needed to consolidate our national independence." He acknowledged that some observers would criticize the publication as an example of the "totalitarian press," but he argued that it was a truly "free" and "responsible" media outlet: *Argentina* was decreed by the government, but not directed by it. In his view the magazine upheld the principles of the "Commission on Freedom of the Press" created by academics in the United States *and* sought to further the goals of "economic and intellectual independence" proclaimed by Perón's government.[11]

The tortured logic of the editorial reveals much about the meaning of propaganda in this historical moment. The intellectuals gathered around Ivanissevich sought to incorporate their project within the Peronist movement at an ideological and institutional level. At the same time they feared that these ties exposed them to the charge of propaganda making and a lack of independence. One way out of this bind was to establish a parallel with an august historical antecedent, the *Gaceta de Buenos Ayres*, which lent gravitas to the new magazine. But this comparison was made in passing and not elaborated in subsequent issues. Instead Ivanissevich's team appears to have sought legitimacy by mirroring the established format and practices of commercial culture. Although its producers could fall back on the deep pockets of the state, *Argentina* was sold and distributed at newsstands alongside other magazines. Thus Ivanissevich courted the very same "mass" audience already created by commercial culture in preceding decades. *Argentina* represented an attempt to introduce a variant of Peronist politics within an ostensibly commercial sphere of civil society, adapting the familiarity of the latter to advance the hegemony of the former.

This approach was viable given the inroads already established by magazines and other commercial forms in Argentine society. The combination of high literacy rates, the prevalence of the printed word in public life, and the concentration of working- and middle-class consumers in urban areas set the foundation for the emergence of print culture on a mass scale by the early twentieth century.[12] In this period the circulation of newspapers such as *La Nación* and *La Prensa* surpassed that of dailies in all other Latin American countries and many European countries.[13] Argentine kiosks were crammed with scores of smaller newspapers and magazines, and widening distribution networks connected media outlets in Buenos Aires with audiences on a national scale. The mid-1940s witnessed an intensification of these trends, but also new problems: greater spending power enjoyed by the working class early in Perón's presidency expanded access to magazines, but shortages of paper and labor conflicts hampered private sector publishers. Likewise, the national government expanded its regulatory authority over the press from the 1930s onward. What made *Argentina* stand out was the approach employed in entering the cultural marketplace directly as a rival to commercial producers. In essence officials like Ivanissevich sought to bolster their nationalist project by rejecting overt, state-distributed (and free) propaganda and to draw legitimacy from the voluntary act of purchasing and consuming the printed word.

This strategy explains the great attention given to the question of the audience for *Argentina*. Although the magazine did not depend on sales alone for its survival, articles in virtually every issue examined circulation and readership. Naturally this information should be taken with a grain of salt, as the editors had an interest in stressing the popular appeal of *Argentina*, both to further the image of Peronism as a mass movement and to justify their publication's existence to other Peronist officials. The editors noted that the low price of the magazine, at just one peso, made it possible to reach a wide audience: echoing the rhetoric of Peronist leaders, they pronounced that this "is a price that breaks with the idea of a luxurious magazine; it is a price that is not oligarchic."[14] In fact the cost was quite reasonable, as daily newspapers such as *La Prensa* sold for approximately 40 centavos by the late 1940s. Given the high production value of the magazine, with fine paper, colorful cover art, and extensive illustrations, the price was a steal—one, incidentally, that would not have been economically feasible for a commercial magazine without state support at a time of high paper costs and shortages.

The circulation figures that *Argentina* itself maintained seemed to confirm the popular appeal of the publication. By its count monthly circulation averaged 55,000 copies during the first year, and the magazine claimed that many more could be sold, but for a worldwide paper shortage (thus sidestepping the polemical issue of how the government controlled access to newsprint stocks). If one compares this estimate to media figures from 1945 (the last date for which reliable ones exist) a more modest picture emerges: in that year the Socialist Party newspaper *La Vanguardia* sold 70,000 copies a day and two Yiddish-language papers (*Di Presse* and *El Diario Israelita*) sold around 45,000 each. After Perón's fall magazines such as *Qué Sucedio en 7 Dias* circulated 200,000 copies a week.[15] Regardless of how many issues of *Argentina* actually sold, what mattered to the editors was stressing the large and popular audience it had developed in such a short time. One article argued somewhat clumsily that there was a frenzied buzz about *Argentina* on the street, as people sought with desperation to borrow a copy from their friends or literally fought to get their hands on the latest issue: "We will not comment on the fights, on the readers who go to the police station to complain about the seller who sold the magazine's issue that should have been reserved for them. We will not comment on merchant profiteering [*agio*]."[16] It was ironic that a magazine with such close ties to the government would use commercial disputes and usurious merchants as evidence of popular success, for the mid-1940s witnessed a series of campaigns organized by state and party institutions against so-called *agiotistas*, or commercial speculators, which ended at times in the imprisonment of suspected merchant profiteers.[17] Such inconsistencies were less important to the editors, it would appear, than creating an image of this state-funded magazine as commercially viable and "non-oligarchic."

This goal was advanced as well through a survey conducted by the magazine of its own readership, which stressed the supposedly popular, national, and diverse character of its audience. According to extended coverage of this survey in the magazine, the readership was split almost evenly between men and women. About two-thirds of readers were adults and one-third were youths under the age of twenty; a quarter lived in the capital Buenos Aires, with the remainder in the "cities and countryside" of the interior—a distribution matched roughly by the population as a whole, and thus making the magazine representative of a truly national public. In accordance with the prevailing logic of commercial publication, the survey focused on the "buying power" of readers both as individuals and as households, providing some sense of their class background. It concluded that the clear majority (68 percent) of families that read *Argentina* earned less than 1,000 pesos a month (with an additional 16 percent earning less than 1,500), which placed them within the ranks of the blue-collar and modest white-collar sectors. This conclusion was confirmed by the employment profile of the audience: public employees, professionals, and merchants, with clerks (*empleados de comercio*, 15 percent) and workers (*obreros*, 13 percent) as the largest categories. In addition, more than one-third of the readers of *Argentina* did not earn a salary, including housewives (14 percent) and students and recruits (21 percent).[18] Brief descriptions from survey participants complemented the data, as in this typical example: "I am Argentine, single, 27 years old, *comerciante* [in this case, a women's shoe seller] . . . this magazine is read in my home where we are seven brothers, my father and mother, that is nine persons, and later I bring it with me to my business where many clients read it." Other respondents offered words of encouragement, declaring the magazine "*formidable*" and asserting that "Reading *Argentina* one feels more Argentine"—no doubt music to the editors' ears.[19]

In the style of a marketing report, the survey also assessed which sections of the magazine were read by which types of audiences. Although only one-third of respondents claimed to read each issue in its entirety, a clear majority (67 percent) completed the nonfiction articles (where the editors most explicitly advanced their political objectives), while half read the fashion section and slightly less the poems and stories.[20] Readers described passing the magazine along to friends and others, and the editors asserted that on average thirteen people read each copy, which was held up as a sign of the extraordinary draw of the magazine compared to others in the marketplace. After multiplying the thirteen readers by the circulation of 55,000, the editors concluded that *Argentina* had a massive readership of 715,000. Naturally this numerical sleight of hand placed the magazine in the best light, and it was likely an exaggeration; after all, the population of the entire nation was 14 million. Information on the size of the audience and its buying power was published in full-page announcements within the magazine to entice commercial advertisers. By placing an ad in *Argentina*, these announcements claimed, businesses would be certain to reach hundreds of thousands of potential consumers.[21]

As these examples suggest, the editors of *Argentina* felt it necessary to provide evidence of the popular and commercial appeal of their publication. It is possible that the magazine's survey was accurate and that a devoted public of working- and middle-class readers did exist. The reality was that this readership was most likely smaller than the editors let on, and at the very least the publication appears not to have defeated its private-sector competitors. Setting aside the issue of social reception for the moment, what emerges is the magazine's imperative to boost legitimacy by crafting an image of commercial viability and mass appeal. Popularity mattered in the context of Peronist politics, especially for leaders who staked their authority on representing the majority's will. Equally important for Ivanissevich, Martínez Zuviría, and their collaborators, a large readership was crucial to cement their own status as cultural mediators. In the media sphere in which these intellectuals and officials chose to operate, legitimacy could not be separated from the logic of the marketplace, nor political loyalties from the supposedly voluntary choices of buyers and sellers.

THE IMPORTANCE OF BEING CULTO

While consumption was not the exclusive focus of *Argentina*, it did occupy a place of prominence in the "commercialized" genre of propaganda. The overtly partisan purpose of broadcasting Peronist accomplishments was intertwined with a cultural agenda, designed to align the behavior of readers with moral, tasteful norms of conduct. The most obvious target audience was the working-class base of the Peronist movement, which not coincidentally, according to *Argentina* itself, constituted the majority of the readership. From this vantage the magazine can be placed alongside other campaigns by state authorities to mobilize these sectors, including by shaping their quotidian behavior and habits. Yet the taste-making ambitions of *Argentina* were also aimed at a higher level of "cultural" polish, which suggests that the publication was also aimed

more broadly, to encompass middle-class readers. Based on the opinions and advice offered in its pages, it sought to convince this public that "good taste" and Peronism were not incompatible, as anti-Peronist critics asserted. Its editors outlined a nationalist, Catholic worldview that responded to a social climate marked by overlapping class and partisan divisions; as tastemakers, they would seek unsuccessfully to transcend these tensions by providing models of proper comportment for the "masses," while solidifying existing cultural hierarchies.

For the contributors to *Argentina*, the question of taste was defined largely in terms of what it meant to be *culto*. This term captured a set of understandings regarding how educated, proper individuals should behave in society, in an implicit contrast to those seen as backward, uncouth, and barbaric.[22] The definition of *culto* was subject to contestation, but it centered on the idealized practices of the urban, upper middle class—often labeled "bourgeois" values. Drawn from the more socially conservative ranks of *nacionalista* circles, the magazine's editors positioned themselves as defenders of established cultural hierarchies against modern, corrupting influences. *Argentina* highlighted the importance of familiarity with the "high" arts, literature, and music as markers of taste, while cultural products with a "low-class" or popular valence, such as the tango, were ignored in the magazine's commentary. Rural themes and populations received occasional attention through romanticized treatments of folk art and national lore. In keeping with their overall political goals, the editors made frequent mention of the religious dimension of comportment, and articles were sprinkled with references to the importance of Catholicism to social life. In short, in their role as authorities on cultural taste, the magazine's contributors had no interest in pursuing an avant-garde project. They presented themselves instead as possessing expertise in what society already deemed respectable, beautiful, and good, which in their view was compatible with Perón's political mission to create a New Argentina.

A key attribute of being culto was knowing how to act in public and private. The magazine's suggestions regarding politeness were tailored to everyday situations. For instance, one editorial on the loosening of civility in Buenos Aires complained that young men no longer gave up their seats to ladies on the subway; another lamented the problem of trash-laden streets in the city.[23] Articles instructed readers on correct *cos-*

tumbres and *modales* (loosely, customs and comportment) at home as well. A feature on "The Well-Set Table" by "Tatiana" informed readers on proper place settings, decorative centerpieces, and recipes for *tomates a la hortelana* and other delicacies.[24] These discussions assumed a degree of affluence: the accompanying photos showed elegant dining rooms with white tablecloths, china, and silver for many courses. In these kinds of articles the magazine targeted women specifically, though not exclusively, in discussing what constituted good taste, especially with regard to the home and personal appearance. One article noted with mild annoyance the trend of *sinsombrerismo* among men, who increasingly felt it no longer necessary to wear a hat in public. In seeking to court a mixed audience, the magazine offered both male and female models of sociability that reinforced prevailing understandings of what it meant to be culto in Argentina of the 1940s.

The emphasis overall was on maintaining proper traditions while being flexible enough to adapt to changes in fashion. In this regard the magazine's paradigm of good taste was not drastically different from those of many other general interest and women's magazines. In other respects, however, the editors of *Argentina* adjusted their didactic messages to the political context of Peronism and the initiatives of the government and party. This tendency can be most clearly seen in a handful of articles on the daily routines of workers. These representations were similar to the regime's visual and print propaganda, profiling the typical day of an industrial worker who moved seamlessly from productive laborer in his factory to contented family man. The workers portrayed in the pages of *Argentina* were "disciplined" and "well behaved" (at least according to prevailing middle-class norms): they were clean, friendly, and dressed in a "respectable" manner. No stereotypical proletarians, they offered models of how even the humble-born could aspire to be culto members of society.

One of the most suggestive portrayals of working-class tastefulness in *Argentina* was a profile of Mr. Fortini, a thirty-six-year-old former tire factory laborer who had become mayor of the Buenos Aires suburb of Lomas de Zamorra. The article and accompanying photographs took pains to show Fortini hard at work in his new job as a public servant, whether eating breakfast in his office at 7 a.m., personally supervising the construction of new roads in the suburb, or visiting sick children at the local hospital on the weekend. Fortini was an ideal subject for *Argentina*, and he was depicted as emblematic of the "new Argentine worker" created by Perón. The author of this profile, Margot Guezúraga, called him a "complete man," and she praised his agreeable appearance: "I am in admiration of how he dresses well and I ask myself where he discovered the secret of true elegance and how he did not fall into the *snobismo* of those recently ascended from their habitual sphere." This passing dig at social climbers aside, the article extols Fortini not only for his much deserved upward mobility and accomplishments as mayor but also for his manners. Naturally, that Fortini was married with children resonated with the Catholic tone of this publication, as did his measured tastes and "nationalist" preferences: "Fortini smokes little. At the table he drinks a good glass of Argentine wine. His favorite dish is steak [*churrasco*] . . . although he gets up at the official argentine hour, sometimes due to his work at city hall he returns home at 3 a.m." Moreover, that he is concerned with the landscaping of his suburb shows his "soul as a poet." As Guezúraga concludes, he is certainly not one of those "workers who runs around with a bomb hidden under a hirsute beard"; he was instead an exceptional representative of the Peronist worker.[25]

The female working-class received more oblique treatment by the editors of *Argentina*, no doubt because their conservative vision of the family stressed a gendered division of labor, with a stay-at-home mother and male breadwinner.[26] Working-class women appeared, if at all, in the guise of housewives. These depictions were shaped by the government's growing attention to ordering consumption in the late 1940s, which formed part of so-called anti-*agio* campaigns that attracted considerable propaganda coverage. Lending support to the regime's strategy to reduce inflation, the magazine encouraged popular women to be thrifty and disciplined consumers.[27] It is worth stressing that these were mainly passing references, fewer in number than advertisements enticing women to spend on beauty products and other consumer goods. Moreover, calls for thrift were contradicted by pages of illustrations for lavish garments of taffeta, lace, and silk, suggesting the challenges faced by the magazine's contributors in coupling their notions of taste to the political context of Peronism. Designs for floor-length evening gowns, complete with jeweled accessories, seemed of scant practical use for transforming working-class women into disciplined consumers. Class biases regarding taste crept into these columns, as in an article on the pressing issue of whether women should wear fur coats. According to the magazine's resident fashion expert, Eugenia de Chikoff, the fur coat was the "dream of all women," and now even secretaries and others of modest means could afford them. But not all women had the appropriate body type to wear them. Some simply lacked the right silhouette—tall and slender, like the elegant, fair-skinned models depicted in the illustrations—and instead were too small and stocky (*redonditas*), body traits that in this era had negative class connotations.[28]

These examples point to a central tension in the magazine's model of cultured taste. The creators of *Argentina* stressed the popular, commercial appeal of their publication. But the magazine paid no attention to educating its readers on the starting point of becoming culto, such as acquiring elementary literacy and basic hygiene (washing with soap, not spitting in public, and so on). Instead they pitched their articles toward a slightly higher stratum, to those already familiar with the parameters of "bourgeois" norms, who knew how to make use of de Chikoff's fashion tips or to nod approvingly at the biographical sketch of Mr. Fortini. Thus the magazine sought at once to include a popular audience within the realm of respectability, offering advice to readers to further elevate their standing, while disavowing those practices deemed excessively vulgar and low-class.

The Peronist regime did not ignore the task of ameliorating the supposedly "backward" customs of the population and creating a more "cultured" citizenry. Like centralizing states elsewhere in the world, the Peróns' government made the inculcation of hygiene part of health care, education, public housing, and other social programs.[29] The dramatic increase of these programs under Peronist rule meant that the dependencies of the state took on a more ambitious role in shaping more orderly subjects and molding "cultured" behavior (a facet of the history of Peronist social welfare that has yet to receive full scholarly attention). Although the magazine focused on refinement, this civilizing mission was reflected in occasional reports on state social programs. One article, titled "Ancianos en libertad," showed the low-income elderly being cared for in a state facility, devoting their free time to attending regular church services and reading books. Similar images of a cultured, disciplined, and Catholic populace were offered in descriptions of Ciudad Evita and other housing projects, which catered (in theory at least) to the working class; they showed well-scrubbed children on their way to school or church, families tending their neat houses—a healthy and happy working class living peacefully under the aegis of the planning state.[30]

In terms of media strategy, the courting of the lower strata was left to other branches of the Peronist movement. Neighborhood-level *unidades básicas*, labor organizations, and other institutions acted as channels for propaganda, while mass circulation newspapers like *Democracia* supplied descriptions of life in the New Argentina written in an accessible style for popular audiences. By comparison, *Argentina* provided another form of propaganda. The magazine's purpose was to inspire loyalists and attract new members to the Peronist camp, but it avoided the more heavy-handed methods of its counterparts—a subject that Ivanissevich, as author of the anthem "Los muchachos peronistas" and other verses knew a great deal about. The regime's leaders stepped up efforts to define a partisan doctrine from 1949 onward (it was in this year, for instance, that concepts such as the "Organized Community" were first unveiled).[31] But *Argentina* was intended to add another layer of gloss to the cultural polish of the population, a fact that necessarily limited its audience to those with a minimal understanding of what it meant to be culto and an interest in hearing the opinions of self-styled cultural authorities in matters of taste.

It remains an open question why these Peronist intellectuals devoted considerable attention to matters of taste, when they could have focused on other aspects of consumption and daily comportment more suited to popular audiences. One possible answer is their desire not just to attract supporters but also to combat the criticisms of anti-Peronists. Opponents often stressed the brutish, "un-cultured" nature of the movement, in some cases by drawing historical analogies to the nineteenth-century contest between civilization and barbarism.[32] Eva Perón was a major target of scorn for her crass taste, low social origins, blatant social climbing, and all-around tackiness—characteristics that were imputed to her followers as well. *Argentina* offered a rejoinder to many of these claims. By contrast, the magazine presented the working class as orderly, and it suggested that workers shared the same standards of taste as their middle-class counterparts. The men and women who produced this publication clearly wanted to be taken seriously as public intellectuals.

Moreover, it is likely that the intellectuals assembled around *Argentina* were also concerned about their own legitimacy in the eyes of the largely anti-Peronist middle and upper classes and thus had a personal stake in crafting a paradigm of Peronism as culto. From this vantage *Argentina* can be seen as part of the larger "culture wars" of the Peronist era, a struggle among competing factions within the middling strata of society.[33] Traditional historical accounts tend to stress the vertical conflicts between a predominately Peronist working class and the anti-Peronist middle and upper classes. But too often the upheavals of Peronism within the middle class get lost. The majority of government officials and the intelligentsia were drawn from these ranks, which also represented the core of the anti-Peronist bloc. By stressing good taste, the editors sought to counter the interclass accusations of barbarism heaped upon them by fellow intellectuals and social peers.

In addition, it is possible that models of "proper" culture did in fact appeal to more popular audiences. The portrayals of respectable workers carried in the magazine might have been attractive to some readers who saw their own aspirations reflected in these pages. At the very least, audiences encountered similar images of the ordered Peronist working class in newsreels and other forms of state propaganda. Working Argentines by no means mindlessly emulated the aesthetic choices, artistic tastes, and norms of conduct of their social "superiors," but neither were they immune from the pull of conventional standards of comportment and beauty. In a society characterized by the promise of upward mobility, one did not have to be a member of the Argentine bourgeoisie to identify with so-called bourgeois taste.[34] Gauging responses to these overtures is difficult, and no doubt varied individually and by categories of gender, region, and age (to name a few factors). One of the characteristics that makes Peronism such a complex social phenomenon is that supporters were also drawn to its more heretical elements. In gaining a better appreciation of how Peronist officials embraced cultural respectability, there is a risk that the heretical side of Peronism may be underemphasized, as propaganda makers tended to favor ordered, positive depictions of life in the New Argentina. For evidence of "bad taste" one must look elsewhere than official propaganda, including in the responses of anti-Peronists to the actions of the government and its supporters. Most cultural expressions no doubt fell somewhere between these extremes and cannot be placed easily into binary categories of heresy and orthodoxy.

In the specific case of *Argentina*, however, the heretical side of Peronism was subordinated to issues of tasteful conduct. The magazine editors sought to convince a national audience that prevailing cultural norms were valid, despite those who feared that the growing prominence of the working class as citizens, laborers, and consumers threatened the value of being culto. Its creators offered a paradigm for respectability through individual improvement, which at once reinforced existing class hierarchies and validated those among the popular sectors who struggled to emulate their more "cultured" superiors. The magazine *Argentina* envisioned an order that did not dismiss the possibility of social mobility but rather stressed cultural emulation of middle-class norms as the path to individual progress for the pueblo. It focused attention on problems of taste, ones that would continue to justify further didactic interventions by intellectual tutors. The working class would continue to exist, for to erase status differences and embrace true egalitarianism would threaten the hierarchy upon which the authority of the magazine's interlocutors depended. Instead laboring people would strive to become culto and adopt commensurate consumption practices—without ever quite reaching the elusive final goal of total respectability, one suspects. After all, as this Peronist publication's fashion expert noted, not everyone was born to wear fur.

NATIONALIZING TASTE

Given that the magazine *Argentina* mirrored the format of its mainstream commercial counterparts, the question arises: What, then, set its content apart? The editors highlighted the importance of nationalism, Catholic religion, and morality in their discussions of taste; these topics were hardly ignored by commercial magazines, but the coverage was more overt in the pages of *Argentina*. Contributors distinguished their project by voicing criticisms of the excesses of commercial culture, such as corrupting foreign influences. At times, however, the magazine's explicit cultural nationalism clashed with its defense of being culto. Defining a distinctively "Argentine" style was tricky, for the country had long been saturated with foreign influences and commercial culture. Local understandings of respectable behavior demanded openness to international trends, which even conservative intellectuals were unwilling to abandon. The editors failed to resolve these contradictions on more than one occasion, pointing to the limits of nationalizing taste in Peronist Argentina. These cultural dynamics were part of the larger problem of asserting sovereignty in a twentieth-century age of mass consumption, where commercial flows and consumer practices regularly transgressed the borders of nation-states. In Argentina as elsewhere in Latin America, this challenge was fraught with additional difficulties by the historical weight of colonialism and underdevelopment; these were societies in which dominant paradigms of "civilized," "modern," and "fashionable" conduct had long been rooted in the appropriation, if not outright emulation, of western European trends and other foreign models.[35]

Nevertheless, the magazine's contributors complained about the public's tendency to embrace "Anglo-Saxon" commercial culture over national offerings. As far as foreign influences were concerned, they preferred the two pillars of *latinidad*, Italy and Spain (like many cultural conservatives in the region).[36] According to *Argentina*, most commercial entertainment was rife with excessive foreignness. An article by Eleonora Pacheco in the February 1949 issue was typical of this critique; titled "What Do Argentine Children See?," this piece expressed dismay that the nation's youth were exposed to Hollywood gangster films, imported comic books, and other threats to public morality. While Pacheco noted that adults could handle strong subject matter, children were susceptible to passionate love scenes and violent shootouts between the police and criminals. Like moralists in other times and places, she stressed the importance of Christian family values to offset pernicious practices: "One must destroy the multiple-headed hydra that is corrupting our children, one must inundate with light the new lives of the Homeland [*Patria*] so that tomorrow they will be upstanding and free men and women in the sense given to these words by the Christian civilization of which we are proud to belong."[37] For outside observers of the Argentine situation, these critiques were seen as further parroting of the anti–United States rhetoric of Peronist leaders; in reality, however, the magazine's editors saw themselves as attempting to articulate an alternative to the dangers of the marketplace.[38]

Argentina was an attempt to replace unsavory commercial culture with more wholesome, patriotic fare. Defining the exact profile of a nationalist alternative was no easy task for Ivanissevich and his team. Unlike intellectuals elsewhere in the region, they had little interest in latching onto an indigenous civilization of the ancient past to distinguish their country's greatness. Rather they worked within currents of nationalism in Argentina, which often erased any sense of an indigenous element in the nation's composition (or for that matter, any African contribution), offering instead a Hispanophile paradigm of a whitened criollo identity.[39] With their roots in the *nationalista* movements of the early twentieth century, the editors of *Argentina* distanced themselves from cultural forms associated with heavily immigrant urban areas. These conservatives saw the provinces and rural areas as the repository of national authenticity. Their patriotism overlapped with the official nationalism of the state and its ritualized worship of the "founding fathers" of Argentine independence, refracted through the ideological prism of Peronism. For *Argentina* the challenge was adapting this nationalism to the mass circulation magazine, which itself was permeated with international elements and often patterned on foreign models. Local publications such as *Para Ti* and *Mundo Argentino* juxtaposed features on local movie stars and social events with stories about celebrities and styles in the United States and Europe; in some cases the articles printed in these publications were translated directly from foreign magazines.

This problem can be most clearly seen in the attempts by *Argentina* to define a nationalist fashion in clothing. De Chikoff's fashion section was supposedly one of the most popular parts of the magazine; according to surveys, all but 2 percent of women readers pored over this section in each issue. De Chikoff saw herself as creating a style based on her country's "history, in its tradition, in its incomparable landscapes, in its picturesque styles, in its old legends and current life."[40] This patriotism was manifested in the designs for women's dresses, which worked within the overall parameters of international styles while seeking to give them a "*sentido argentino.*" Therefore de Chikoff mirrored the output of Europe's fashion capitals: patterned dresses and blouses, knee-length skirts set off with wide belts, fur coats for the winter season, and long, elaborate gowns for formal events. Her nationalist pride translated mainly into the names of her designs: "Tucumana," "Tigrense," "Chiripá," and so on. Sketches highlighted national character by placing models in settings that evoked the countryside or in front of outlines of maps of Argentine provinces.[41] For de Chikoff these heavy-handed references to national imagery were enough to justify her mission to capture the spirit of the Peronist era: as she proclaimed in the magazine's inaugural issue: "we must argentinize fashion, because the country strengthens everyday more its *argentinisimo* in all other respects."[42] But like other contributors to *Argentina*, de Chikoff seemed trapped between an alternative to foreign commercial influences and conventional understandings of what constituted good style. She claimed that her women's coats, inspired by the styles worn by Argentina's "founding fathers"—including a high-collared outfit called the "Belgrano," after the illustrious nineteenth-century leader—were evidence of a new nationalism in fashion, while noting that these designs were similar to a revolutionary era or "Directory" style coming out of Paris. At times she stressed that what mattered was not only a patriotic style but also employing materials domestically manufactured by Argentina's *obreros*, thus combining an aesthetic nationalism with Peronist economic nationalism. And on occasion de Chikoff's patriotic imaginings were a bit bolder: an unusual men's winter outfit called the "Antártida" combined gaucho pants (*bombachas*) and a top patterned with the map of Argentina's Antarctic territories! But these were exceptions.[43] In most cases the nationalist staff of *Argentina* strove for a more modest reconfiguration of taste.

This apparent contradiction was even starker in advertisements for consumer goods. The ads that ran in *Argentina* were integral to conveying the illusion that this magazine was more than state-orchestrated propaganda. Thus aside from occasional ads from government ministries, the bulk of the advertising was from the private sector. Unfortunately, little is known about how *Argentina* secured advertisers, but given the editors' ideological inclinations it is surprising to encounter numerous ads in *Argentina* for foreign consumer products and services. In fact most were for luxury goods well outside the price range of the "average" reader of the magazine (at least as determined by the magazine's own survey) and for products that clashed with the economic nationalism of the Peronist regime. Full-page ads for Morris automobiles imported from Britain seemed out of place in a magazine committed to Argentine values and domestic manufacturing, and it certainly clashed with the reality of Peronist economic controls to restrict car imports.

Likewise, what was an advertisement for springtime vacations to the United States on Pan American World Airways doing in the very same issue of a magazine that contained articles on Peronist tourism programs for poor children? To be sure, Argentine-made goods were also advertised, sometimes in ways that made reference to nationalist themes. But at the same time domestic businesses enticed Argentine consumers with the allure of the foreign. An ad for a perfume called Bohemia (most certainly produced locally) stressed that it was manufactured with French "essences." The accompanying illustration departed from the moralistic tone of the magazine's editorials and articles, as it portrayed a high society party, with men in tuxedos and women in ball gowns sipping champagne and cavorting happily.[44]

The decision-making process behind the paradoxical juxtapositions of "foreign" ads in a staunchly nationalist magazine is unclear. It is possible that Martínez Zuviría and his fellow intellectuals were simply lazy editors, who cared more about their own writing and left business affairs to others. This reasoning is undercut by the statement appearing near the table of contents of each issue: "*Argentina* does not accept ads whose products or claims are damaging to spiritual or physical health. It also does not accept ads in poor taste [*mal gusto*]." One explanation for the contradiction may be found by comparing *Argentina* to other mid-twentieth-century Latin American attempts to regulate the foreign content of the commercial media. Recent studies of Mexico have illustrated the bind facing PRI government officials entrusted with regulating the mass media and commerce. On the one hand they sought to shield the nation from foreign threats posed by immoral comic books, music, and film; in this case the origin of these artifacts in the United States upped the patriotic stakes. On the other hand, officials associated foreign goods and imported commercial practices with modernity and saw them as useful in helping Mexico to become a truly "advanced" industrialized nation on a par with its northern rival.[45] Discounting the specific historical dynamics of Mexico, Argentine peers encountered a similar pull between an anti-foreign nationalism and a desire to appear modern. The editors of *Argentina* would at once criticize those aspects of commercial culture that they considered immoral and excessively foreign and allow space for those deemed proper and tasteful—even if it meant running ads for British cars in a pro-Peronist magazine.

This ambiguous compromise between the magazine's political and cultural impulses can be seen in advertisements of Argentine-made consumer goods. In this Peronist publication many advertisements were for luxury items. Ads placed by furniture stores in Barrio Norte for ornate Spanish Baroque chairs were obviously aimed at a more affluent tier of consumers than the dutiful workers profiled in the magazine's articles, or the supposed core of readers who earned less than a thousand pesos a month. The same held true for ads from the jewelry shop Casa Escasany, which sold silver-plated *bombillas* and eighteen-carat *mate* gourds for 590 pesos.[46] These pieces were patriotic, creole symbols that would have pleased nationalist intellectuals, but the farce of such an "oligarchic" take on quotidian implements is obvious.

As suggested by these advertisements, the creators of *Argentina* saw themselves as communicating to an audience with an appreciation for the goods things in life. Even readers who could not afford these products might derive satisfaction from window shopping through the magazine, and at least they could entertain the fantasy of living like the rich and famous. The magazine's staff was certainly not against understandings of luxury rooted in existing class relations. From their perspective good taste meant admiring quality, while rejecting the immoral enticements of sex and violence in mass-produced, commercial culture. Notwithstanding the obvious contradictions, *Argentina* represented an attempt to advance a moralistic brand of cultural nationalism, with sporadic appeals to economic nationalism. In this case a cohort of Peronist intellectuals was unable to resolve a central problem: they sought through a commercial medium to gain the loyalty and attention of a wide public, in keeping with the identification of Peronism as a national, popular movement; yet they upheld existing hierarchies of taste, shielding them not only from foreign threats but also from the pressures of crass commercialization.

Argentina was an experiment cut short after less than two years, but the magazine did not fail because of a lack of commercial viability or a limited audience. Rather, an internal power struggle within the Peronist high command stopped the presses, as Ivanissevich stepped down from his position as minister of education in May 1950. Why he was forced out is unclear. In addition to his other duties Ivanissevich was the personal doctor to Juan and Eva Perón, and he was among the first to become aware of the First Lady's cervical cancer. He advocated a hysterectomy, a procedure that Evita rejected and, so the theory goes, caused her to turn against this Peronist of the first hour.[47] In any event, with Ivanissevich's departure from the administration the magazine *Argentina* lost its most powerful ally, and soon after it vanished from sight. This was a fitting demise. Despite its commercial pretensions, the publication depended on the financial backing, access to paper stocks, and distribution channels provided by the regime.

Nevertheless, *Argentina* set a crucial precedent in media and propaganda policies. In the years that followed, Peronist authorities pursued other attempts to reach audiences through commercial culture, including in magazine form. By the late 1940s the mantle of propaganda making passed to Raúl Apold in the Subsecretaria de Informaciones and to other branches of the regime.[48] Apold and his collaborators created a successor to *Argentina*, the magazine *Mundo Peronista*. This new publication was a blunt tool of propaganda for a popular, pro-Peronist audience. Most articles extolled the government's accomplishments or the leading couple; the format paralleled loosely that of general interest magazines, but its heavily partisan tone made it more like Peronist newspapers. The emphasis shifted from issues of taste and mainstream cultural legitimacy to generating enthusiasm among supporters and indoctrination. As a reflection of the worsening economic climate, *Mundo Peronista* stressed other themes related to consumption—above all, the need for thrift and coordination between consumers and political authorities—prevalent in Peronist propaganda during the early 1950s.

What conclusions can one draw about the cultural history of Peronism from the story of the magazine *Argentina*? There are at least two possible interpretations. First, this magazine is suggestive of the larger pattern of Peronist interventions in commercial culture. In general, Peronist authorities were reluctant to condemn the commercial media and popular entertainments as inherently depraved, corrupting, or immoral. Perhaps Eva Perón's background as a radio and film actress made this an untenable position. Rather than launch rebukes, propaganda makers attempted to use the loyalties and traditions of mass audiences to new partisan ends; even the intellectuals responsible for *Argentina* decided to work through the genre of a consumer good to critique aspects of mass consumption. In other words, what is noteworthy is not the magazine's moralizing about irreligious, foreign influences but the editors' inability to make these themes more central to Peronist cultural policies. The growing antagonism between Perón and the Catholic Church in the 1950s no doubt made the religious nationalism of *Argentina* less attractive to propaganda makers. During the remaining years of Perón's presidency few officials rushed to condemn Hollywood films and other dangers to the nation with the same vigor. (In 1954, for instance, the government helped to organize an international film festival in Mar del Plata, which invited Errol Flynn and numerous foreign stars of the silver screen, the type of entertainers who had been critiqued in *Argentina*.)[49] Certain aspects of mass consumption mattered more than others to political authorities. The approach to consumer moralizing typified by *Argentina* paled alongside other Peronist state campaigns in the field of mass consumption, such as imposing an ethical and partisan order on daily commerce ("anti-speculation") or encouraging thrifty household spending.

However, there were limits to the regime's cultural populism. Peronist authorities stressed the empowerment of the popular sectors and exhibited relative tolerance of commercial culture, but this did not mean that all aesthetic choices, modes of conduct, or practices were equally worthy. This is the second conclusion: that *Argentina* was well within the Peronist mainstream in emphasizing the importance of being culto. It may be tempting to question exactly how "Peronist" this magazine was, given that the Catholic nationalists involved in publishing it had stressed the importance of cultured behavior in the past. But as the chapters in this book illustrate, there was no single Peronist cultural project, and the movement's intellectuals and officials drew from multiple influences. Several experiments occurred simultaneously under the Peronist tent, occasionally in competition with one another but frequently with unexpected commonalities. Although the magazine's perspective on luxury consumer goods was somewhat unusual, a similar emulation and adaptation of a "high-class" orthodoxy informed Peronist cultural policies and propaganda. Representations of tidy "bourgeois" laborers in *Argentina* also appeared in *Mundo Peronista* and other propaganda. Orthodox styles and aesthetics were not limited to matters of consumption but could also be found in the architecture favored by Peronist builders, the décor of social welfare facilities, and state policies toward the arts.[50] In all these areas officials acknowledged markers of social distinction associated with the liberal order, including those of economic elites, and attempted to bend them to the political circumstances of Peronism. Even Eva Perón combined nationalistic and populist rhetoric with a fondness for foreign designers and a desire to conform to the latest fashions. Of course it is hardly fair to equate *Argentina* to the powerful First Lady; after all, Evita's appropriation of a luxurious aesthetic contained a potentially subversive thrust, in that a humbly born woman enjoyed lavish finery and in so doing rejected the monopolization of comfort by the wealthy. That said, one can appreciate a similar sensibility in the magazine *Argentina* and other Peronist efforts to assert cultured taste, which led at times to exaggerated, even kitsch versions of bourgeois styles.

In this regard Perón's government resembled other regimes in the mid-twentieth century that crafted new forms of mass politics while largely accepting established notions of tastefulness. To take the most extreme case, Stalinist rule in the Soviet Union witnessed a shift in the 1930s from avant-garde experimentation on the cultural front to an accommodation with earlier understandings of educated comportment and taste. Fascist rulers appropriated elements of cultural orthodoxy to solidify their legitimacy, as did many "populist" regimes in Latin America (that of Vargas in Brazil, for instance). Naturally many of these actors broke with tradition by creating new political subcultures, and they sought to imprint their own socialist, fascist, or partisan characteristics onto existing cultural practices. Historians have suggested that the pursuit of cultural orthodoxy serves different political purposes: in some cases it offers a means for a new state elite to shore up ties with intellectual and managerial strata (as in the Soviet Union of the 1930s and Brazil under Vargas), and in others it provides leaders with a means to protect "national values" against threats to sovereignty and social hierarchy posed by mass cultural imports (as in postwar Mexico and Fascist Italy).[51] Peronist authorities adopted similar strategies as they tapped into established understandings of taste to forge a stronger political hegemony, guided by a combination of intraclass negotiations and nationalist impulses.

Although more research is needed on the broader pursuit of orthodoxy in the Peronist era, the magazine *Argentina* reveals how a group of top officials and prominent intellectuals envisioned their role as cultural interlocutors. Their publication countered critiques of Peronism as a barbaric, low-class threat to the social order and broadcast a model of respectability for its audience to follow. It assumed a didactic mantle, hoping to keep foreign threats at bay and articulate a moralizing variation on commercial culture. The continued resentment of anti-Peronist sectors—especially those in the middle class, who were best positioned to appreciate the magazine's overtures—points to the ultimate failure of *Argentina* in realizing its aims, notwithstanding the resources at its disposal. If anything, the "culture wars" between anti- and pro-Peronists mapped more forcefully onto class antagonisms in the 1950s and intensified over subsequent decades. The cross-class alliances that did emerge within the Peronist ranks centered either on nationalist paradigms of development or more radical visions of change, rather than matters of cultural tastefulness. But the paths blazed by *Argentina* and other experiments in the 1940s did not disappear entirely: longings for a conventional respectability continued to shape Peronist visions of the good life, and the movement's leaders appropriated orthodox norms to new ends. Wedded to conservative notions of propriety and reliant on mercurial forms of state patronage, the editors of *Argentina* were unable to complete their cultural project, but the problem of Peronism and taste endured long after their magazine stopped being sold at the nation's newsstands.

NOTES

1 Continuities with an earlier cultural order were important, and Peronists drew on influences as varied as the nationalism of the Catholic right and the labor iconography of the secular left. Plotkin, *Mañana es San Perón*, xi. Other inquires in this vein include Ciria, *Política y cultura popular*; and Gené, *Un mundo felíz*, 11–28.

2 Gené, *Un mundo felíz*, 117–30; Ballent, *Las huellas de la política*, 19–29.

3 James, *Resistance and Integration*, 7–40; de Ípola, "Ruptura y continuidad. For an analysis of Peronism and anti-Peronism as two clashing cultures see Natalia Milanesio's chapter in this volume.

4 Plotkin, *Mañana es San Perón*, 35–36.

5 In this chapter "commercial culture" refers to film, music, print materials, and other media produced on a mass scale, distributed commercially, and consumed by broad sectors of the Argentine population.

6 Studies of Peronism and the media include Plotkin, *Mañana es San Perón*; Ciria, *Política y cultura popular*; Cane-Carrasco, *The Fourth Enemy*; Sirven, *Perón y los medios de communicación*, 122–27; Haussen, *Rádio e Política*, 61–102; Capelato, *Multidões em cena*.

7 Oscar Ivanissevich, *Rindo Cuenta, 1893–1973*, vol. 2 (Buenos Aires: Ministerio de Cultura y Educación, 1973), 319–20.

8 Juan Carlos Moreno, *Gustavo Martínez Zuviría* (Buenos Aires: Ediciones Culturales Argentinas, 1962); Flavia Fiorucci, "La cultura, el libro y la lectura bajo el peronismo: el caso de las bibliotecas" (unpublished paper).

9 Plotkin, *Mañana es San Perón*, 95–99. Joseph A. Page, *Perón: A Biography* (New York: Random House, 1983), 225, 235–37.

10 Ivanissevich, *Rindo Cuenta*, 397. For more on the regime's relationship with intellectuals in this period see Fiorucci, "Between Institutional Survival and Intellectual Commitment."

11 *Argentina*, January 1949, 1.

12 National literacy rates were near 90 percent by the 1950s. Torre and Pastoriza, "La democratización del bienestar," 296–97. Ulanovsky, *Paren las rotativas.*

13 I would like to thank James Cane-Carrasco for sharing circulation figures and other findings from his book on Peronism and the press, *The Fourth Enemy.*

14 *Argentina*, August 1949, 54.

15 Cane-Carrasco, *The Fourth Enemy.*

16 *Argentina*, August 1949, 54.

17 For more on anti-speculation and the Peronist regime see my article "Peronist Consumer Politics and the Problem of Domesticating Markets in Argentina"; and Milanesio, " 'The Guardian Angels of the Domestic Economy."

18 *Argentina*, September 1949, 70–72.

19 *Argentina*, August 1949, 66–67.

20 *Argentina*, September 1949, 71

21 *Argentina*, September 1949, 70; November 1949, 63.

22 My discussion here is influenced by Bourdieu's treatment of cultured taste in mid-twentieth-century France. Bourdieu, *Distinction.*

23 *Argentina*, February 1950, 4.

24 *Argentina*, July 1950, 33; February 1949, 70.

25 *Argentina*, January 1950, 22–24.

26 On related gender dimensions of Peronism see Ramacciotti and Valobra, eds., *Generando el peronismo*; Mirta Zaida Lobato, ed., *Cuando las mujeres reinaban: belleza, virtud y poder en la Argentina del siglo XX* (Buenos Aires: Biblos, 2005); Cosse, *Estigmas de nacimiento.*

27 *Argentina*, February 1949, 71; July 1949, 56.

28 *Argentina*, June 1949, 56.

29 Relevant works on social policy include Ballent, *Las huellas de la política*; Berrotarán, Jáuregui, and Rougier, *Sueños de bienestar en la Nueva Argentina*; Aboy, *Viviendas para el pueblo.*

30 *Argentina*, May 1949, 68–71; March 1950, 5–8.

31 Carlos Altamirano, "Ideologías políticas y debate cívico," *Nueva Historia Argentina*, vol. 8, ed. Carlos Torre (Buenos Aires: Sudamericana, 2002), 231–39.

32 Sebastiani, *Los antiperonistas en la Argentina peronista*. See also James, "October 17th and 18th, 1945."

33 Williams, *Culture Wars in Brazil*; Plotkin, *Mañana es San Perón*, 19–58.

34 For an analysis of consumption, class, and emulation in the early twentieth century see Rocchi, *Chimneys in the Desert*, 49–85.

35 Arnold Bauer, *Goods, Power, History*; Benjamin Orlove, ed., *The Allure of the Foreign: Imported Goods in Postcolonial Latin America* (Ann Arbor: University of Michigan Press, 1997).

36 *Argentina*, January 1949, 4.

37 *Argentina*, February 1949, 4.

38 In a brief article on Ivanissevich, *Time* magazine noted the appearance of *Argentina* on Buenos Aires newsstands; this "slickest and newest" publication, "packed with pictures and color," was derided by *Time* for its attacks on the "inequities of U.S. comic strips" aimed mainly to satisfy the anti-American "intelligentsia." *Time*, 24 January 1949.

39 For more on this type of *criollo* nationalism see Oscar Chamosa's chapter in this volume.

40 *Argentina*, January 1950, 41

41 *Argentina*, June 1949, 56; December 1949; July 1950, 44.

42 *Argentina*, January 1949, 4.

43 *Argentina*, April 1949, 61–69; June 1949, 56.

44 *Argentina*, May 1949, 81; February 1949, 56; January 1949, 9.

45 Rubenstein, *Bad Language, Naked Ladies, and Other Threats to the Nation*; Eric Zolov, *Refried Elvis: The Rise of the Mexican Counterculture* (Berkeley: University of California Press, 1999); Moreno, *Yankee Don't Go Home!*; Joseph, Rubenstein, and Zolov, eds., *Fragments of a Golden Age*.

46 *Argentina*, September 1949; May 1949, 25.

47 Page, *Perón*, 235. Shortly after Ivanissevich left, *Time* magazine published a brief note that suggested another cause. In this version of the story Ivanissevich crossed Perón when he refused to order an hour of mandatory speeches in public schools to criticize the actions of Juan Casella Piñero, a Radical Party deputy in the provincial legislature of Buenos Aires, who during an act celebrating the Liberator San Martín refused to rise from his seat. Ivanissevich, as minister of education and chairman of the Year of San Martín celebrations, took a principled stand not to use the schools in railing against Piñero's "insult." While possible, this version of the events seems unlikely given Ivanissevich's unwavering loyalty to the Peronist cause and few qualms

about introducing partisan doctrine into the curriculum and student organizations. *Time*, 29 May 1950.

48 Plotkin, *Mañana es San Perón*, 78–82; Gené, *Un mundo felíz*, 29–64.

49 Hugo Gambini, *Historia del peronismo*, 153–55.

50 For a probing look at how architects adapted existing fashions and aesthetic conventions to new political ends see Ballent, *Las huellas de la política*.

51 On the Soviets and orthodoxy see Sheila Fitzpatrick, *The Cultural Front: Power and Culture in Revolutionary Russia* (Ithaca: Cornell University Press, 1992). On Italian fascist distrust of commercial culture see de Grazia, "Nationalizing Women." As suggested earlier in this chapter, there are similarities between the moralizing impulses of the editors of *Argentina*, nationalist intellectuals under Vargas in Brazil, and post-revolution governments in Mexico. See Williams, *Culture Wars in Brazil*; and Joseph, Rubenstein, and Zolov, eds., *Fragments of a Golden Age*.

César Seveso

....

POLITICAL EMOTIONS AND THE ORIGINS
OF THE PERONIST RESISTANCE

Perón's return was the return of decency and dignity for us workers, to get the *patrón* off our backs, it was the return of happiness, it was the end of all the sadness and bitterness that had weighed upon millions of regular men, it was the end of persecution for so many who, like me, had never dreamed of getting into politics or getting involved in revolutions, but who had gotten involved because there was no other remedy, and if we didn't get involved it was only because we were *cagones*.[1]

"CRÓNICAS DE LA RESISTENCIA"

In 1955, during what the writer Jorge Luis Borges called "the epic rains of September," the formidable state built around Juan Perón crumbled behind him as he marched into exile on a Paraguayan seaplane.[2] General Eduardo Lonardi led the military uprising—known as the Revolución Libertadora—which the *New York Times* called "the most sanguinary of all the revolts against Perón."[3] As he would repeatedly say, Perón feared the destruction of valuable infrastructure and did not want to plunge the country into a civil war by giving arms to his descamisados. Still fresh on his mind was the massacre of 16 June 1955, when navy planes attacked the Casa Rosada and the Plaza de Mayo, killing nearly 350 people, most of them civilians, in an attempt to oust him from power.[4] "The city was a desert," Perón wrote, describing his last hours in Buenos Aires. "The fog spread across the lower parts of the buildings just as it covers tree trunks in the forest. In this blurry setting of rain and fog, it all seemed unreal."[5]

This chapter analyzes the clash between Peronists and anti-Peronists after Perón's overthrow and argues that emotions were inextricable from the exercise and contestation of power. Emotions not only helped produce, and were created by, a repertoire of tactics but also translated new gender roles and legitimated new political identities in the context of collective action. To elucidate the emotional culture of Argentina in the mid-1950s, this chapter begins by examining the explosion of upper- and middle-class political vengeance after the Libertadora's triumph and re-creates the great humiliation suffered by Peronist militants and sympathizers. Although the brutality of the dictatorships of the 1960s and 1970s has diminished in our eyes the atrocities committed after the coup of 1955, Peronists who lived through this period experienced it as a nightmare. Humiliation was further worsened by a sense of loss and desperation since individual identities and, more generally, class status, social relations, and work culture were tied to and made possible by the Peronist regime. It was the end of the populist emotional climate—the destruction of *un mundo felíz* (a happy world).[6] I next focus on a poem written by a Peronist woman to examine how popular political poetry channeled the process of mourning and the socialization of suffering. In examining her poem, I elaborate on the collective construction of another emotional climate, one in which—as in the juxtaposition of sadness, bitterness, and agency in the words of the militant quoted in the epigraph above—the humiliation and shame that settled in after the coup coexisted with a desire to speak up and fight back. I conclude the chapter by analyzing the relationship of politics, emotions, and memory. It has been argued that "retrospective accounts of activists often privilege cognitive dimensions of decision making and suppress emotional dynamics regarded as less politically legitimating."[7] In contrast, I show how emotions structure the memories of those who participated in the only major pro-Perón popular uprising that followed the September coup. The three discussions in this chapter thus follow an emotional metamorphosis, from humiliation and shame to anger and pride.

Throughout this chapter I deploy emotions as a category of analysis to understand what propels political struggle in highly antagonistic societies such as Argentina in the 1950s. Crucial in the origin, maintenance, and decline of political action, emotions are the invisible force pushing people to the streets, even in the absence of likely success and favorable structural conditions.[8] In dialogue with a burgeoning scholarship on the sociology of contentious politics, philosophy, and cultural studies, I define political emotions as a culturally and socially produced range of feelings that both create and are the result of political agency. Emotions —such as anger, hope, regret, sympathy, and hatred—entail an interpretation of the power relations that political actors face, changes in bodily sensations, and a display of expressive gestures to nurture political mobilization.[9] By turning our attention to the emotional cultures of political action, we can gain a better understanding of the nonmaterial, non-ideological basis for mobilization and explain how both Peronists and anti-Peronists *felt* in the face of political upheaval.

The study of political violence and emotions has yet to capture the attention of historians of Latin America. Political violence and more specifically popular violence have usually appeared as residues of power relations and struggles; their existence has been recorded, but the meanings embedded in violence and the ways violence intertwined with emotions and fueled both representations and practices have rarely been examined. Most commonly, scholarship has more directly addressed the many facets of state violence or explained violence in instrumental terms.[10] Instead I study the cultural dimensions of violence "as a changing form of interaction and communication, as a historically developed cultural form of *meaningful* action."[11] The historiography of the Peronist resistance in particular has remained anchored around three main issues: a close connection between shop floor struggles and violence, an emphasis on the spontaneity and anarchic nature of violence, and finally the exhaustion and demoralization of militants because of state repression.[12] Drawing on Raymond Williams's concept of "structures of feeling," Daniel James explained how bitterness, pride, and a sense of class solidarity shaped working-class consciousness after 1955.[13] My analysis expands on James's insights by reframing the struggles between Peronists and anti-Peronists not only as an activity propelled by emotions but also as a source of individual and collective emotional dynamics. As an interpretive tool, emotions allow for an understanding of Argentine politics that goes beyond vested interests and ideological foundations to engage with the very same terms by which military officers, workers, and political militants made sense of violence, persecution, and empowerment.[14]

Y otra vez han de oírse los clarines,

que anuncien la nación reconquistada,

por la sangre valiente de sus hijos,

que prefieren morir, a verla esclava![15]

"A PERÓN"

Anti-Peronist violence, both physical and symbolic, had two objectives. It most immediately sought to produce the rejection of Peronism as a legitimate political ideology, and it strove to eradicate Peronism from individual and collective memory. To be effective, coercion and more generally the construction of the anti-Peronist hegemony had to be accompanied by the socialization of shame and humiliation among Perón's followers. While both shame (*vergüenza*) and humiliation (*humillación*) targeted the Peronists' public self, shame was more clearly a commentary on their lack of honor and reputation while humiliation aimed at their pride. The production of shame stigmatized Peronism by reinterpreting it as an immoral and corrupt phenomenon. As such, shame was meant to function as a backward-looking feeling. In contrast, humiliation, the byproduct of feelings of powerlessness and the erosion of dignity, was not related to what Peronists had been but to what they had become after the coup, and even to what they could aspire to be. To paraphrase William Ian Miller, shame was the consequence of not having lived up to what Peronists ought to be, while humiliation was the consequence of trying to live up to what they had no right to be.[16]

Military skirmishes were not over, as the spaces and images through which Juan and Eva Perón had asserted their power became the epicenter of a battle of another kind. This was a symbolic battle, fought mainly among civilian contenders, that would produce a myriad of foundational moments and contentious landmarks. Across the country anti-Peronist crowds stormed government buildings and trade union headquarters to destroy furniture and official documentation and danced on, insulted, and spat on the busts, paintings, and photographs of Juan and Eva Perón. Two statues of Evita in one railway station in Buenos Aires were toppled, roped to automobiles, and dragged through the city's main streets, while street signs named after the presidential couple were replaced with hand-made paper signs honoring the heroes of the Libertadora.[17] It was an expression of a vengeful and joyful violence that even allowed for a champagne toast, while hands and white handkerchiefs waved from balconies and in the streets, to honor the triumph of the coup.

Feelings of hate, vengefulness, righteousness, and the affirmation of manhood thus shaped the anti-Peronists' "emotional economy."[18] In a drastic reversal of power relations, Peronists were taunted and mocked in the streets and public places. Civil commandos, consisting of anti-Peronist Catholics and activists drawn from the Socialist Party and the Radical Party, drove around neighborhoods displaying guns, shouting offensive slogans, and searching houses to hunt down Peronists. Penitentiaries were stormed to free anti-Peronist detainees who were received at the gates by crowds chanting the national anthem and the "Marcha de la Libertad," the war song of the Revolución Libertadora. In the Plaza de Mayo "elated young men" dug up a casket containing the written history of the Peronist movement, dedicated by Perón himself to the youth of 2000, and paraded it through the streets, finally offering it as a trophy to the anti-Peronist newspaper *La Nación*.[19] In the seaside resort of Mar del Plata an anti-Peronist crowd waving the Argentine flag attacked the 17 de Octubre hotel—which was owned by the Oil Workers Union—the Peronist Party headquarters, and the police station, freeing many detainees.[20] The alliance between anti-Peronist soldiers and the Catholic Church—together self-appointed arbiters of a new, post-Peronist morality—gave birth to sacred symbolic violence, as in the Air Force School in Córdoba, where rebel troops tore out a bust of Perón and put a crucifix in its place.[21]

How crucial these emotional and physical struggles over symbols were to Peronists and anti-Peronists alike is revealed by the many stories of militants rescuing Peronist icons from the anti-Peronist hordes, such as when a worker at the Hospital Provincial in Rosario ran away with a bust of Evita to keep it safe in his home, where he hid it for seventeen years until Perón returned to Argentina in 1972. The bust became an improvised altar and neighbors visited it daily to pray to Evita, who represented the most pure, authentic expression of what Peronism had been.[22] What were militants trying to save when they put away a bust of

Perón or physically protected a statue of Evita? This was undoubtedly a reflex action, a process set in motion when anti-Peronists first converted the Peronist iconography into a field of confrontations where politicized objects could be exhibited as war booty. Yet it was more than that. In a moment of lawlessness, both the success of the revolution and loyalty to Perón came to be embodied by a political material culture made of busts, statues, flags, monuments, and emblems. As in other contentious scenarios, "the destruction of the symbols of the old regime was, at least for the revolutionaries, the destruction of the old regime itself."[23]

In a coordinated de-Peronizing campaign, General Eduardo Lonardi and then more vehemently General Pedro Aramburu abolished the celebration of October 17 as a national holiday, ordered the confiscation and public burning of Peronist reading manuals used in schools, set up a special commission to investigate the fallen regime's misdeeds, and authorized the demolition of Palacio Unzué, Perón's official residence in Buenos Aires.[24] Simultaneously, in an attempt to uncover corruption during the Peronist government, public expositions were organized to show the houses, apartments, cars, furniture, and jewelry owned by Perón, Evita, and other well-known politicians, who had either been arrested or were hiding from the police.[25] It was a double policy that sought both to expose and to hide the legacies of Peronism to Argentine political history by destroying what was visible and exposing what was not. Either way the implicit goal was to liberate anger toward the past regime and generate shame among the vanquished as part of the larger effort to mark the end of the "emotional regime" of Peronism"[26]

No other image better illustrates the extent of the de-Peronizing campaign than a photograph taken in November 1955 showing three statues atop the unfinished building of the Eva Perón Foundation. Next to the imposing statue of General José de San Martín, Argentina's national hero of independence are two thirty-ton spectral figures wrapped in black burlap. The ghostly, even ominous contours hide the Carrara marble statues of Juan and Eva Perón—two involuntary actors in the Libertadora's mise-en-scène awaiting their forceful removal from the city's urban and political landscape. Their final destination was still uncertain when the photograph was taken, but in what would have been one of the Peróns' biggest and most ironic contributions to Argentina's high culture, art professors had already requested portions of the figures to use as raw material in their classes.[27] The removal of the statues at the Eva Perón Foundation was the Libertadora's most grandiose political spectacle, yet it followed in the path set by rank-and-file anti-Peronists' desecration of many other small symbols, busts, and monuments. As a political tool, the goal was to expose and increase the humiliation of the vanquished. As a material confirmation of the anti-Peronist victory, it was a very palpable means to impose a definitive closure on the struggle, burn all bridges with the past, and signal the beginning of a new epoch.[28]

Rumors, misinformation, and disbelief fueled feelings of bewilderment and disorientation, so pervasive in the narrations of old-time Peronists when recalling the aftermath of Perón's fall. In Argentina's small towns and major industrial centers, particularly those that had been spared the fighting between loyal and revolutionary troops, the Libertadora's victory came as "a blow to the head."[29] Indeed, almost until Lonardi officially took power in Buenos Aires on 23 September the official radio and the press kept portraying the uprising as insignificant while positively describing the succession of government victories.[30] Fifty years after the coup, recalling that fateful week of September 1955, Ema Lucero, a Peronist militant from Rosario, told me: "I just couldn't believe it was true. I thought that Perón would be back again soon. I couldn't accept that he was gone . . . I thought the world was ending."[31] The cataclysmic imagery, also conveyed by other rank-and-file Peronists through the metaphor "heaven fell upon us," not only underscored a sense of loss, impotence, and rage but also denoted what they perceived as the end of an epoch and, perhaps more ominously, the coming of Judgment Day. Shame produced a sense of isolation from community that was accompanied, as Jack Katz has remarked in another context, by feelings of moral inferiority and personal vulnerability.[32] The experience of inversion was so drastic that it could only be described by evoking the unreal nature of a nightmare, as in the recollection of one of the leaders of the resistance: "The world we knew, the day-to-day world, changed completely. People, facts, work, streets, newspapers, the air, the sun, life was turned on its head. All of a sudden we entered a nightmare world in which Peronism didn't exist. Everything was abnormal."[33]

Si ésta es la libertad, la democracia
que ha venido a implantar la oligarquía
pedimos al Señor como una gracia
que nos traiga otra vez la tiranía.[34]

"EL TIRANO"

The same day that Lonardi took power, the Peronist Adelma Martínez de Amarante wrote a poem reflecting her own emotions in a context of persecution and disorientation. Until 1955 Amarante had been a lukewarm sympathizer who disliked "the excesses within our party," such as the use of the Peronist insignia and the obligatory national mourning after Evita's death.[35] A seventy-four-year-old woman when I met her, she participated in the demonstrations against the coup of 1955 and then had become a fervent conspirator in the campaign to bring Perón back to Argentina. She was recounting how she felt in the first days after the coup when she reached into her black purse for two yellowish, legal-size pages folded into a tiny square: a poem simply titled "Juan Domingo Perón." I claim that Amarante's poem is a particular example of the emotional dynamics forged after the anti-Peronists' triumph. Here I analyze it to explain how the socialization of shame and humiliation gave rise to an emotional, counter-hegemonic discourse that sought to make sense of Perón's fall. These are the poem's first three stanzas:

Llegó la hora funesta, argentinos . . .
la hora de la ingratitud tremenda
la hora en que el corazón más grande y sensitivo
renunciando a su derechos nos ofrenda
la paz, que no podrá ser paz sin su presencia
Sólo de corazón tan noble e intachable
gesto tan grande de amor brotar pudiera.
Sólo de pecho tan viril, que tanta ingratitud
como pago a su bondad infinita recibiera
podría nacer decisión más digna, más loable.
Todo lo diste por tu pueblo y hoy, ingratos,
te dejamos marchar, sin un gesto siquiera,

que detenga tu marcha INCONCEBIBLE.

Pero no estarás nunca solo; dondequiera

te encuentres, el alma de tu pueblo será tu compañera.[36]

The first line, by using the noun "Argentines" rather than the more obvious choice "Peronists," implicitly excludes the anti-Peronists from membership in the national community. However, in what is one of the poem's most striking features, Amarante avoids more directly confronting the "others who will rule our destinies"—as she refers to the Revolución Libertadora authorities—to directly address Perón and an invisible audience of descamisados. Her caution, perhaps dictated by a concern for her personal safety, contrasts with the irreverent remarks toward the "oligarchy" that I found in other poems, such as the one seized from a *unidad básica* in Capital Federal by the commission investigating the Peronist regime's wrongdoings:

Todos los oligarcas,

Muy contentos están,

Pero no se alegren tanto,

Que pronto llega el final.[37]

On one level Amarante's poem exalts Perón's many virtues—his goodness, his love for the people, and even his manliness. In the last stanzas she swears eternal loyalty and assures the deposed president that future generations would ultimately recognize his good deeds. In Amarante's writing Peronism—as a memory—was immediately idealized: it became more egalitarian, less contradictory, and even powerful and just. Written in a simple, very accessible style, the poem thus echoes a genre most commonly employed to pay homage to Argentina's nineteenth-century heroes of national independence. However, Amarante complicates the characteristically deferential, martial style with a melodramatic twist that allows her to more easily explore her own political emotions and those of her fellow Peronists.[38] As such, her poem is representative of what I call popular political poetry, in which obscure metaphors, complex stylistic techniques, and other abstract poetic figures—the frivolous, "sophisticated" language of the upper classes—are almost absent, replaced by an effort to master a transparent, direct, and accessible language.[39] The goal was to replicate in poetry what the writer, as an agent of the popular classes, stood for in real life: simplicity and honesty. This is, furthermore, a poem that eschews falling into the profanity, irreverence, and parody that Luisa Passerini has uncovered in the poetry of the antifascist working class of Turin in the 1930s to bring about a sadder emotional climate characterized by feelings of bitterness, anger, and sorrow.[40] In this sense Amarante's piece avoids the irony of other poetry post-1955, such as "El Tirano," the poem cited in the epigraph above, in which the author ridicules the upper class's association of Peronism and totalitarianism. In "El Tirano" the inversion of meanings, which characterized the new language of democracy coined by the Libertadora in its attempt to mask the suffering and repression of everyday life, translated to almost every aspect of reality, as is exemplified by these two stanzas:

> Con él se fue la paz, vino el terror
> llenan las calles bélicos pertrechos
> y el arma que forjó nuestro sudor
> se vuelve apuntada a nuestro pechos.
> Que hay libertad nos dicen diariamente
> en discursos, arengas y sermones
> y lo afirma una prensa complaciente
> mientras llenan de gentes las prisiones.[41]

Another anonymous poem that circulated after 1955 conveys an even more sardonic version of what seems to be the product of a masculine sensibility:

> Fumando un puro
> me cago en Aramburu
> y si se enoja
> también me cago en Rojas.[42]

In contrast, Amarante's inspiration is rather within the moral universe that Daniel James has encountered in the poem that the Peronist activist María Roldán wrote after a fellow worker died of tuberculosis because of the harsh conditions at the Swift meatpacking plant in Berisso.[43] But if harsh labor conditions led Roldán to address gender oppression at work and denounce social inequalities, political turmoil and Perón's fall gave Amarante an opportunity to shed light on the Peronist militancy's failure to rise above the disorientation and impotence that followed the coup.

In Amarante's poem the recurrence of the word "ingratitude" has two meanings: on the one hand it underscores how militants had failed Perón by so easily resigning to the triumph of the oligarchic revolution, and on the other it constitutes a veiled reproach of the ideological foundations of Peronism itself. Lines such as "Llegó la hora funesta, argentinos . . . / la hora de la ingratitud tremenda" and "Todo lo diste por tu pueblo y hoy, ingratos / te dejamos marchar, sin un gesto siquiera" express a feeling of contrition and self-reproach and, at the same time, channel a critique toward the ideological inadequacy of Peronism when forced to deal with a physical, violent confrontation. The critique is most openly expressed in the following stanza:

No tuviste a tu lado un esfuerzo leal
una ayuda sincera que igualara tu ardor
y tras años de lucha, solitaria, implacable
tu semilla de amor no pudo germinar.
¡Cómo habría de ser si hubo solo UN PERON![44]

In exalting Perón's larger-than-life attributes, which are exemplified by his renunciation of the presidency as a means of sparing the country a full-blown civil war, the poem troublingly blames both the viciousness that plagued Argentine politics by the mid-1950s and Peronists themselves for the revolution's success. The destruction of dreams and lives brought about by the coup first developed into impotence and rage, eventually producing a sensation of speechlessness, typically compared to drowning or suffocation. As Amarante told me: "I cried like a baby [when the coup took place]. I wrote a poem—I don't know if you can call it a poem, because it was the first thing I wrote, something expressing my feelings at that moment. I put it down on paper because I felt like I was suffocating, like I was dying, that I had to explode, that I had to hit the streets screaming. I felt like what was happening was simply not possible." Beyond the individual satisfaction of recovering speech, her poem and other emotionally charged writings—such as Catholic-inspired prayers eulogizing political martyrdom, most commonly written by nationalist and left-wing militants in the 1960s and 1970s—also served another specific purpose. By merging individual tragedy with collective suffering, they catalyzed a healing process within a political community of victims and survivors.[45] In articulating the emotional reactions to the suffering and despair that ensued after the coup, poems like Amarante's helped to define a Peronist "mourning genre."[46] The act of writing allowed Amarante to rework the events and start making sense of what had happened. In turn, this mourning genre made possible the manifestation of emotions that could not have been fully explored in other forms of written or oral expression. It was furthermore an act that defied shame, to the extent that it rescued Peronism from public illegitimacy and stigmatization.

In Amarante's case individual and collective emotions met when she overcame her fears and started to read her poem aloud on the street corners of her working-class neighborhood. "People cried like it was a funeral," she said when describing the range of emotions stirred by the poem. Characteristically, this was not poetry written for the sole private consolation of its author but rather a work that aspired to promote the formation of a new political identity. As Anne McClintock put it in her study of African oral poetry, "the focus is on the performance in its social context, on the function of the performance in society, almost to the exclusion of transmission of the text over time."[47] Jean Franco has called this type of poetry a civic and public form of address, a poetry of communion that when read aloud functions as a public performance of political resistance.[48]

The infamous Decree 4161 of March 1956 specifically targeted the oral and written transmission of the Peronist past that political poems and other ideologically charged objects and narratives were trying to effect after the coup. Memories of the recent past were an offense to the political values that the Libertadora was promoting, since they evoked "an epoch of mockery and pain," and by stirring up what had become disturbing emotions caused a breach of the internal peace. As a result, General Aramburu prohibited images, symbols, signs, doctrines, articles, and artistic works that could be construed by the government as propagating Peronist ideology. The decree banned the use of photographs, portraits, and sculptures of Peronist public officials and their relatives, especially Juan and Eva Perón; the Peronist pin and flag; Perón's name and the names of his relatives; the expressions *peronismo, peronista, justicialismo, justicialista,* and *tercera posición,* and the acronym "P.P." (as in Partido Peronista); the holidays observed during the Peronist regime; the music and lyrics from the "Marcha de los muchachos peronistas" and "Evita capitana"; Evita's autobiography *La razón de mi vida*; and the speeches of Juan and Eva Perón. The punishment for not observing the decree included from thirty days to six years of imprisonment, a fine of up to one million pesos, and a prohibition against working in the public sector, serving in public office, or acting as a trade union leader for a period twice as long as the prison time served.[49]

The decree's far-reaching aims, which made it conceivable to incarcerate every Peronist in Argentina, more realistically attempted to erase any public trace of Peronism from the country's political system and collective memory forever. But the raids carried out by the civil commandos and the police in their daily harassment of rank-and-file Peronists extended the effects of Decree 4161 into the private realm. Peronists still remember the bonfires in working-class backyards consuming the *Mundo Peronista* magazine or the hurried digging of a pit in the hen run to bury a poster of Perón. Some militants challenged the repression by keeping Evita's portrait on the wall and resorted to word of mouth and anonymous leaflets in a war of positions against the state. The poem "El Tirano," for instance, was circulated among friends and close confidants —it could even be argued that it became one of the many hidden transcripts that militants created during the Libertadora's reign.[50] Replicating the anti-Peronists' tactics before the coup of 1955, even to the point of claiming God as the interlocutor, Peronists also made carbon copies of "El Tirano" and sent them randomly through the mail.[51]

Decree 4161 did not put an end to Amarante's public performance of her poem. It is rather in the poem itself that I find the conditions making it an untenable narrative. To put the blame of Perón's fall on the beleaguered descamisados was a disturbing message that few if any wanted to hear in the aftermath of the coup. Indeed, the emotional climate that Amarante sought to create could not but increase the shame and humiliation the Peronists were already suffering. But as time went by, the poem's cautionary tale would eventually gain legitimacy among other critical discourses condemning the abdication of supposedly loyal party bureaucrats and military officers.[52] In the meantime a more violent story was being written in the streets of Rosario.

For many months, I kept a flyer where the people of a tiny, suffering, working-class neighborhood, Villa Manuelita, challenged the world in more or less these words: "The United States, Russia, England recognize Lonardi. Villa Manuelita recognizes Perón." To me, Rosario had a symbolic dimension. I can assure you that if the gunboat had taken the Paraná [River], my passage through Rosario would have had the effect of a spark before a keg of gunpowder.[53]

JUAN PERÓN

The Peronists who rowed small boats out to catch a last glimpse of the deposed president waited in vain, since the Paraguayan gunboat on which Perón first sought refuge before flying to exile never left the Buenos Aires harbor.[54] Yet despite Perón's wishes, there was no need for the spark; Rosario was already in flames. A city of 600,000 inhabitants on the Paraná River about two hundred miles northwest of Buenos Aires, Rosario was the only place in Argentina where massive pro-Perón protests against the coup took place. The uprising's symbolic dimension was so compelling that the city immediately became known as the "birthplace of the Peronist resistance." It was, I argue, a formative event, powerful enough to shape the emotional climate—a mixture of suffering, anger, indignation, resentment, and hatred—of later confrontations between Peronists and the state. The uprising allowed for the construction of a political myth through which militants projected a sense of victimization and heroism to legitimize the exercise of violence in the confrontation with the post-Peronist state. As Alessandro Portelli argues in his study of the Italian resistance to the German occupation, "a myth is not necessarily a false or invented tale; rather it is a story that becomes significant as it amplifies the meaning of an individual event (factual or not) into a symbolic and narrative formalization of a culture's shared self-representations."[55]

Fifty years after the coup the story of the uprising received a new layer of meaning when Rosario's councilmen voted unanimously to pay homage to the victims of 1955 and had a memorial plaque installed at the intersection of two main avenues where a fierce clash between Peronists and revolutionary soldiers had erupted. The text is brief but powerful:

"On September 16, 1955, the people of Rosario took to the streets, all across the city, against the anti-popular coup. On this corner, on September 24, a heroic battle was fought."[56] It was an overdue commemoration that marked the incorporation of the uprising into the city's official history and legitimized the memories of those who had fought against the Libertadora. How emotions shape what memories are made of is indeed the topic of this discussion.

Scattered newspaper accounts and historical witnesses concur that columns of working-class people converged on the city's downtown area as soon as the news of Perón's resignation started to spread, although the "news" was more properly a rumor that Peronists circulated but did not entirely believe. One activist described the early stages of the demonstration as follows: "It was like a collective shiver, as if a secret voice were speaking to each human being, moving the masses like an irresistible hypnotic force. At the same time, groups began to come together in the different working class neighborhoods that surrounded the city on three of its cardinal points, though no one had summoned them. The masses moved, like a living unit that was fueled by a collective consciousness. In all the neighborhoods, a single voice was heard: 'Downtown! Downtown!' And downtown thousands of people headed, tens of thousands of adults, young people, old people, women, and entire families dragging their children and grandparents behind them."[57] Policemen—most of them Peronists—hesitantly and unsuccessfully tried to stop the marchers. The lack of repression, the city's compact layout and wide avenues, and the mobilizing efforts of activists, whose role is not recognized in the epic account cited above, quickly put Rosario at the mercy of the incensed Peronists. The soldiers from the 11th Infantry Regiment, who were returning from Córdoba, where they had been sent to repress Lonardi's uprising, entered the city singing the Peronist anthem "Los muchachos peronistas" while handing out bullets to the people who greeted them on the streets.[58] It is interesting to note that according to most accounts demonstrators were not armed, so the troops' gesture could only imply a symbolic refusal to fire on the people.[59] José Mármol, a municipal worker who was in the barricade erected at the corner of 27 de Febrero Boulevard and Ovidio Lagos Avenue, where the city council put up the plaque, told me that they were only armed with their "fists, mouths, and hearts."[60] While the mention of fists most obviously implies a lack of guns while exalting working-class courage and bravery, "hearts" here is a metaphor for the emotions fueling the militants' loyalty to Perón. Likewise, the mouth was the instrument that made this loyalty clear when shouting the slogan "¡la vida por Perón!" (our lives for Perón!) on the march downtown. Accordingly, explaining the rationale behind the demonstrations in emotional terms, as fueled by a feeling of love for the deposed president, implicitly denies the credibility of the claim by the reactionary press that rank-and-file Peronists were used as pawns by professional agitators seeking to destabilize the Libertadora's hegemony in the rest of the country.[61] The mention of love, though, relegates to the background other emotions such as anger and hatred—alluded to by the use of fists—that additionally informed the protesters' judgment and agency during those days.

While some marchers set up barricades to obstruct police and military reinforcements arriving from Buenos Aires, others kept walking toward downtown while repeatedly clashing with anti-Peronists over the possession of the national flag and Peronist placards.[62] It could be argued that this was a demonstration without a specific target, since marchers did not want to seize a police station or attack the opposition parties' headquarters. However, it was not meaningless. As had happened before during the Perón government, marchers wanted to show both the elite and the state that poor Peronists from working-class neighborhoods would not vanish from the public space so easily. The resistance they faced was fierce, as is clear from the many violent and potent images that they recall, even including that of planes dropping tear-gas bombs on the columns approaching downtown. Most dramatically, Peronists always highlight in their recollections that snipers from the civil commandos shot at them from the rooftops of buildings and shops.[63] Years later a Peronist newspaper claimed—stressing the alliance between the oligarchic soldiers and the anti-Peronist clergy—that snipers fired from churches and the diocese.[64] Mármol, who tried to block the troops' advance by wrapping himself in an Argentine flag, was shot in the shoulder and lost a kidney after an officer hit him with the butt of a rifle as he lay bleeding on the street.

The fusion between his body and the flag—a risky, ambiguous gesture that could either be an appeal to the anti-Peronists' patriotic feelings or a way to show them that Peronists were the only real Argentines in that corner of Rosario—underscores the use of bodies in the production of gendered emotions. In the working-class neighborhood of El Saladillo, which surrounded the Swift meatpacking plant, soldiers sent to remove a statue of Evita had to first pull off a group of women who were protecting it with their own bodies. The most significant detail of what already was a marvelous story of gender dynamics and power relations came when according to one account those enraged women tore off their blouses and shirts to expose their breasts in a defiant gesture toward the troops.[65] While unique, the scene reverberates nonetheless with other violent, gendered encounters between women and the state in which the female body enacted the Peronists' cultural construction of emotions. A middle-class anti-Peronist woman recalled that when Perón was overthrown "tons of people roamed the streets cheering for him, and the women walked the streets bearing their chests [con el pecho desnudo] . . . bearing their breasts [las tetas desnudas], with Perón's picture on their chests."[66] Interestingly, stories told about the Peronist resistance to the failed coup of June 1955 also mention a woman marching near Plaza de Mayo waving an Argentine flag before being gunned down by revolutionary troops.[67] In another account centered on the struggles of September 1955 in Rosario, a group of women and children confronted and disarmed the soldiers sent to take down a banner whose text vowed to disobey the Lonardi government—the same banner that Perón so vividly recalled in exile.[68]

The Saladillo incident together with these three moments doubtless echo Eugène Delacroix's famous painting Liberty Leading the People (1830), in which a bare-breasted woman carrying the tricolor in one hand and a bayoneted musket in the other marches over dead bodies alongside a boy holding pistols. The gender dynamics at play show that Peronists used those clashes in their favor as a symbol of working-class female solidarity and the people's victimhood and sacrifice vis-à-vis the brutality of the Revolución Libertadora. The absence of Peronist males in the narratives avoids projecting a self-emasculating image by directing the attention toward the anti-Peronist troops. Indeed threatening, marching, shirtless women exposing their breasts can be interpreted as a regendered, transvestite version of the descamisados, a version that masculinizes women at the same time that it feminizes the hopeless, impotent soldiers. In particular, the Saladillo incident tells an even more complex tale by pointing to the savagery and lewdness of the Libertadora as embodied in the young troops who entered a terrain where the line between repression and sexual attack had been blurred. The trope of rape, which is evoked by the torn clothes, the bare breasts, the bayonets, the blood, and the charging motion that the soldiers executed when pushing the women back, is counterbalanced by the women's nude torsos as a weapon that causes repulsion and disgust in an army so strongly identified with religious values and puritan morality.[69]

While clashes continued, soldiers from Buenos Aires and Corrientes arrived in Rosario to put an end to the demonstrations, but workers only retreated on 25 September, two days after Lonardi officially took power.[70] Protesters claimed that soldiers used blank cartridges and intentionally aimed high to spare people's lives, but they have also asserted that there were a great number of casualties. Although the exact figure was never provided, participants have argued there were hundreds of deaths and have even used the words "massacre" and "genocide."[71] In reality, both accounts highlight different points along a continuum: soldiers stationed in Rosario, most of them conscripts born and raised in the city, were intentionally ineffective, while the nonlocal reinforcements did not hesitate to shoot at the crowd to put an end to the demonstrations. To my knowledge it was by far the bloodiest uprising the city had ever experienced. When a newspaper reported fifteen deaths and fifty-five persons wounded, Rosario's working-class neighborhoods were still not totally subdued.[72] Although Sherman tanks and troop transport trucks patrolled the streets, scattered groups of militants still tried to stop the circulation of streetcars and buses and painted cars with pro-Perón slogans. Disobeying the call to order issued by trade union leaders, workers congregated around factories and refused to walk in.[73]

The images and memories evoked by the rebellion in Rosario led some Peronists to establish a parallel with October 1945, when a massive working-class demonstration converged upon the Plaza de Mayo to force the release of Perón from the penitentiary on Martín García Island. These writers pointed to the reemergence in September 1955 of a mass of leaderless and confused militants struggling to protect Perón from his enemies and bring him back to power.[74] Yet this comparison did not convince most of those who provided written and oral accounts of the days following the coup. Amarante does not even register the demonstrations in her otherwise telling poem. The marchers' defeat, to the extent that the demonstrations did not reinstall Perón to power, was so painful —and perhaps even so embarrassing—that it could not immediately become the subject of a poem. Most likely, the historical parallel attempted to use the patina of the success of 1945 to cover the disaster that took place ten years later, but it was precisely the humiliation that Peronists suffered and the impotence ultimately manifested in Perón's exile that made that kind of comparison impossible. In fact, the uprising was not characterized by the carnivalesque behavior and secular iconoclasm that infused the events of October 1945.[75] The symbolic but brief fraternizing with the police and conscripts from the 11th Regiment quickly dissipated under the rain of bullets from anti-Peronist guns. The shots, the deaths, and an overwhelming sense of frustration led more easily to a pessimistic evaluation.

A very intriguing story that a marcher told me about anti-Peronist planes firing real bullets toward a dense column of marchers in Rosario made me aware that there was perhaps yet another meaning to the narratives of the uprising. The story's puzzling fact was that the bullets coming from the planes surprisingly missed their targets, not even wounding one of the marchers. The adamant claim that Peronists did not carry weapons, engage in physical violence, or attack public and private property confirmed that poor, working people were again on the losing side, even as it highlighted the savagery of those who won. The shame of not being able to avoid the death of so many marchers—which was in the end inevitable owing to the overpowering attack launched by anti-Peronists—was replaced by an emphasis on the peaceful spirit shown by demonstrators and the courage with which they faced enemy fire. The weeklong uprising was endowed with the attributes that would make it a formative event, in the sense that it encapsulated what Peronists already knew about the *gorilas*. With the benefit of hindsight, as the story of the uprising was told and retold, it anticipated—amplified, in the sense that Portelli uses the word in his definition of myth—as a tragic omen the violence that would befall the *sufrido pueblo peronista* (long-suffering Peronist people).[76] The insistence on portraying themselves as the only legitimate victims, in contrast to the claims made by the anti-Peronist middle and upper classes regarding their own suffering under Perón, sometimes obscures the other lesson that Peronists extracted from the battles of Rosario. This was an empowering lesson that turned victims into heroes and suffering into courage by portraying the Peronist working class engaged together as a "living unit" in the first battle against the repressive apparatus of the Revolución Libertadora. In a reversal of the events' emotional makeup, the telling itself, like Amarante's reading of her poem, was an act of resistance that proved how ineffective the repression was, just like the planes firing from the sky. Emotions articulated the narratives, gave meaning to the confrontations, and provided the language through which people passed on the memories of the uprising. In the end, bullets would not kill as long as the story of those days was not forgotten.

EMOTIONAL PERONISM

> Even now, I command more than the dictatorship, because I command over so many millions of hearts.[77]
>
> LETTER FROM PERÓN TO RONALD HILTON

The "onset of an episode of contention," Ron Aminzade and Doug McAdam claim, "is associated with, and partially dependent upon, the collective mobilization of heightened emotion."[78] But is it only about mobilizing something already existing, or does the collective mobilization also imply an act of creation and learning? Can we speak of a repertoire of emotions that can be involuntary—say, anger just happens to us when we see an injustice being committed—but can also be taught in stories told among militants and printed in the partisan press? The essence of such stories would claim, "Something grave has occurred, this is the way you should feel about what has happened, and when you feel this way this is what you must do." Emotions, as I have shown, are judgments—deeply implicated in the exercise of power and its contestation—connected to choice, intention, and purpose.[79] In the words of Stephanie A. Shields, "the discourse of emotion is fundamentally concerned with judgments about the authenticity and legitimacy of experience."[80] Hence it is possible to assert that the production and circulation of certain emotions—anger, pride, and resentment, for example—can facilitate and legitimate the identity and agency of political actors.

The intimate relationship between emotions and political mobilization is revealed in a manuscript that Perón received in early 1967, when he was exiled in Spain. José Julio Jáuregui, a writer and actor who had been corresponding with Perón, sent him the draft of his novel, hoping that Perón would offer editorial comments and even "administer a bit of plastic surgery," cutting out the superfluous parts.[81] As Jáuregui explained in a letter accompanying the novel, his story was about the moral imperatives that drove common men without political militancy to stand up against oppression. After the September coup the protagonist, named José Páez, starts organizing a clandestine cell, convinced that he cannot passively watch while the Argentina that he knew under Perón slowly fades away. "I have to get involved, because something in my loins is ordering me too; yes, something right here, and it tells me, get involved; and you'll see I can't ignore it," Páez tells three close friends with whom he created the cell.[82] The confession doubtless echoes the words at the beginning of this chapter from the anonymous militant who claimed that not joining the resistance would imply being a *cagón*—it points also to the role of emotions in translating the new gender roles that Peronists were forging in their confrontation with an authoritarian state. In Jáuregui's novel, however, emotions are misleading and prove ultimately to be a great obstacle to the success of the resistance. In a meeting with a military officer and two dock workers who were also conspiring against the Libertadora, a young professor, who plays the part of a Gramscian organic intellectual, tells Páez and his group that emotions are Peronism's Achilles heel. The professor laments that while Peronists' agency is fueled by emotions, Peronism's internal and foreign enemies more effectively gave primacy to rationality and cold calculations. Emotions, in the professor's view, blur the perception, distort the analysis, and hinder the construction of a cohesive strategy to power. The authoritative words strike the small working-class audience with the force of an epiphany.

Perón, in contrast, must have been unpleasantly surprised by the professor's warning, since the tactical use of emotions, or "commanding over the men's hearts," had long been in his view the most important condition for successful leadership.[83] Indeed, after 1955 hate and resentment toward the "*canalla dictatorial*" were the leitmotif of his letters from exile. He conceived of hate as a malleable weapon, powerful enough to singularly drive the clandestine struggle against the dictatorship. Hate, furthermore, gave intensity to the militants' everyday efforts and complemented the soft pressure exercised by ideals and moral imperatives. In Perón's own words: "The process [of resistance] is slow because compounding the difficult task of integral organization itself is the secrecy factor, which makes things harder. Nonetheless there is a factor which is fundamental for acceleration: it is enthusiasm and hate, which have begun to work determinedly. I've learned that although the ideal is a powerful force that gives the effort continuity, hate is no less powerful, because it gives it intensity. Hate is precisely what we were lacking, but now we have it, and 'by the ton.' "[84] If hate was something new within the emotional universe of Peronism, a byproduct of both the state's repression and an equally oppressive social climate at work and in public, where millions of rank-and-file de-Peronizers continued the drive to oust Perón from memory, it was nonetheless easily nurtured and socialized. Love, political love—as in love toward the have-nots, as in the love of Evita toward Perón and her grasitas, or the love that Amarante felt for Perón—was what defined, together with pride, loyalty, and dignity, the Peronist's hegemonic emotional regime almost until its fall. In exile Perón trusted more what Robert C. Solomon has described as "nasty and double-edged emotions" than any other more "positive" emotions.[85] Certainly political engagements are always affective engagements, and the events I have described were part of a war of positions in which the confronting factions sought to produce, circulate, and consume a wide array of emotions. After all, the discourse of emotions was straightforward, appealed to what seemed a very "natural" characteristic of human beings, and was not tarnished by the suspicion of corruption and duplicity that shadowed formal political speech. Thus the emphasis on hearts in the first two stanzas of Amarante's poem, in Mármol's telling of the Rosario uprising, and in Perón's claim that his command from exile was over the hearts of his followers. It should not be surprising then to read in today's newspaper the matter-of-fact statement that Peronism is a feeling.[86]

In the wake of the September coup emotions became a basis for political action. Anti-Peronists took to the streets to humiliate Perón's followers, while Lonardi and Aramburu guaranteed the expansion of that humiliation by removing monuments, prohibiting certain words, or more crudely by sheer repression. In their hands Peronism was turned into a shameful object. In contrast, militants and the Peronist press quickly reversed the profound frustration and bitterness that settled in after the coup by launching a resistance embedded with new emotional meanings. The deaths, *la sangre derramada*, gave rise to "memories of bloodshed." In contrast to historical contexts in which remembering was a form of healing and reconciliation, in Argentina remembering led to the confirmation and coherence of political hatred in the everyday struggle. In the ensuing months, as more suffering fell upon the Peronist working class, the battles of Rosario and other smaller gestures of resistance, like the shout "*¡viva Perón, carajo!*" (fucking long live Perón!) in the middle of the night, helped to awaken what had remained a dormant heretical memory within Peronism.

James has used the idea of "heresy" to describe how Peronism provided a narrative to working-class people that allowed them to question traditional authority—be it politicians, bosses at work, or the Argentine elite.[87] As manifested in popular political culture, the heresy that the regime channeled specifically entailed the production of working-class pride and self-esteem. Before the coup of 1955 Perón's government encapsulated the heretical challenge it had unleashed, controlling and demarcating the mobilization of workers under the tutelage of the party and the trade union. It was an ideological corset—which ultimately emphasized social harmony and good relations between capital and labor—meant to avoid, or control, the proliferation of conflict and physical violence. However, Peronism entered a period of accelerated transformations immediately after September 1955. Without the party's ideological corset, under fierce state repression, and with a sense of working-class despair fueled by impotence and desertion, militants revitalized the heresy in Peronism. The treason committed by party bureaucrats and military officers who did not rise up in defense of Perón during and after the coup was painful to rank-and-file militants but ultimately was processed as a necessary purification of the party's lines. State repression, moreover, was perceived as a confirmation of collective identity. Understood in class terms, persecution and incarceration were framed as the concrete manifestations of upper-class hatred and as a means to curtail the sense of manliness and womanhood that Peronism had instilled in working-class people.

I do not think that the revitalization of the heretical discourse simply consisted of its exhumation exactly as it had existed before the September coup. It was as much an act of daily creation infusing the heretical narrative with new meanings and practices. Pierre Bourdieu claims that a heretical discourse not only helps subjects detach their thoughts and actions from the prevailing common sense but also produces a new common sense that incorporates previously repressed practices and experiences. In turn, public expression and collective recognition legitimize this repressed knowledge.[88] In Argentina emotions—humiliation, shame, and anger—together with the exercise, and the suffering, of violence shaped the new common sense that Bourdieu is talking about. Those massacred in June 1955, those killed during the September coup, and those who met their death anonymously on any given day while being tortured in a police station gave something new and tragic to Peronism. The memories of survivors—stories of familiar and unknown faces speaking of oppression, whispering revenge—weighed "like a nightmare on the brain of the living."[89] Peronism thus became more resentful, and Peronists stopped looking for social harmony where only repression and mockery could be found.

NOTES

I would like to thank Oscar Chamosa, Kevin Coleman, Konstantin Dierks, Lessie Jo Frazier, Jeffrey Gould, Peter Guardino, Daniel James, Matthew Karush, Natalia Milanesio, Antonius Robben, and the two anonymous reviewers for their comments on drafts of this chapter. The research and writing were funded by a Doris G. Quinn Foundation Dissertation Fellowship and the Department of History and the College of Arts and Sciences of Indiana University, Bloomington.

1 "Crónicas de la Resistencia," *Antropología* 3er *Mundo* 11 (August–September 1972), 17.

2 Jorge Luis Borges, "Oda compuesta en 1960," *Obras completas*, vol. 9, *El hacedor* (Buenos Aires: Emecé, 1960), 88.

3 "Revolt against Perón," *New York Times*, 18 September 1955, E, 10.

4 On the massacre of June 1955 see Carbone, *El día que bombardearon Plaza de Mayo*; Chaves, *La masacre de Plaza de Mayo*; Cichero, *Bombas sobre Buenos Aires*.

5 Juan Domingo Perón, "Del poder al exilio: cómo y quiénes me derrocaron" (1958), *Los libros del exilio, 1955–1973*, vol. 1 (Buenos Aires: Corregidor, 1996), 162.

6 Gené, *Un mundo feliz*.

7 Ron Aminzade and Doug McAdam, "Emotions and Contentious Politics,"

Silence and Voice in the Study of Contentious Politics (New York: Cambridge University Press, 2001), 49.

8 A recent study has identified at least twenty-eight emotions relevant to political action. See the introduction to Jeff Goodwin, James M. Jasper, and Francesca Polletta, eds., *Passionate Politics: Emotions and Social Movements* (Chicago: University of Chicago Press, 2001), 1–26.

9 The theoretical framework I use to analyze political emotions is based on Aminzade and McAdam, "Emotions and Contentious Politics"; Ahmed, *The Cultural Politics of Emotion*; Robert C. Solomon, *True to Our Feelings: What Our Emotions Are Really Telling Us* (New York: Oxford University Press, 2007).

10 For a few exceptions within Argentine studies see Robben, *Political Violence and Trauma in Argentina*; Graziano, *Divine Violence*; Auyero, *Contentious Lives*; and the chapters by Jeffrey M. Shumway and Donna J. Guy in Johnson, ed., *Body Politics*.

11 Anton Blok, "The Enigma of Senseless Violence," *Meanings of Violence: A Cross Cultural Perspective*, ed. Goran Aijmer and Jon Abbink (Oxford: Berg, 2001), 24 (emphasis in original).

12 James, *Resistance and Integration*, chapter 2; Amaral, "El avión negro"; Melón, "La Resistencia Peronista."

13 James, *Resistance and Integration*, 97–100.

14 Throughout the chapter my emphasis on certain kinds of emotions should not be read as excluding other possible emotions in the making of collective action. I only want to stress that the emotions I analyze were preponderant in the formation of a specific emotional climate.

15 "And the bugles will be heard again / pronouncing the nation re-conquered / by the valiant blood of the nation's sons / who would rather die than see it enslaved!" From an anti-Peronist poem entitled "A Perón" that originally circulated as a pamphlet and was later published in Felix Lafiandra, ed., *Los panfletos: Su aporte a la Revolución Libertadora*, 2nd edn (Buenos Aires: Itinerarium, 1955), 297.

16 William Ian Miller, *Humiliation and Other Essays on Honor, Social Discomfort, and Violence* (Ithaca: Cornell University Press, 1993), 145. My idea of humiliation does not imply the existence in the person being humiliated of pretentiousness or vanity, as in Miller's book. One more caveat: the analytic distinction between shame and humiliation should not mean that both cannot result from the same action.

17 "Revolt Topples Perón's Regime," *New York Times*, 20 September 1955, 3; Hugo Gambini, *Historia del peronismo*, 391.

18 Martin Francis, "Tears, Tantrums, and Bared Teeth: The Emotional Econ-

omy of Three Conservative Prime Ministers, 1951–1963," *Journal of British Studies* 41, no. 3 (July 2002), 354–87.

19 "El mensaje de Perón a la juventud del año 2000 fue retirado," *Crónica* (Rosario), 24 September 1955, 1. Even though *La Nación* declined the offer, the casket was finally accepted by Gendarmería Nacional.

20 "Argentines Fled Navy Rebel Guns," *New York Times*, 21 September 1955, 3.

21 Photograph published in Bonifacio del Carril, *Crónica interna de la Revolución Libertadora* (Buenos Aires: Emecé, 1959), no page.

22 On Evita's legacies see Guy, "Life and the Commodification of Death in Argentina"; Hall, "Evita Perón."

23 Orlando Figes and Boris Kolonitskii, *Interpreting the Russian Revolution: The Language and Symbols of 1917* (New Haven: Yale University Press, 1999), 48.

24 "Peronist Holiday Voided in Argentina," *New York Times*, 10 October 1955, 11; Spinelli, *Los vencedores vencidos*, chapter 2.

25 The first public sale of Perón's personal possessions, which the National Wealth Recovery Board set to coincide with the anniversary of the "día de la lealtad," attracted more than four thousand potential buyers and curious onlookers in only one day. See "Argentina Opens Perón 'Loot' Sale," *New York Times*, 18 October 1957, 8; "Argentina to Sell Perón's Jewel Hoard," *Los Angeles Times*, 26 November 1957, 10.

26 The concept of emotional regime, which implies a set of normative emotions and their concomitant prescribed performance, was coined by William M. Reddy in *The Navigation of Feeling: A Framework for the History of Emotions* (New York: Cambridge University Press, 2001).

27 "Anti-Perón Drive Extends to Shrouding Statues," *New York Times*, 27 November 1955, 1.

28 The resignification of monuments by partial obliteration, resulting in "disavowed sites," was also common in post-Soviet contexts. See for example Benjamin Forest and Juliet Johnson, "Unraveling the Threads of History: Soviet-Era Monuments and Post-Soviet National Identity in Moscow," *Annals of the Association of American Geographers* 92, no. 3 (2002), 524–47.

29 Interview with Adelma Martínez de Amarante, Rosario, 27 December 2005.

30 See for example "En nuestra provincia, como en el resto del país, reina la calma," *La Capital*, 19 September 1955, 4.

31 Interview by author, Rosario, 3 November 2005.

32 Jack Katz, *How Emotions Work* (Chicago: University of Chicago Press, 1999), 142–74.

33 César F. Marcos, "La cosa fue así," *Peronismo y liberación* 1 (August 1974), 23.

34 "If this is freedom, the democracy / that the oligarchy has come to instate / we ask by the grace of the Lord / bring the tyranny back." From the poem

"El Tirano" in Roberto Baschetti, ed., *Campana de palo: antología de poemas, relatos y canciones de 35 años de lucha, 1955–1990* (La Plata: de la Campana, 2000), 12.

35 Interview by author, Rosario, 27 December 2005.

36 "The hour of death is near, Argentines . . . / the hour of tremendous ingratitude / the hour in which the biggest, most sensitive heart / giving up his rights offers us / peace, which will not be peace without his presence / Only from such a noble and irreproachable heart / could a gesture of love so great spring / Only from such a virile chest, that received / so much ingratitude in payment for his infinite kindness / could a decision so worthy and laudable be born / You gave everything for your people and today, ungrateful, / we let you depart, without even lifting a hand, / to stop your UNCONCEIVABLE departure. / But you will not be alone, wherever / you find yourself, the soul of your people will always be your *compañera*."

37 "All the oligarchs, / are very happy, / but don't get too cheerful, / for the end will soon come." "El reencuentro," Comisión no 2, caja 1, Expediente 12855 A56, Fondo Comisión Nacional Investigadora, Archivo Intermedio del Archivo General de la Nación.

38 I am espousing here a vision of melodrama as a counterhegemonic, potentially subversive narrative. See James, *Doña María's Story*, 253–61; Karush, "The Melodramatic Nation." For a similar approach uncovering the use of victimage rhetoric within melodramatic discourses see Michael Blain, "Power, War, and Melodrama in the Discourses of Political Movements," *Theory and Society* 23, no. 6 (December 1994), 805–37.

39 For a comparative perspective see Paul Lauter, "Under Construction: Working-Class Writing," *New Working-Class Studies*, ed. John Russo and Sherry Lee Linkon (Ithaca: Cornell University Press, 2005), 63–77; Paula Rabinowitz, *Labor and Desire: Women's Revolutionary Fiction in Depression America* (Chapel Hill: University of North Carolina Press, 1991).

40 Luisa Passerini, *Fascism in Popular Memory: The Cultural Experience of the Turin Working Class* (New York: Cambridge University Press, 1987), 70–95.

41 "With him went peace, terror came / war gear fills the streets / and the weapon that our toil forged / is turned upon our breasts. / Freedom is here, they tell us daily / in lectures, speeches, and sermons / and a complacent press confirms it / while the prisons fill up with people."

42 "Smoking a cigar / I shit on Aramburu / and if he gets angry / I'll shit on Rojas too." The stanza can be found in Jorge Pinedo, *Consignas y lucha popular en el proceso revolucionario argentino, 1955–1973* (Buenos Aires: Freeland, 1974), 53.

43 James, *Doña María's Story*, 244–80.

44 "You did not have a loyal force by your side / sincere aid to match your ardor / and after years of struggle, alone, relentless / your seed of love could not germinate. / How could it be otherwise if there was ONLY ONE PERÓN!"

45 It should be noted, though, that the above stanza does not allude to Evita, as could be wrongly assumed by taking it as a denunciation of Evita's failure to measure up to the high standards set by Perón or as a metaphor for the presidential couple's childless marriage and the consequent lack of a political heir.

46 An early insinuation of this genre can be found in what Ernesto Goldar calls the "elegiac poetry" written after Evita's death in 1952. See his "La literatura peronista."

47 Anne McClintock, *Imperial Leather: Race, Gender and Sexuality in the Colonial Contest* (New York: Routledge, 1995), 345.

48 Franco, *The Decline and Fall of the Lettered City*, 72–74.

49 Decree-Law no. 4161, *Documentos de la Resistencia Peronista, 1955–1970*, ed. Roberto Baschetti (La Plata: de la Campana, 1997), 80–82.

50 The classic reference is still James C. Scott, *Domination and the Arts of Resistance: Hidden Transcripts* (New Haven: Yale University Press, 1990).

51 In February 1956 Perón himself sent a copy of the poem to Ronald Hilton, a professor of Romance languages at Stanford University and editor of the monthly journal *Hispanic American Report*. See Amaral and Ratliff, eds., *Juan Domingo Perón*, 180–85.

52 Juan M. Vigo, *¡La vida por Perón! Crónicas de la Resistencia* (Buenos Aires: A. Peña Lillo, 1973), 46, 84; Marcos, "La cosa fue así," 24; "Crónica por un resistente," *Antropología 3er Mundo* 10 (June 1972), 12.

53 Enrique Pavón Pereyra, *Coloquios con Perón* (Buenos Aires: n.p., 1965), 147.

54 The story of Peronists battling the waters of the Paraná River to meet the gunboat on its way up to Paraguay is mentioned in Councilman Gentili's project. A well-known lawyer of the meatpacking workers' trade union also mentions it in Garulli et al., *Nomeolvides*, 67.

55 Alessandro Portelli, *The Battle of Valle Giulia: Oral History and the Art of Dialogue* (Madison: University of Wisconsin Press, 1997), 153. For a discussion of myths as ideologically marked narratives see also Christopher G. Flood, *Political Myth: A Theoretical Introduction* (New York: Routledge, 2002).

56 Project presented by councilman Fabio Gentili, Municipal Council of Rosario, 15 September 2005. Copy in author's possession.

57 Vigo, *¡La vida por Perón!*, 78.

58 "Aceptamos el desafío," *Soberanía*, 4 June 1957, 3; Garulli et al., *Nomeolvides*, 85.

59 At another level, by representing a moment of political brotherhood and bonding between marchers and soldiers the tale offsets the construction of an anti-militaristic discourse within Peronism. Thus it was possible to condemn as anti-patriotic certain military officers but not the whole army.

60 Interview by author, Rosario, 4 November 2005.

61 For an article denouncing the involvement of professional agitators see "Finalidad de los agitadores," *Crónica* (Rosario), 26 September 1955, 1.

62 "El Gral: lugand censura y acusa por intermedio de su esposa," *Soberanía*, 18 June 1957, 1.

63 *Nosotros . . . la Resistencia* (Rosario: n.p., 1998), 95; "Daños de importancia provocaron las manifestaciones de anoche," *Crónica* (Rosario), 23 September 1955, 2.

64 "Aceptamos el desafío," *Soberanía*, 4 June 1957, 3.

65 A similar version appears in Garulli et al., *Nomeolvides*, 81–83.

66 Amelia Foresto, interview by Natalia Milanesio, Rosario, 18 October 2005.

67 Carbone, *El día que bombardearon Plaza de Mayo*, 68; Ramón Prieto, *El pacto: ocho años de política argentina* (Buenos Aires: En Marcha, 1963), 16.

68 Vigo, ¡*La vida por Perón!*, 80.

69 For an introduction to the political uses of the breasts see Marilyn Yalom, *A History of the Breast* (New York: Alfred A. Knopf, 1997), esp. chapter 4. Similar episodes echoing those that I detail here can be found almost everywhere—and Yalom details many of them. For an example from South Africa, where the bare-breasted woman conveys, in the police's eyes, an imagery of social and sexual dread see Robert J. Thornton, "The Shooting at Uitenhage, South Africa, 1985: The Context and Interpretation of Violence," *American Ethnologist* 17, no. 2 (May 1990), 217–36. Daniel James was told, while doing research in Berisso during the late 1980s, that working-class women who participated in the demonstration of October 17, 1945, marched through the streets chanting "la concha por Perón" (our pussies for Perón). Personal communication with author. In Argentine literature an early reference can be found in a novel by Bernardo González Arrili, who vividly describes two moments when women working in a meatpacking plant politically used their "oscuras verguenzas" (private parts)—first to incite male workers to strike and then to deride the "carneros" who did not walk out. See *Los charcos rojos* (Buenos Aires: Eden, 1927), 96–97, 106–7.

70 "El ejército reprime con energía intentos de los manifestantes," *La Tribuna*, 24 September 1955, 1.

71 José Mármol, letter to Councilman Fabio Gentili, not dated. Copy in author's possession.

72 "Quince muertos y 55 heridos hubo por los sucesos de ayer," *Crónica* (Rosario), 24 September 1955, 1.

73 "La normalidad y el orden son restablecidos en nuestra ciudad," *Crónica* (Rosario), 26 September 1955, 2.

74 Américo Barrios, *¿Adónde vamos?* (Ciudad Trujillo: n.p., 1959); Vigo, *¡La vida por Perón!*, 46.

75 James, "October 17th and 18th, 1945."

76 The foundational nature of collective violence, that is, violence as "the basis for the constitution of collective narratives of origin, loss, and recovery," is also stressed in Ussama Makdisi and Paul A. Silverstein, eds., *Memory and Violence in the Middle East and North Africa* (Bloomington: Indiana University Press, 2006). Lessie Jo Frazier in turn has explained how the memory-work demanded by the process of affirming and contesting the Chilean project of nation-state formation was deeply implicated in the production of emotional drive. See *Salt in the Sand*.

77 Perón to Ronald Hilton, Colón, 3 February 1956, in Amaral and Ratliff, eds., *Juan Domingo Perón*, 183.

78 Aminzade and McAdam, "Emotions and Contentious Politics," 17.

79 These reflections are based on Robert C. Solomon, "Emotions, Thoughts and Feelings: What Is a 'Cognitive Theory' of Emotions and Does It Neglect Affectivity?," *Philosophy and the Emotions*, ed. Anthony Hatzimoysis (New York: Cambridge University Press, 2003), 1–18.

80 Stephanie A. Shields, *Speaking from the Heart: Gender and the Social Meaning of Emotion* (New York: Cambridge University Press, 2002), 185.

81 José Julio Jáuregui to General Juan Perón, Buenos Aires, 21 January 1967, Juan Domingo Perón papers, Hoover Institution Archives, box 3.

82 José Julio Jáuregui, untitled novel, Juan Domingo Perón papers, Hoover Institution Archives, box 3, 36.

83 See Juan Perón, *Conducción política* (Buenos Aires: Freeland, 1971 [1952]), 54–55.

84 *Perón-Cooke: Correspondencia*, vol. 1 (Buenos Aires: Papiro, 1972), 42; see also 17, 20. More examples of Perón's comments on the use of hate and other emotions such as love and resentment can be found in Marta Cichero, *Cartas peligrosas de Perón* (Buenos Aires: Planeta, 1992), 293; Amaral and Ratliff, eds., *Juan Domingo Perón*, 86, 140, 161, 163, 183.

85 Solomon, *True to Our Feelings*, 101. Both the interlocutor and the occasion greatly determined Perón's specific choice of emotions.

86 The phrase "el peronismo es un sentimiento" was recently used by Gerónimo Venegas, secretary general of the orthodox trade union confederation 62 Organizaciones. See " 'El que convoca es Perón desde la muerte,' aseguró

Lorenzo Pepe," *La Capital*, 17 October 2006. The movie director and long-time Peronist Leonardo Favio has similarly titled his hagiographic documentary on the history of Peronism *Perón, sinfonía del sentimiento* (1999) And the former senator Antonio Cafiero once said that Peronism is "a sentimiento que se vota" (a feeling that you vote for).

87 James, *Resistance and Integration*, 30–40.
88 Pierre Bourdieu, *Language and Symbolic Power* (Cambridge: Harvard University Press, 1991), 129.
89 Karl Marx, "The Eighteenth Brumaire of Louis Bonaparte," *Marx's "Eighteenth Brumaire": (Post)modern Interpretations*, ed. Mark Cowling and James Martin (London: Pluto, 2002), 19.

Mariano Ben Plotkin
....

FINAL REFLECTIONS

Peronism has been by far the most studied phenomenon, if not the best studied, of twentieth-century Argentina, and as the publication of this book shows, it continues to attract the interest of scholars both foreign and national. To this day the study of Peronism generates fruitful questions about the country's (and by extension Latin America's) political, social, and cultural evolution. It is almost a commonplace to say that the Perón regime was a watershed in contemporary Argentine history. Perón and his regime became an object of analysis by scholars and political militants very early on. Barely one year had passed since the fall of Perón when Fritz Hoffmann published a review article in the *Hispanic American Historical Review* summarizing the already substantial body of work devoted to "the leader" and his regime. Just three years later a second review by the same author showed that the corpus on Peronism had expanded impressively.[1] For political scientists Peronism became a yardstick, almost an "ideal type" against which other "populist" experiences in Latin America could be measured and compared.

In Argentina Peronism has been much more than an object of scholarly interest. The ten years of the first Perón government deeply divided Argentine society; more precisely, it dramatically deepened an ideological polarization that already existed. Even more important, Peronism redefined the system of political and even nonpolitical identities in Argentina.[2] Peronism politicized the system of social identifications. For decades the line that divided Peronism from anti-Peronism cut across Argentine society, generating a political system of classification that articulated other forms of social identification. It could be said that the distinction between Peronism and anti-Peronism permeated into and subordinated other forms of social identity.[3]

If Peronism transformed Argentine collective identities in such a profound manner, then the study of its symbolic dimension is crucial. Peronism inaugurated new forms of the exercise of power. The anthropologist Clifford Geertz has shown that "investigations into the symbolics of power and into its nature are very similar endeavors."[4] Therefore an analysis of the system of symbolic exchange originated by the Perón government constitutes an unavoidable starting point for understanding the nature of that political regime and its aftermath. Of course this does not mean that its social, political, or economic aspects should be ignored. I simply mean that Peronism generated a strong system of symbolic exchange that cannot and should not be overlooked. As the editors of this volume emphasize, in agreement with Geertz, this cultural and symbolic side of Peronism is inherently linked to the process of state formation and therefore has an important political dimension.

During Perón's government but particularly after its fall, Peronism also became an epistemological problem for Argentine intellectuals, particularly but not only for those of leftist orientation whom Peronism deprived of contact with the working class. The Peronist experience forced many intellectuals to revise their previous certitudes and to confront a reality that escaped their analytic tools. As Carlos Altamirano has pointed out, one of the effects of Peronism was to generate an unbridgeable gap between "the people" and the intellectuals.[5] Searching for the explanation of Peronism became almost an obsession for social scientists, historians, and public intellectuals. From the sociologist Gino Germani to cultural and literary critics and writers like the brothers Ismael and David Viñas and many others, Peronism became a big incognita, the "dark continent" of Argentine politics and culture: that which needed an explanation that proved to be always elusive. It has even been argued that Argentine sociology was constructed around the need to explain Peronism.[6] If Peronism had generated an unbridgeable gap between its supporters and its detractors, similar chasms separated the different and contradictory interpretations of the regime and of its origins. Who supported Perón? Why? What kind of bond did Perón create with its followers? What is the revolutionary potential, if any, of the movement created by Perón? Could Peronism be considered a creole form of fascism? These questions were being asked, and alternative answers provided, even before Perón took power, and I would argue that Peronism as a cultural phenomenon was constituted by the discourses it generated. Exploring the nature of Peronism is an enterprise that cannot be distinguished from exploring the "layers" of interpretation that it generated. As a case in point, the events of October 17, 1945—the founding episode of Peronism—inspired wildly divergent contemporary interpretations. For Perón's supporters the workers who mobilized in the Plaza de Mayo were "the people," the incarnation of nationality, while for others, most notoriously socialists and communists, the Peronist masses were a lumpen-proletariat who had little in common with the "real working people."

Although those who overthrew Perón believed that the removal of the "leader" would end the allegiance that his movement had generated among the working class (in Peronist Argentina and for decades after Perón's fall, the word "worker" was almost a synonym of "Peronist"), the fact is that Peronism and Perón himself during the rest of his lifetime continued to play a central role in Argentine politics. Moreover, through its multiple metamorphoses, Peronism became identified successively, and sometimes simultaneously, with a social movement, a working-class political party, a left-wing armed revolutionary movement, a right-wing paramilitary organization aimed at destroying the left wing (and also Peronist) revolutionary guerrilla, the "neoliberal revolution," and the forces that opposed the "neoliberal revolution." Today Argentina is under a Peronist government that claims to represent exactly the opposite values from those held by the previous Peronist government (1989–99). Thus it seems that it is not at the level of ideology where one should look for coherence in Perón's creation.

Although Peronism brought undeniable benefits to workers and the poor in general, it is very difficult, despite the efforts of some intellectuals, to characterize the Peronist experience in any of its incarnations as a social revolution, in the classical sense at least. During Perón's terms in office the share of the national GDP represented by wages increased from 37 percent to 47 percent, while real wages increased by 40 percent between 1946 and 1948.[7] Workers received other material benefits in the form of social legislation that included paid vacations, access to social and medical services, and a broad menu of other social services.[8] Furthermore, as a result of Perón's policies the organized working class became, and has remained until the present day, a crucial actor, a "factor of power" in Argentina, so important that both the civilian and the military governments succeeding Perón had to take it very seriously. Peronism empowered the working class and redefined citizenship. Yet Perón never disputed the existence of private property, nor did he ever question capitalism or suggest the possibility of socializing the means of production. In fact, if there was one single constant factor in Perón's political ideas, it was his uncompromising anticommunism. As Perón himself suggested in a much cited speech delivered at the Buenos Aires Chamber of Commerce in 1944, the social reforms that he was introducing from his position as secretary of labor and welfare were aimed at stopping more violent changes otherwise certain to result from the inevitable communist revolution that he believed would follow the end of the Second World War. And there are reasons to believe that he was sincere.

Nevertheless, it is also difficult to deny that there has been a Peronist revolution in Argentina. Post-Peronist Argentina resembled very little the country of pre-1945. It is true that the world had also changed, but in Argentina those changes had a particular overtone. This Peronist revolution could be better understood in "cultural" terms, which of course does not mean that it did not have crucial social and economic consequences.[9] As the editors of this book point out, emphasizing the cultural dimension of Peronism does not mean denying the importance of other transformations introduced by the Peronist experience in Argentina (in the sense that it was "just" a cultural phenomenon, not a "real" revolution). Quite the opposite, underlining this aspect of Peronism highlights some of its most creative and unique facets.

Perón and his movement subverted the accepted system of social classification existing in Argentina, and this was probably one of its most traumatic effects for those who opposed it. As the sociologist Pierre Bourdieu points out, "what is at stake in the struggles about the meaning of the social world is power over the classificatory schemes and systems which are the basis of the representations of the groups and therefore of their mobilization and demobilization."[10] One of the consequences of Peronism was precisely an alteration in the "rules of the game" of social classification. This disruption was in part the result of a system of political socialization organized by the Peronist state and in part the consequence of more spontaneous factors associated with the dynamics of the movement and its conditions of origin. It is not by chance that to this day one of the most powerful iconic elements of the origins of Peronism (both for Peronists and for anti-Peronists) is a photograph taken on October 17, 1945, showing Perón's supporters dipping their feet in the fountain of the Plaza de Mayo. These people were doing the wrong thing in the wrong place. Peronism nevertheless reformulated the symbolic meaning of the Plaza de Mayo, one of the "places of memory" (lieux de mémoire) of Argentina. To some extent the plaza, surrounded by the governmental palace, the cathedral, and the Cabildo, became associated with Peronism in the years to come. One feature of the picture has always surprised observers: the men in the fountain were wearing jackets, as was expected in the 1940s of men who visited downtown. This evidence of respect for social etiquette from people who otherwise were breaking a sacred rule of behavior (civilized people don't wash their feet in the fountain) reveals that Peronists could not be characterized as completely "other," since even at this moment of social subversion the "new barbarians," as they were portrayed by Perón's opponents from both the right and the left, submitted to some form of social regulation. In the view of many anti-Peronists, any porosity in the "us-them" distinction was disturbing. "Invasion"—meaning people out of place, doing things out of place—became a recurring trope in anti-Peronist imagery. To this image should be added an ethnic component. In a city that prided itself on being a "white enclave" in Latin America, the presence of masses of mestizo workers from the interior of the country, the so-called cabecitas negras, introduced an additional element of discomfort for elites. As happened in other cases, the originally derogatory name of cabecitas negras was reappropriated by Peronists and became a kind of trademark for them.

Even before Peronism's official birth on October 17, 1945—that is to say, even before this trope could be formulated ideologically—it emerged as a "structure of feelings" (using Raymond Williams's concept) articulated around the themes of barbarian invasion and the degradation of good taste. In the short novel *Sábado de Gloria* (1944), for example, Ezequiel Martínez Estrada interweaves a narrative set in the present day with images of the invasion of Buenos Aires in 1820 by caudillos from the interior, an episode characterized in official Argentine historiography as a takeover of the city by barbarians and the collapse of the national project. Later the topic of invasion would appear more explicitly in works by Julio Cortázar, Jorge Luis Borges, Adolfo Bioy Casares, and others.

Many intellectuals conceptualized Peronism in a political but also an aesthetic fashion. Peronism conjured up a dichotomous understanding of Argentine reality that had existed among intellectuals since the nineteenth century. Not all writers of fiction conceived of Peronism in the same way. Cortázar, for instance, through the use of metaphors, was able to problematize his own perception of Peronism, most notoriously in such short stories as "Las puertas del cielo." In a way that recalls Sarmiento's writings one century earlier, the new phenomenon evokes in Cortázar's characters a mixture of repulsion and fascination. Although the trope of invasion was present in some of the stories that Cortázar wrote during Perón's time, most notoriously in "Casa Tomada," the ambiguities present in the narrative leave open the possibility of multiple interpretations. This was definitely not so for Borges and Bioy Casares, whose short story "La fiesta del Monstruo," a catalogue of monstrosities committed by the followers of "the Monster," shows to what extent Peronism constituted a limit for the authors' comprehension of Argentine reality. For some prominent intellectuals Peronism became the "total other," almost an epistemological limit, a catastrophe.

The clash between Peronists and anti-Peronists created a situation that could be described as "mutual de-legitimation." Each party refused to see in the other a legitimate contender in the political arena, as was clear, for instance, from the appropriation by both Peronists and anti-Peronists of specific words like "resistance." During the process that took Perón to power, coinciding with the final phase of the Second World War, intellectual anti-Peronists called themselves the "Resistencia." Later, after the fall of Perón, this name was appropriated—as la Resistencia Peronista—by groups of Peronists who carried out terrorist attacks. Needless to say, in both cases the symbolic association was the French Resistance that had fought against the Nazis during the war. Peronists were not only reappropriating the term "resistencia" but by doing so also likening the military government that overthrew Perón (the so-called Revolución Libertadora) to the Nazis. And that was exactly what the anti-Peronist opposition had done with Perón and the military government from which he emerged.

Studying the cultural and symbolic aspects of a historical phenomenon poses serious methodological challenges that the "new cultural history" has begun to address. In addition to the usual difficulties of this task, Peronism presents an even more complicated case, since the political passions and emotions that played such a central role in motivating political behaviors during the 1940s and 1950s, as César Seveso shows in this volume, persist today. Moreover, as Emilio de Ípola has pointed out, Peronism is a phenomenon "mediated" by a diversity of discourses, including those that Peronism has been constructing about itself during the last sixty years.[11] In a country like Argentina, where governments and other social groups have routinely made use of history to justify current political positions, contrasting images of Peronism have become weapons in a symbolic struggle, and sometimes not just a symbolic struggle. The chapters in this book show, in my view, the potential but also the difficulties inherent in a cultural approach to Peronism.

How can such a complex topic be studied? In what follows I wish to emphasize three methodological steps which to some extent have been taken into consideration by the authors of this collection:

1. TAKING PERONISM SERIOUSLY. Peronism can be characterized as a machine of symbolic production. During Perón's first two terms in office an enormous propaganda machinery was set in motion in the service of generating some form of ideological consensus that could not be created through other means.[12] Since his time as a professor at the Argentine military school in the 1930s, Perón showed an obsession with obtaining what he called "spiritual unity." This concept, originally the idea that the thinking of the commander in chief should be the thinking of the whole army, was gradually extended to the whole society. As Perón pointed out in a speech delivered in 1944: "In the political objective derived from people's feeling of nationality, because it is single and indivisible, no divergent opinions are acceptable."[13] Years later the "Peronist Doctrine" would be declared "National Doctrine" by law of Congress. However, the nature of the movement created by Perón and the circumstances that took him to power not only annulled the possibility of generating a broad consensus but deepened an already existing ideological polarization. In fact Perón's program, which included industrialization and social programs for the workers, had several points in common with social projects formulated by industrialists and others since the 1930s, whom he neverthless

failed to convince of the imminent communist threat that he perceived and therefore of the need for such extensive reform. Perón's style was deemed subversive by the capitalist sector. Therefore Perón was forced to create the *illusion* of a consensus that he was unable to create in reality. With this purpose the Perón regime gradually generated an imagery aimed at monopolizing the social symbolic space. This became evident in the evolution of political rituals associated with the successive commemoration of the October 17. If during the first commemorations the emerging Peronist iconography shared space with elements taken from other symbolic systems such as Catholicism (let us remember that Perón won the elections of 1946 as the Catholic candidate), soon these elements external to Peronism were displaced from the celebration. In the first anniversary of October 17, in 1946, a *misa de campaña* (open-air Mass) at the Plaza de Mayo was an essential element of the celebration. One year later the altar for the Mass was placed under an arch depicting political allegories of October 17, thus subordinating the religious celebration to the political one. In 1948 the Mass was held for the last time, but now the religious ceremony started with the raising of the national flag by the general secretary of the Confederación General del Trabajo. From that point on the political rituals and iconography associated with the celebration of October 17 became more elaborate, and any symbol foreign to Peronism disappeared from the event.[14]

At the center of this symbolic production was the glorification of the Peronist state and of Perón and Eva. One room in each school and one school in each district had to bear the name of one or the other. Provinces and cities throughout the country were renamed after the ruling couple. During Perón's second term in office (1951–55) the state implemented a broad educational reform aimed at turning primary schools into centers of dissemination of the "Peronist Doctrine." The new textbooks approved by the recently created Ministry of Education included a proliferation of images of Perón and Eva. Standard phrases traditionally used to teach children to read, such as "Mommy loves me," were replaced by "Evita (or Perón) loves me." A wave of Peronist publications printed by state-operated publishing houses multiplied, including the magazine *Argentina*, analyzed here by Eduardo Elena. These magazines and journals were supposed to appeal to a wide range of publics, including children. *Mundo Infantil* was probably the first "modern" children's magazine published in Argentina, but it was loaded with Peronist propaganda. During the Perón regime a whole system of political socialization for children was set in place. Perón was quoted as saying that he had won his first presidential election with the votes of men, his second election with the votes of women, and that he would win his third presidential election with the votes of children. This statement contains a grain of truth. In fact Perón won his first election with the votes of men exclusively, since women were only granted the franchise in 1947. In the first presidential election in which women could participate (that of 1951), they voted especially strongly for Perón. Finally, Perón's third successful presidential election took place in 1973, and many of the people who voted for him—certainly most young people between twenty-five and thirty at that time, who massively cast their votes for Perón—had been children during Perón's first two terms in office. Of course we cannot know to what extent the votes of "Peronist children" were the result of the policies of political socialization carried out in the 1950s, which included not only the revision of school textbooks but also state-sponsored soccer championships (the Campeonatos Evita) and many other things, but the question is worth considering. The propaganda effort was not limited to the written or spoken word. A Peronist iconography and even a Peronist architecture (analyzed by Anahi Ballent in this volume and in her book)[15] were promoted by the state.

It is easy and tempting to dismiss this enormous discursive production as nothing more than a massive and homogeneous glorification of the regime. Anyone who has worked with Peronist publications knows very well to what extent the repetitive and routine nature of the glorification of Perón and Eva can try one's patience. Precisely one of the problems of analyzing the reception of this enormous propaganda effort is that the kind of ritualized discourse promoted by the regime was to some extent internalized. Vestiges of this discourse can be found in the stereotyped responses given by the former Queens of Labor to their interviewers in the chapter by Lobato, Damilakou, and Tornay.

Nevertheless, more recent scholarship, of which this volume is a fine example, has started to "deconstruct" Peronist discourse: that is to say, to take it seriously. What do I mean by this? First, I mean that the scholarship places the discourse in its time and place, historicizing it. Perón was a child of his time, and the time when he lived and ruled was defined by the aftermath of the Second World War, the beginnings of the cold war, Stalin's Russia, and the memory of the New Deal. As Marcela Gené has shown in a work often cited in this volume, Perón's iconography of work and workers owes a lot to Mussolini and Hitler, but also to all these other sources.[16] Perón's propaganda was perhaps not too democratic, but it was not out of place historically speaking.

Second, any serious study of the Peronist discourse and symbols should go underneath the surface to find how the Peronist message was constructed and what it was meant to convey. A close analysis shows first of all that beyond glorification of the regime, Peronist discourse was a heterogeneous conglomerate of different and sometimes complex ideological elements full of ambiguities. This conglomerate also changed over time. As I have analyzed elsewhere, the "Peronist textbooks" mentioned above, beyond the ritual mentions of Perón and Eva, contained other important elements, including a redefinition of the role of the state, of national history, and of class relations in Argentine society.

2. QUESTIONING "NATIVE" CATEGORIES AND SELF IMAGES. Although for opposite reasons, Peronists and anti-Peronists agreed that the Perón government was a complete novelty that did not fit into the accepted historical narrative of the country. While Peronists emphasized the "revolutionary" nature of the Peronist experience and its rupture with the past, for anti-Peronists the regime was a kind of pathology that could not be connected to the glorious history of the country. For Peronists Peronism marked the beginning of a new era; for anti-Peronists it was a parenthesis in Argentine history, something that could and should be encapsulated and extirpated. Peronism, it was said, provoked a cultural revolution. But like any other historical phenomenon it combined truly original elements with others from a more or less distant past. Several of the chapters in this book emphasize this characteristic of Peronism as it related to folklore (Chamosa), architecture (Ballent), and good taste (Elena).

The example of *Argentina*, the magazine that was published during Oscar Ivanissevich's tenure as minister of education, is a case in point. Eduardo Elena investigates how through this publication a populist movement adapted orthodox norms of good taste. Beyond Dr. Ivanissevich's idiosyncrasies (as minister he used to write some of his speeches in verse), the fact is that through different means the Peronist state tried to establish the myth, shared by its opponents, that it constituted a complete rupture with the past. This can be seen in the way it reformulated the narrative about Labor Day to turn a socialist commemorative date into a Peronist celebration.[17] This supposedly revolutionary transformation of the order of things included also the idea of establishing a new system of symbolic social hierarchies. Yet the movement's alluvial character and its ideological heterogeneity, together with the openly and strongly anti-intellectual discourse and policies of the regime, made this task very difficult. *Argentina* was a failed attempt at constructing a "Peronist alternative system of good taste." The failure to form a new consensus and a new system of social classification was in some opportunities implicitly or explicitly recognized. A publication of the Subsecretaría de Prensa y Difusión of 1952 titled *Síntesis de las letras argentines* named Jorge Luis Borges and Victoria Ocampo, both fierce anti-Peronists, as two of the best Argentine writers and intellectuals. It is worth remembering that Borges had been publicly humiliated by the Perón government when he was forced out of his position of head of the Municipal Library and appointed instead inspector of chicken and *aves de corral*, while Ocampo was briefly jailed without charges. The inclusion of these well-known anti-Peronists in a list of top Argentine writers can be understood as a recognition that the Peronist regime had failed to create an alternative "Peronist culture" and to attract renowned intellectuals to its cause. In this sense as in many others, Peronism was very far from fascism. As the Peronist writer Manuel Gálvez recalled, the Asociación Argentina de Escritores, an organization of pro-Perón writers formed in opposition to the largely anti-Peronist Sociedad Argentina de Escritores (SADE), contained "an abundance of school-text writers and a shortage of men of real prestige, most of whom were in SADE."[18]

The "dragging" of elements of the past was not passive; it involved reappropriation and reformulation. Nevertheless these existing elements were a constitutive part of Peronist imagery. Tulio Halperin has emphasized that even Perón's political style owed much more to an ancient tradition (which according to him could be traced back to General Mitre) than he would ever have been willing to admit.[19] Looking for elements of continuity is not just an exercise in historical demythification but a step in the process of historicizing Peronism, returning it to the flow of history. The idea that Peronism represented a total rupture with the past should be treated as a "native" image that must be analytically questioned and analyzed as part of the process of historical construction of Peronism, not taken for granted.

3. UNDERSTANDING THE CONDITIONS AND THE PROCESS OF RECEPTION OF THE PERONIST MESSAGE. As the editors of this volume recognize, understanding the construction of the Peronist discourse is dealing with only part of the problem. Citing Daniel James's work, Chamosa and Karush emphasize the importance of carefully considering "the ways rank and file workers understood Peronism." Focusing only on the "emission side" of the Peronist message may lead us to ignore the agency of the Peronist masses. If, as the editors point out, "very few studies have emulated James's innovative reconstructions of popular reception," this failure is due partly to the intrinsic difficulty of doing this kind of analysis and partly to the fact that the task of defining the "Peronist message"—what I have called "taking Peronism seriously"—is methodologically previous to studying the conditions of reception of that message. Until it was determined that the Perón regime had an intelligible discourse that went beyond glorification of the ruling couple, it was impossible to analyze how this discourse was received and understood by the masses. And I would like to highlight here the word "intelligible." One of the big achievements of recent scholarship has been to return Peronism to the realm of intelligibility. If for many intellectuals of the post-Peronist era, the Peronist experience had been something that fell outside the history of the country, like a parenthesis in the normal historical development of Argentina—and the obsession with the origins of Peronism shown by the early scholarship discussed in the introduction to this volume reflected the need to "explain" something that was

inherently unintelligible—one of the merits of recent work has been precisely to return Peronism to the realm of history. And historicizing a phenomenon implies rendering it intelligible.

Focusing on the reception of the Peronist message is probably the most difficult part of the job. As the editors point out, it is a question not of finding an "uncontaminated" grassroots perspective but rather of looking at intersections: intersections between the process of state formation, mass culture, and state propaganda and its multiple appropriations and reformulations. Once again, the chapters in this book show the potential and also the problems implicit in this approach. Thus Matthew Karush shows that Perón appropriated creatively many elements of popular melodrama and tango, which had been widespread since the 1930s, but we are still wondering how those elements were reprocessed by the Peronist masses. Similarly, Elena provides a fascinating analysis of the magazine *Argentina*, but we know very little about how this magazine was read and by whom, except for what the magazine said about itself and its readership. We know something about the intentions, but comparatively little about the results. Likewise, the chapter on the Queens of Labor by Lobato, Damilakou, and Tornay reveals what the regime expected from the crowning of the queens but provides only a partial view of what the participants in the ceremony (or even the queens themselves) thought.

The chapter by Natalia Milanesio on how social stereotypes were constructed during Peronism is different. Drawing from an impressive corpus of sources, including works of fiction, oral testimonies, and newspapers, Milanesio points to the multiple sources of those stereotypes that would be one of the foundations of the dichotomy between Peronism and anti-Peronism. Similarly, César Seveso's chapter points to the role of emotions in political mobilization, showing how under Peronism emotions articulated political identity. Although Seveso never really discusses how he defines emotions, or where they are located (In the individual? Is there something that can be considered "social emotion"?), he makes a convincing argument about the role of emotions in promoting concrete political action.

One methodological problem remains in analyzing the "reception side": the uses of memory in history. Although a great deal has been written on this topic, I would like to add just a few thoughts, starting with the obvious: memory is not the same as history. Oral testimonies cannot and should not be used as if they reflect an immediate truth, whether objective (about the facts) or subjective ("unmediated" thoughts or recollections). As Daniel James points out, "oral historians are increasingly aware of the limits of oral testimony as a source for expanding our stock of historical facts about the recent past."[20] In oral sources, or in the poems analyzed by James and Seveso, historians search for material related to the subjective elements that constitute sources of identity. Less obvious are the additional complications of studying a phenomenon like Peronism from this perspective, a topic that requires particular care on the part of the historian. Memory is filtered by successive memories, and as Elizabeth Jelin (following Paul Ricoeur) points out, personal recollections are immersed in collective narratives that are reinforced in group rituals and commemorations.[21] The problem with Peronism is that it is still very much present. The memories of the "first Peronism" are filtered by the memories of its successive reincarnations; the passions that they have generated connect the experience of the 1940s and 1950s to the present through the memory of previous Peronist governments (1973–76, 1989–99). Peronism in Argentina refuses to be locked up in the past. It could be argued that for Argentines Peronism is still associated with a "structure of feelings," something in the making, at least in cultural terms. Of course this characteristic of Peronism should not prevent the use of oral sources or other kinds of memory analysis. But as the chapters of this volume show, special care must be exercised.

It is clear that Peronism, perhaps more than any other Argentine historical processes (although I would recommend this approach for the study of any historical phenomenon), requires what I would call an anthropological approach. Geertz defines the object of ethnography as "a stratified hierarchy of meaningful structures."[22] What is required of the historian of Peronism is precisely the identification or construction of such a stratified hierarchy out of behaviors and memories, what Geertz characterizes as "thick description."[23] Of course there are differences between a historian and an anthropologist, not least that while the anthropologist typically sees his or her subjects, the historian must content himself or herself with vestiges (in the form of historical evidence) left by the object of analysis. However, my point is that the scholar's attitude should be the same, since both anthropology and history are interpretive disciplines. Daniel James's classic article on October 17, 1945, is an excellent example of, and a starting point for, this kind of analysis. The issue at stake (citing Geertz once more) is to look at grand problems such as Power, Change, Faith, Oppression, and Work, but "in contexts obscure enough. . . . To take the capital letters off them."[24] The chapters in this book constitute an important step forward in this direction.

Although the cultural history of Peronism, or rather the cultural approach to the history of Peronism, is a booming field, and this volume is an excellent example of that, I would like to end by proposing two areas of research that have been virtually ignored so far. The first concerns the actual day-to-day working of what I would characterize, for lack of a better term, as the "bureaucrats of the symbolic." If the celebrations of October 17 and May Day became elaborated rituals, who was in charge of organizing them? Who designed the ceremonies and how? If school textbooks had to convey a particular message, who were the bureaucrats in charge of selecting texts, defining the message, and approving it, and how were these bureaucrats recruited? An analysis of the second and third level of Peronist bureaucracy in these and other areas would provide material for a better understanding of the day-to-day dynamics of the Peronist state.

Finally, another kind of research that would shed light on the "reception side" discussed above would explore the impact of the politicization introduced by Peronism in everyday life and particularly at the level of the families. How, for example, did the policies that the Peronist government implemented toward the political socialization of children, which included the political use of schools, but also children's magazines, sports competitions, distribution of gifts, and the like, affect non-Peronist or even anti-Peronist families? When examined by means of the anthropological approach discussed above, new sources that became available to scholars only very recently, as well as oral-history and other unconventional sources, are changing our vision of Peronism. This volume is a fine example of the possibilities opened up by applying new approaches to a well-studied topic.

NOTES

I would like to express my appreciation to Matthew Karush for his careful copy editing and comments, to Oscar Chamosa for his comments, and to Elisa Grandi for her suggestions.

1. Fritz Hoffmann, "Perón and After: A Review Article," *Hispanic American Historical Review* 36, no. 4 (November 1956); 39, no. 2 (May 1959).
2. See Caimari and Plotkin, "Pueblo contra anti-pueblo."
3. See James, *Resistance and Integration*, esp. chapter 1.
4. Geertz, "Centers, Kings and Charisma: Reflections on the Symbolics of Power," *Local Knowledge: Further Essays in Interpretative Anthropology* (New York: Basic, 1983), 124.
5. Altamirano, "¿Qué hacer con las masas?"
6. Neiburg, "Ciencias sociales y mitologías nacionales"; Neiburg, *Los intelectuales y la invención del peronismo*.
7. Gerchunoff and Antúnez, "De la bonanza peronista a la crisis del desarrollo," 145.
8. Torre and Pastoriza, "La democratización del bienestar," 257–313.
9. See Tulio Halperin Donghi, *Argentina en el callejón* (Monetevideo: ARCA, 1964), and also his *La larga agonía de la Argentina peronista* (Buenos Aires: Ariel, 1994).
10. Bourdieu, *Distinction*, 479.
11. De Ípola, "Ruptura y continuidad." See also his *Ideología y discurso populista* (Mexico City: Folios, 1982).
12. The need to generate a consensus and its consequences is discussed in my *Mañana es San Perón*.
13. Plotkin, *Mañana es San Perón*, 22
14. Plotkin, *Mañana es San Perón*, chapter 4.
15. See Ballent, *Las huellas de la política*; and Aboy, *Viviendas para el pueblo*.
16. Gené, *Un mundo feliz*.
17. See Viguera, "El Primero de Mayo en Buenos Aires." See also Plotkin, *Mañana es San Perón*, chapter 3.
18. Manuel Galvez, *Recuerdos de la vida literaria*, vol. 4 (Buenos Aires, 1965), 176.
19. Halperin Donghi, "El lugar del peronismo en la tradición política argentina."
20. James, *Doña María's Story*, 123.
21. Jelin, *Los trabajos de la memoria*, 21.
22. Clifford Geertz, *The Interpretation of Cultures* (New York: Basic, 1973), 7.
23. James, "October 17th and 18th, 1945."
24. Geertz, *The Interpretation of Cultures*, 21.

BIBLIOGRAPHY

Aboy, Rosa. *Viviendas para el pueblo: espacio urbano y sociabilidad en el Barrio Los Perales, 1946–1955*. Buenos Aires: Fondo de Cultura Económica, 2005.

———. " 'The Right to a Home': Public Housing in Post–World War II Buenos Aires." *Journal of Urban History* 33, no. 3 (2007), 493–518.

Acha, Omar. "Sociedad civil y sociedad política durante el primer peronismo." *Desarrollo Económico* 44, no. 174 (2004), 199–230.

Adelman, Jeremy. "Reflections on Argentine Labour and the Rise of Perón." *Bulletin of Latin American Research* 11, no. 3 (1992), 243–59.

Aelo, Oscar. "Apogeo y ocaso de un equipo dirigente: el peronismo en la provincia de Buenos Aires, 1947–1951." *Desarrollo Económico* 44, no. 173 (2004), 85–107.

Ahmed, Sara. *The Cultural Politics of Emotion*. New York: Routledge, 2004.

Altamirano, Carlos. "¿Qué hacer con las masas?" *La batalla de las ideas (1943–1973)*, ed. Beatriz Sarlo. Buenos Aires: Ariel, 2001.

Amaral, Samuel. "El avión negro: retórica y práctica de la violencia." *Juan Domingo Perón: Del exilio al poder*, ed. Samuel Amaral and Mariano Plotkin. Buenos Aires: Eduntref, 2004 [1993].

Amaral, Samuel, and William E. Ratliff, eds. *Juan Domingo Perón: Cartas del exilio*. Buenos Aires: Legasa, 1991.

Archetti, Eduardo P. *Masculinities: Football, Polo and the Tango in Argentina*. Oxford: Berg, 1999.

Armus, Diego. "Tango, Gender, and Tuberculosis in Buenos Aires, 1900–1940." *Disease in the History of Modern Latin America*. Durham: Duke University Press, 2003.

Auyero, Javier. *Poor People's Politics: Peronist Survival Networks and the Legacy of Evita*. Durham: Duke University Press, 2000.

———. *Contentious Lives: Two Argentine Women, Two Protests, and the Quest for Recognition*. Durham: Duke University Press, 2003.

Ballent, Anahi. "All about Eve: Eva Perón y los equívocos de la biografía." *Punto de Vista* 58 (1997), 9–14.

———. *Las huellas de la política: vivienda, ciudad, peronismo en Buenos Aires, 1943–1955.* Buenos Aires: Prometeo y Ed. Universidad Nacional de Quilmes, 2006.

Barnes, John. *Eva Perón.* Buenos Aires: Pleamar, 1987.

Bauer, Arnold. *Goods, Power, History: Latin America's Material Culture.* Cambridge: Cambridge University Press, 2001.

Beasley-Murray, Jon. "Peronism and the Secret History of Cultural Studies and the Substitution of Culture for State." *Cultural Critique* 39 (1998), 189–217.

Belej, Cecilia, Ana Martín, and Alina Silveira. "La más bella de los viñedos: trabajo y producción en los festejos mendocinos." *Cuando las mujeres reinaban: belleza, virtud y poder en la Argentina del siglo XX,* ed. Mirta Lobato, 45–74. Buenos Aires: Biblos, 2005.

Belli, Elena, Ricardo Slavutsky, and Pantaleón Rueda, eds. *Malón de la Paz: "una historia, un camino."* Tilcara: University of Buenos Aires, Facultad de Filosofía y Letras, 2008.

Benjamín, Walter. *The Work of Art in the Age of Its Technological Reproducibility and Other Writings on Media,* ed. Michael Jennings, Brigid Doherty, and Thomas Y. Levin. Cambridge: Harvard University Press, 2008.

Berhó, Deborah. "Working Politics: Juan Domingo Perón's Creation of Positive Social Identity." *Rocky Mountain Review of Language and Literature* 54, no. 2 (2000), 65–76.

Berrotarán, Patricia, Aníbal Jáuregui, and Marcelo Rougier. *Sueños de bienestar en la Nueva Argentina: Estado y políticas públicas durante el peronismo, 1946–1955.* Buenos Aires: Imago Mundi, 2004.

Bianchi, Susana, and Norma Sanchís. *El Partido Peronista Femenino.* Buenos Aires: Centro Editor de América Latina, 1987.

Billorou, María José, and Ana María Rodríguez. "Reinas y campesinas: las 'hijas de los colonos' en escena." *Cuando las mujeres reinaban: belleza, virtud y poder en la Argentina del siglo XX,* ed. Mirta Zaída Lobato. Buenos Aires: Biblos, 2005.

Bourdieu, Pierre. *Distinction: A Social Critique of the Judgment of Taste.* London: Routledge and Kegan Paul, 1986.

———. *Language and Symbolic Power.* Cambridge: Harvard University Press, 1991.

Bravo, Anna. *Il fotoromanzo.* Bologna: Il Mulino, 2003.

Briones, Claudia. *La alteridad del Cuarto Mundo: una deconstrucción antropológica de la diferencia.* Buenos Aires: Ediciones del Sol, 1998.

———. "Formaciones de alteridad: contextos globales, procesos nacionales y provinciales." *Cartografías argentinas: políticas indígenas y formaciones provin-*

ciales de alteridad, ed. Claudia Briones, 9–40. Buenos Aires: Antropofagia, 2005.

Buchrucker, Cristián. *Nacionalismo y peronismo: la Argentina en la crisis ideológica mundial (1927–1955)*. Buenos Aires: Sudamericana, 1987.

——. "Interpretations of Peronism: Old Frameworks and New Perspectives." *Peronism and Argentina*, ed. James Brennan, 3–28. Wilmington, Del.: SR, 1998.

Caimari, Lila, and Mariano Plotkin. "Pueblo contra anti-pueblo: la politización de las identidades no políticas en la Argentina peronista (1943–1955)." *Facultad de Derecho y Ciencias Políticas, Documento de Trabajo n° 3*. Buenos Aires: Universidad Católica Argentina. 1997.

Calinescu, Matei. *Five Faces of Modernity: Modernism, Avant-Garde, Decadence, Kitsch, Postmodernism*. Durham: Duke University Press, 1987.

Cane-Carrasco, James. *The Fourth Enemy: Journalism and Power in the Making of Peronist Argentina, 1930–1955*. University Park: Penn State University Press, forthcoming.

Capelato, Maria Helena. *Multidões em cena: propaganda política no varguismo e no peronismo*. São Paulo: Fapesp, 1998.

Carbone, Alberto. *El día que bombardearon Plaza de Mayo: 16 de junio de 1955*. Buenos Aires: Vinciguerra, 1994.

Carrasco, Morita. "Hegemonía y políticas indigenistas argentinas en el Chaco centro-occidental." *América Indígena* 51, no. 1 (1991), 63–122.

Carrasco, Morita, and Claudia Briones. *La tierra que nos quitaron*. Buenos Aires: IGWIA y Lhaka-Honhat, 1996.

Caruso, Marcelo. "El año que vivimos en peligro: izquierda, pedagogía, y política." *Discursos pedagógicos e imaginario social en el peronismo*, ed. Adriana Puiggrós, 43–106. Buenos Aires: Galerna, 1995.

Chamosa, Oscar. "Indigenous or Criollos? The Myth of White Argentina in Tucumán's Calchaquí Valley, 1900–1945." *Hispanic American Historical Review* 88, no. 1 (2008), 71–106.

Chaves, Gonzalo. *La masacre de Plaza de Mayo*. La Plata: De la Campana, 2003.

Cichero, Daniel. *Bombas sobre Buenos Aires*. Buenos Aires: Vergara, 2005.

Cichero, Marta. *Cartas peligrosas de Perón*. Buenos Aires: Planeta, 1992.

Ciria, Alberto. *Política y cultura popular: la argentina peronista, 1946–1955*. Buenos Aires: De la Flor, 1983.

Ciucci, Giorgio. "Linguaggi classicisti negli anni Trenta in Europa e in America." *L'estetica della politica: Europa e America negli anni Trenta*, ed. Maurizio Vaudagna and Gianpiero Brunetta, 45–57. Bari: Laterza, 1989.

Claxton, Robert Howard. *From Parsifal to Perón: Early Radio in Argentina, 1920–1944*. Tallahassee: University Press of Florida, 2007.

Cohen, Colleen Ballerino, Richard Wilk, and Beverly Stoelje, eds. *Beauty Queens on the Global Stage: Gender, Contest, and Power.* New York: Routledge, 1996.

Conti, Viviana, Ana Teruel de Lagos, and Marcelo Lagos, eds. *Mano de obra indígena en los ingenios de Jujuy a principios de siglo.* Buenos Aires: Centro Editor de América Latina, 1988.

Cosse, Isabella. *Estigmas de nacimiento: peronismo y orden familiar, 1946–1955.* Buenos Aires: San Andrés / Fondo de Cultura Económica, 2006.

D'Arino Aringolli, Guillermo E. *La Propaganda Peronista, 1943–1955.* Ituzaingo: Maipue, 2006.

de Grazia, Victoria. "Nationalizing Women." *The Sex of Things: Gender and Consumption in Historical Perspective,* ed. Victoria de Grazia and E. Furlough. Berkeley: University of California Press, 1996.

De Imaz, José Luis. *La clase alta de Buenos Aires.* Buenos Aires: University of Buenos Aires, 1965.

de Ípola, Emilio. "Populismo e ideología (a propósito de Ernesto Laclau: Política e ideología en la teoría marxista)." *Revista Mexicana de Sociología* 41, no. 3 (1979).

——. "Ruptura y continuidad: claves parciales para un balance de las interpretaciones del peronismo." *Desarrollo Económico* 29, no. 115 (1989), 331–59.

de la Cadena, Marisol. *Indigenous Mestizos: The Politics of Race and Culture in Cuzco, 1919–1991.* Durham: Duke University Press, 2000.

de la Fuente, Ariel. *Children of Facundo: Caudillo and Gaucho Insurgency during the Argentine State Formation Process (La Rioja, 1853–1870).* Durham: Duke University Press, 2000.

Delaney, Jeanne. "Making Sense of Modernity: Changing Attitudes toward the Immigrant and the Gaucho in Turn of the Century Argentina." *Comparative Studies in Society and History* 38, no. 3 (1996), 434–59.

del Campo, Hugo. *Sindicalismo y peronismo: los comienzos de un vínculo perdurable.* Buenos Aires: CLACSO, 1983.

Delgado, Sergio. "Realismo y región: narrativas de Juan Carlos Dávalos, Justo P. Sáenz, Amaro Villanueva y Mateo Booz." *El imperio realista,* ed. María Teresa Gramuglio, 345–64. Vol. 6 of *Historia crítica de la literatura argentina,* ed. Noé Jitrik. Buenos Aires: Emecé, 2002.

Delrio, Walter *Memorias de expropiación: sometimiento e incorporación indígena en la Patagonia, 1872–1943.* Buenos Aires: Universidad Nacional de Quilmes, 2005.

De Paoli, Pedro. *Función social de la radiotelefonía.* Buenos Aires: El Ateneo, 1945.

Di Liscia, María H. B. *Mujeres y Estado en la Argentina: educación, salud y benefincencia.* Buenos Aires: Biblos, 1997.

Di Liscia, María H. B., and Ana M. Rodríguez. "El cuerpo de la mujer en el marco del Estado de bienestar en la Argentina: la legislación peronista, 1946–1955." *Boletín Americanista* 54 (2004), 63–85.

Di Núbila, Domingo. *La época de oro: historia del cine argentino*, vol. 1. Buenos Aires: El Jilguero, 1998 [1960].

Di Tella, Torcuato. *Perón y los sindicatos: el inicio de una relación conflictiva*. Buenos Aires: Ariel, 2003.

Donatello, Luis Miguel. "Manuel Romero y el peronismo: una lectura a través de 'Gente Bien.'" *Cine e imaginario social*, ed. Fortunato Mallimacci and Irene Marrone, 93–107. Buenos Aires: University of Buenos Aires, 1997.

Doyon, Louise. "La formación del sindicalismo peronista." *Los Años Peronistas (1943–1955)*, ed. Juan Carlos Torre, 355–403. Vol. 8 of *Nueva Historia Argentina*, ed. Juan Suriano. Buenos Aires: Sudamericana, 1998.

Dyer, Richard. *Las estrellas cinematográficas: historia, ideología, estética*. Buenos Aires: Paidós, 1979.

Elena, Eduardo. "Peronist Consumer Politics and the Problem of Domesticating Markets in Argentina, 1943–1955." *Hispanic American Historical Review* 87, no. 1 (2007), 111–49.

España, Claudio, ed. *Cine argentino: industria y clasicismo, 1933–1956*. Buenos Aires: Fondo Nacional de las Artes, 2000.

Falicov, Tamara. "Argentine Cinema and the Construction of National Popular Identity, 1930–1942." *Studies in Latin American Popular Culture* 17 (1998), 68–72.

Félix-Didier, Paula. "Soñando con Hollywood: los estudios Baires y la industria cinematográfica en Argentina." *Studies in Latin American Popular Culture* 21 (2002), 77–103.

Ferioli, Néstor. *La Fundación Eva Perón*. Buenos Aires: Centro Editor de América Latina, 1990.

Fiorucci, Flavia. "Between Institutional Survival and Intellectual Commitment: The Case of the Argentine Society of Writers during Perón's Rule, 1945–1955." *Americas* 62, no. 4 (2006), 591–622.

Foss, Clive. "Selling a Dictatorship: Propaganda and the Peróns." *History Today* 50, no. 3 (2000), 8–14.

Franco, Jean. *The Decline and Fall of the Lettered City: Latin America in the Cold War*. Cambridge: Harvard University Press, 2002.

Franco, Marcela, and Nora Pulido. ¿Capitanas o guardianas del hogar?: deseos y mandatos en la Argentina peronista." *Boletín Americanista* 37, no. 47 (1997), 113–25.

Fraser, Nicholas, and Marysa Navarro. *Evita: The Real Life of Eva Perón*. New York: W. W. Norton, 1996.

Frazier, Lessie Jo. *Salt in the Sand: Memory, Violence, and the Nation-State in Chile, 1890 to the Present*. Durham: Duke University Press, 2007.

Fürstenberger, Nathalie. "Güemes y los de abajo: fabricación y alcance del heroismo en La guerra gaucha." *Revista Iberoamericana* 71, no. 213 (2005), 1109–19.

Gallo, Ricardo. *La radio: ese mundo tan sonoro*, vol. 2. Buenos Aires: Corregidor, 2001.

Gambini, Hugo. *Historia del peronismo*, vol. 2. Buenos Aires: Planeta, 2001.

Garulli, Liliana, et al. *Nomeolvides: Memoria de la Resistencia Peronista, 1955–1972*. Buenos Aires: Biblos, 2000.

Gené, Marcela. *Un mundo feliz: imágenes de los trabajadores en el primer peronismo, 1946–1955*. Buenos Aires: Fondo de Cultura Económica, 2005.

Gerchunoff, Pablo, and Damián Antúnez. "De la bonanza peronista a la crisis del desarrollo." *Los años peronistas (1943–1955)*, ed. Juan Carlos Torre. Vol. 8 of *Nueva Historia Argentina*, ed. Juan Suriano. Buenos Aires: Sudamericana, 2002.

Germani, Gino. "El surgimiento del Peronismo: el rol de los obreros y de los migrantes internos." *Desarrollo Económico* 13, no. 51 (1973), 432–88.

Godio, Julio. *Perón: regreso, soledad y muerte (1973–1974)*. Buenos Aires: Hyspamérica, 1986.

Goldar, Ernesto. "La literatura peronista." *El Peronismo*, ed. Gonzalo Cárdenas et al., 162—68. Buenos Aires: CEPE, 1973.

——. *Buenos Aires: vida cotidiana en la década del 50*. Buenos Aires: Plus Ultra, 1980.

Goodwin, Jeff, James M. Jasper, and Francesca Polletta, eds. *Passionate Politics: Emotions and Social Movements*. Chicago: University of Chicago Press, 2001.

Gorelik, Adrian. *La grilla y el parque: espacio público y cultura urbana en Buenos Aires, 1887–1936*. Buenos Aires: Universidad Nacional de Quilmes, 1998.

Graziano, Frank. *Divine Violence: Spectacle, Psychosexuality, and Radical Christianity in the Argentine "Dirty War."* Boulder: Westview, 1992.

Grimson, Alejandro, and Elizabeth Jelin, eds. *Migraciones regionales hacia la Argentina: diferencia, desigualdad y derechos*. Buenos Aires: Prometeo, 2006.

Guivant, Julia Silva. *La visible Eva Perón y el invisible rol político femenino en el Peronismo, 1946–1952*. Notre Dame: Hellen Kellog Institute for International Studies, 1986.

Guy, Donna. "Life and the Commodification of Death in Argentina: Juan and Evita Perón." *Body Politics: Death, Dismemberment, and Memory in Latin America*, ed. Lyman Johnson. Albuquerque: University of New Mexico Press, 2004.

Hall, Linda. "Evita Perón: Beauty, Resonance, and Heroism." *Heroes and Hero Cults in Latin America*, ed. Samuel Brunk and Ben Falaw. Austin: University of Texas Press, 2006.

Halperín Donghi, Tulio. "Algunas observaciones sobre Germani, el surgimiento del peronismo y los migrantes internos." *Desarrollo Económico* 14, no. 56 (1975), 765–81.

———. "El lugar del Peronismo en la tradición política argentina." *Perón: del exilio al poder*, ed. Samuel Amaral and Mariano Plotkin. Buenos Aires: Eduntref, 2004 [1993].

———. *La larga agonía de la Argentina peronista*. Buenos Aires: Ariel, 2006 [1994].

Haussen, Doris Fagundes. *Rádio e política: tempos de Vargas e Perón*. Porto Alegre: EDIPUCRS, 1997.

Healey, Mark. "La trama política de un desastre natural: el terremoto y la reconstrucción de San Juan." *Entrepasados* 11, no. 22 (2002), 49–65.

———. *The Ruins of the New Argentina: Peronism and the Remaking of San Juan after the 1944 Earthquake*. Durham: Duke University Press, forthcoming.

Horowitz, Joel. *Argentine Unions, the State, and the Rise of Perón*. Berkeley: University of California Press, 1990.

Hunt, Lynn. *The New Cultural History*. Berkeley: University of California Press, 1989.

Huyssen, Andreas. *Después de la gran división: modernismo, cultura de masas, posmodernismo*. Buenos Aires: Adriana Hidalgo, 2002.

James, Daniel. *Resistance and Integration: Peronism and the Argentine Working Class, 1946–1976*. Cambridge: Cambridge University Press, 1988.

———. "October 17th and 18th, 1945: Mass Protest, Peronism and the Argentine Working Class." *Journal of Social History* 21, no. 3 (1989), 441–61.

———. *Doña María's Story: Life History, Memory, and Political Identity*. Durham: Duke University Press, 2000.

———, ed. *Violencia, proscripción y autoritarismo (1955–1976)*. Vol. 9 of *Nueva Historia Argentina*, ed. Juan Suriano. Buenos Aires: Sudamericana, 2003.

Jelin, Elizabeth. *Los trabajos de la memoria*. Madrid: Siglo Veintiuno, 2002.

Jelin, Elizabeth, and Victoria Langland, "Introducción: las marcas territoriales como nexo entre pasado y presente." *Monumentos, memoriales y marcas territoriales*. Madrid: Siglo Veintiuno, 2003.

Johnson, Lyman, ed. *Body Politics: Death, Dismemberment, and Memory in Latin America*. Albuquerque: University of New Mexico Press, 2004.

Jorrat, Jorge. "Reflexiones sobre un balance de las interpretaciones del peronismo." *Desarrollo Económico* 30, no. 118 (1990), 277–83.

Joseph, Gilbert, Anne Rubenstein, and Eric Zolov, eds. *Fragments of a Golden*

Age: The Politics of Culture in Mexico since 1940. Durham: Duke University Press, 2001.

Joseph, Gilbert, and Daniel Nugent, eds. *Everyday Forms of State Formation: Revolution and the Negotiation of Rule in Modern Mexico*. Durham: Duke University Press, 1994.

Karush, Matthew. "The Melodramatic Nation: Integration and Polarization in the Argentine Cinema of the 1930s." *Hispanic American Historical Review* 87, no. 2 (2007), 293–326.

Kindgard, Adriana. "Procesos sociopolíticos nacionales y conflictividad regional: una mirada alternativa a las formas de acción colectiva en Jujuy en la transición al peronismo." *Entrepasados* 11, no. 22 (2002), 67–87.

———. "En torno al Malón de la Paz de 1946." *Estudios Interdisciplinarios de America Latina y el Caribe* 15, no. 1 (2004), 165–85.

Kraniauskas, John. "Political Puig: Eva Perón and the Populist Negotiations of Modernity." *New Formations* 28 (1996), 121–31.

———. "Eva-peronismo, literatura, Estado." *Revista de Crítica Cultural* 24 (2002).

Laclau, Ernesto. "Towards a Theory of Populism." *Politics and Ideology in Marxist Theory: Capitalism, Fascism, Populism*, 143–98. London: NLB, 1977.

Lazzari, Axel. "Antropología en el Estado: el Instituto Étnico Nacional (1946–1955)." *Intelectuales y expertos: la constitución del conocimiento social en la Argentina*, ed. Federico Neiburg and Mariano Plotkin, 203–30. Buenos Aires: Paidós, 2004.

León, Carlos A., and Carlos A. Rossi. "Aportes para la historia de las instituciones agrarias en la Argentina: el Consejo Agrario Nacional." *Realidad Económica* 198 (2003).

Lobato, Mirta. "Entre la protección y la exclusión: discurso maternal y protección de la mujer obrera, Argentina 1890–1934." *La cuestión social en Argentina, 1870–1943*, ed. Juan Suriano. Buenos Aires: La Colmena, 2000.

———. "Lenguaje laboral y de género en el trabajo industrial: primera mitad del siglo XX." *Historia de las mujeres en la Argentina*, vol. 2, ed. Fernanda Gil Lozano, Valeria Pita, and Gabriela Ini. Buenos Aires: Siglo XX / Taurus, 2000.

———. *La vida en las fabricas: trabajo, protesta y política en una comunidad obrera: Berisso, 1904–1970*. Buenos Aires: Prometeo / Entrepasados, 2001.

———. "La Política como espectáculo: imágenes del 17 de octubre." *17 de octubre de 1945: antes, durante y después*, ed. Juan C. Torre. Buenos Aires: Lumiere, 2005.

———, ed. *El progreso, la modernización y sus límites, 1880–1916*. Vol. 5 of *Nueva Historia Argentina*, ed. Juan Suriano. Buenos Aires: Sudamericana, 2000.

Luna, Félix. *El Cuarenta y Cinco: Crónica de un año decisivo*. Buenos Aires: Sudamericana, 2005 [1969].

Macor, Darío, and César Tcach, eds. *La invención del peronismo en el interior del país*. Santa Fe, Argentina: Universidad Nacional del Litoral, 2003.

Mafud, Julio. *Argentina desde adentro*. Buenos Aires: Américalee, 1971.

———. *Sociología del Peronismo*. Buenos Aires: Américalee, 1972.

Maranghello, César. *La epopeya trunca: artistas argentinas asociados*. Buenos Aires: El Jilguero, 2002.

Margulis, Mario. *Migración y marginalidad en la sociedad argentina*. Buenos Aires: Paidós, 1968.

Margulis, Mario, and Marcelo Urresti. *La segregación negada: cultura y discriminación social*. Buenos Aires: Biblos, 1999.

Martínez Sarasola, Carlos. *Nuestros paisanos los indios: vida, historia y destino de las comunidades indígenas en Argentina*. Buenos Aires: Sudamericana, 1992.

Matamoro, Blas. *La ciudad del tango*. Buenos Aires: Galerna, 1982.

McCann, Bryan. *Hello, Hello Brazil: Popular Music in the Making of Modern Brazil*. Durham: Duke University Press, 2004.

Melón, Julio César. "La Resistencia Peronista, alcances y significados." *Anuario del IEHS* 8 (1993), 215–46.

Michelini, Pedro, ed. *El 17 de octubre de 1945: testimonio de sus protagonistas*. Buenos Aires: Corregidor, 1994.

Milanesio, Natalia. "'The Guardian Angels of the Domestic Economy': Housewives' Responsible Consumption in Peronist Argentina." *Journal of Women's History* 18, no. 3 (2006), 91–117.

Moffat, Alfredo. *Estrategias para sobrevivir en Buenos Aires*. Buenos Aires: Jorge Álvarez, 1967.

Monsiváis, Carlos. "Se sufre, pero se aprende: el melodrama y las reglas de la falta de límites." *Archivos de la Filmoteca* 16 (1994), 10.

Moreno, Julio. *Yankee Don't Go Home! Mexican Nationalism, American Business Culture, and the Shaping of Modern Mexico, 1920–1950*. Chapel Hill: University of North Carolina Press, 2006.

Murmis, Miguel, and Juan Carlos Portantiero. *Estudios sobre los orígenes del Peronismo: sociología y política*. Buenos Aires: Siglo Veintiuno, 2004.

Navarro, Marysa, ed. *Evita: mitos y representaciones*. Mexico City: Fondo de Cultura Económica, 2002.

Neiburg, Federico. "Ciencias sociales y mitologías nacionales: la constitución de la sociología en la Argentina y la invención del peronismo." *Desarrollo Económico* 34, no. 136 (1997).

———. *Los intelectuales y la invención del peronismo*. Buenos Aires: Alianza, 1998.

Oroz, Silvia. *Melodrama: el cine de lágrimas de América Latina.* Mexico City: UNAM, 1995.

Orquera, Yolanda Fabiola. "Marxismo, peronismo, indocriollismo: Atahualpa Yupanqui y el Norte Argentino." *Studies in Latin American Popular Culture* 27 (2008), 185–206.

Ostiguy, Pierre. "Peronism and Anti-Peronism: Class, Cultural Cleavages, and Political Identity in Argentina." Ph.D. diss., University of California, Berkeley, 1998.

Pastoriza, Elisa, ed. *Las puertas al mar: consumo, ocio y política en Mar del Plata, Montevideo y Viña del Mar.* Buenos Aires: Biblos, 2002.

Pellettieri, Osvaldo. "Cambios en el sistema teatral de la gauchesca rioplatense," *Gestos* 4 (1987).

Pittelli, Cecilia, and Miguel Somoza Rodríguez. "Peronismo: notas acerca de la producción y control de símbolos." *Discursos pedagógicos e imaginario social en el peronismo (1945–1955),* ed. Adriana Puiggrós, 209–16. Buenos Aires: Galerna, 1995.

Plotkin, Mariano. "The Changing Perceptions of Peronism: A Review Essay." *Peronism and Argentina,* ed. James Brennan, 29–56. Wilmington, Del.: SR, 1998.

——. *Mañana es San Perón: A Cultural History of Perón's Argentina.* Wilmington, Del.: Scholarly Resources, 2003 [orig. Span. edn 1993].

——. "La 'ideología' de Perón: continuidades y rupturas." *Perón: del exilio al poder,* ed. Samuel Amaral and Mariano Plotkin, 45–67. Buenos Aires: Eduntref, 2004.

Prieto, Adolfo. *El discurso criollista en la formación de la Argentina moderna.* Buenos Aires: Sudamericana, 1988.

Pujól, Sergio. *Jazz al sur: la música negra en la Argentina.* Buenos Aires: Emecé, 1992.

——. *Discépolo: una biografía argentina.* Buenos Aires: Emecé, 1996.

Quijada, Mónica. "Indígenas: violencia, tierras y ciudadanía." *Homogeneidad y nación: con un estudio de caso: Argentina, siglos XIX y XX,* ed. Mónica Quijada and Carmen Bernard. Madrid: Consejo Superior de Investigaciones Científicas, 2000.

Ramacciotti, Karina, and Adriana Valobra, eds. *Generando el Peronismo: estudios de cultura, política y género 1946–1955.* Buenos Aires: Proyecto, 2004.

Ramella, Susana. *Una Argentina racista: historia de las ideas acerca de su pueblo y su población, 1930–1950.* Mendoza: Facultad de Ciencias Políticas y Sociales, UNCuyo, 2004.

Ratier, Hugo. *El cabecita negra.* Buenos Aires: Centro Editor de América Latina, 1971.

Rein, Raanan. *Peronismo, populismo y política*. Buenos Aires: Belgrano, 1998.

——. "Preparando el camino para el peronismo: Juan A. Bramuglia como interventor federal en la provincia de Buenos Aires." *European Review of Latin American and Caribbean Studies* 67 (1999), 35–55.

Robben, Antonius C. G. M. *Political Violence and Trauma in Argentina*. Philadelphia: University of Pennsylvania Press, 2005.

Rocchi, Fernando. *Chimneys in the Desert: Industrialization in Argentina during the Export Boom Years, 1870–1930*. Stanford: Stanford University Press, 2006.

Romero, Luis Alberto. *A History of Argentina in the Twentieth Century*. University Park: Penn State University Press, 2002.

Rubenstein, Anne. *Bad Language, Naked Ladies, and Other Threats to the Nation: A Political History of Comic Books in Mexico*. Durham: Duke University Press, 1998.

Rubinstein, Gustavo. *Los sindicatos azucareros en los orígenes del peronismo tucumano*. Tucumán: Universidad Nacional de Tucumán, 2005.

Saítta, Sylvia. *Regueros de tinta: el diario crítica en la década de 1920*. Buenos Aires: Sudamericana, 1998.

Salvatore, Ricardo. *Wandering Paysanos: State Order and Subaltern Experience in Buenos Aires during the Rosas Era*. Durham: Duke University Press, 2003.

Sarlo, Beatriz. *El imperio de los sentimientos: narraciones de circulación periódica en la Argentina (1917–1927)*. Buenos Aires: Catálogos, 1985.

——. *Una modernidad periférica: Buenos Aires 1920 y 1930*. Buenos Aires: Nueva Visión, 1988.

——. "Eva Perón: algunos temas." *La Argentina en el siglo XX*, ed. Carlos Altamirano, 341–55. Buenos Aires: Ariel / Universidad Nacional de Quilmes, 1999.

——. *La pasión y la excepción*. Buenos Aires: Siglo Veintiuno, 2003.

Saulquín, Susana. *Historia de la moda argentina: del miriñaque al diseño de autor*. Buenos Aires: Emecé, 2006.

Savigliano, Marta. *Tango and the Political Economy of Passion*. Boulder: Westview, 1995.

Scarzanella, Eugenia. "El ocio peronista: vacaciones y 'turismo popular' en Argentina (1943–1955)." *Entrepasados* 14 (1998), 65–84.

Sebastiani, Marcela. *Los antiperonistas en la Argentina peronista: radicales y socialistas en la política Argentina, 1945–1951*. Buenos Aires: Prometeo, 2005.

Sebreli, Juan José. *Buenos Aires, vida cotidiana y alienación*. Buenos Aires: Sudamericana, 2003 [1964].

Senkman, Leonardo. "Etnicidad e inmigración durante el primer peronismo." *Revista Estudios Interdisciplinarios de América Latina y el Caribe* 3, no. 2 (1992).

Serbín, Andrés. "Las organizaciones indígenas en la Argentina." *América Indígena* 41, no. 3 (1981), 407–33.

Shwittay, Anke F. "From Peasant Favors to Indigenous Rights: The Articulation of an Indigenous Identity and Land Struggle in Northwestern Argentina." *Journal of Latin American Anthropology* 8, no. 3 (2003), 127–54.

Sigal, Silvia, and Eliseo Verón. *Perón o muerte: los fundamentos discursivos del fenómeno peronista*. Buenos Aires: Eudeba, 2003 [1986].

Silva, Matilde. "Las políticas económicas y sociales del primer peronismo y sus repercusiones: el caso de la reacción del empresariado azucarero tucumano, 1943–1949." *América Latina en la Historia Económica* 22 (2004), 11–27.

Sirven, Pablo. *Perón y los medios de comunicación (1943–1955)*. Buenos Aires: Centro Editor de América Latina, 1984.

Smith, Peter. "The Social Base of Peronism." *Hispanic American Historical Review* 52, no. 1 (1972), 55–73.

Spektorowski, Alberto. *The Origins of Argentina's Revolution of the Right*. Notre Dame: University of Notre Dame Press, 2003.

Spinelli, María Estela. *Los vencedores vencidos: el antiperonismo y la "Revolución Libertadora."* Buenos Aires: Biblos, 2005.

Stern, Steve J. "Between Tragedy and Promise: The Politics of Writing Latin American History in the Late Twentieth Century." *Reclaiming the Political in Latin American History: Essays from the North*, ed. Gilbert Joseph. Durham: Duke University Press, 2001.

Suriano, Juan. *Anarquistas: cultura y política libertaria en Buenos Aires, 1890–1910*. Buenos Aires: Manantial, 2001.

Tamarin, David. *The Argentine Labor Movement, 1930–1945: A Study in the Origins of Peronism*. Albuquerque: University of New Mexico Press, 1985.

Tandeciarz, Silvia. "Romancing the Masses: Peronism and the Rise of Cultural Studies in Argentina." *Journal of Latin American Studies* 9, no. 3 (2000), 283–303.

Tesler, Mario. *Los aborígenes durante el peronismo y los gobiernos militares*. Buenos Aires: Centro Editor de América Latina, 1989.

Tola, Florencia, and Timoteo Francia. *Historias nunca contadas*. Buenos Aires: Tatú, 2001.

Torrado, Susana. *Estructura social de la Argentina*. Buenos Aires: De la Flor, 1992.

Torre, Juan Carlos. *La vieja guardia sindical y Perón: sobre los orígenes del peronismo* Buenos Aires: Sudamericana, 1990.

——, ed. *El 17 de octubre de 1945*. Buenos Aires: Ariel, 1995.

Torre, Juan Carlos, and Elisa Pastoriza. "La democratización del bienestar." *(1943–1955)*, ed. Juan Carlos Torre, 255–312. Vol. 8 of *Nueva Historia Argentina*, ed. Juan Suriano. Buenos Aires: Sudamericana, 1998.

Tranchini, Elina. "El Cine Argentino y la construcción de un imaginario criollista, 1915–1945." *Entrepasados* 9, nos. 18–19 (2000).

Traversa, Oscar. *Cuerpo de papel: figuraciones del cuerpo en la prensa, 1918–1940.* Buenos Aires: Gedisa, 1997.

Ulanovsky, Carlos. *Paren las rotativas: una historia de grandes diarios, revistas y periodistas argentinos.* Buenos Aires: Espasa, 1997.

Ulla, Noemí. *Tango, rebelión y nostalgia.* Buenos Aires: Jorge Alvarez, 1967.

Valko, Marcelo. *Los indios invisibles del Malón de la Paz: de la apoteosis al confinamiento, secuestro y destierro.* Buenos Aires: Madres de Plaza de Mayo, 2007.

Viguera, Aníbal. "El primero de mayo en Buenos Aires, 1890–1950: revolución y usos de una tradición." *Boletín del Instituto Dr. Emilio Ravignani,* 3rd ser. (1991).

Walter, Richard. "The Right and the Peronists, 1943–1955." *The Argentine Right: Its History and Intellectual Origins, 1910 to the Present,* ed. Sandra McGee Deutsch and Ronald H. Dolkart, 99–118. Wilmington, Del.: Scholarly Resources, 1993.

Williams, Daryle. *Culture Wars in Brazil: The First Vargas Regime, 1930–1945.* Durham: Duke University Press, 2001.

Zanatta, Loris. *Del Estado liberal a la nación católica: iglesia y ejército en los orígenes del peronismo.* Buenos Aires: Universidad Nacional de Quilmes, 1996.

ABOUT THE CONTRIBUTORS

Matthew B. Karush is an associate professor of history and the director of Latin American Studies at George Mason University. He is the author of *Workers or Citizens: Democracy and Identity in Rosario, Argentina, 1912–1930* as well as numerous articles on Argentine political and cultural history. His current research examines mass culture in Argentina in the 1920s and 1930s.

Oscar Chamosa is an assistant professor of history at the University of Georgia. His articles have appeared in the *Hispanic American Historical Review* and *The Americas*. He is currently finishing a book manuscript entitled *Archetypes Of Nationhood: Nationalism, Folklore and the Rural Workers of Northwestern Argentina, 1920–1955.*

Natalia Milanesio is an assistant professor of history at the University of Houston. She has written about consumer culture, Peronism, gender, and social movements in modern Argentina. Her articles have appeared in *Gender and History*, the *Journal of Social History*, and the *Journal of Women's History*. She is currently working on a book manuscript on popular consumer culture and modernity in mid-twentieth-century Argentina.

Diana Lenton teaches anthropology at the University of Buenos Aires and is a researcher at CONICET (the National Council for Scientific and Technological Research). She has published numerous articles and book chapters in both Argentine and international publications. Her work focuses on indigenous rights, indigenous policies, and indigenous militancy in Argentina.

Anahi Ballent is a professor of history at the University of Quilmes in Argentina and a researcher for CONICET. She is the author of numerous books, articles, and book chapters dealing with the history and politics of architecture, housing, and technology in Argentina and Latin America. She is the author of *Las huellas de la política: vivienda, ciudad, peronismo en Buenos Aires, 1943–1955*, from which her chapter in the present volume is drawn.

Mirta Zaida Lobato is a professor of history at the University of Buenos Aires. She has been a visiting scholar at Duke University and at the Institute for Advanced Studies at Indiana University. She has published extensively and received international recognition for her work on class and gender identity among Argentine industrial workers. Her recent publications include *La vida en las fábricas: Trabajo, protesta y política en una comunidad obrera, Berisso (1904–1970)* and *Historia de las Trabajadoras en la Argentina (1869–1960)*.

María Damilakou is a lecturer of Latin American history in the Ionian University in Greece. She has published articles and chapters on the history of nitrate workers in Chile and port workers in Argentina. She is the author of *The Greek Immigration in Argentina: The Process of Construction and Transformations of a Migrant Community, 1900–1970*.

Lizel Tornay is the coordinator of the Museum of the Escuela Normal Superior Mariano Acosta of Buenos Aires and a researcher at the Archive of Women's Images and Voices in the Interdisciplinary Institute of Gender Studies, University of Buenos Aires. Her work focuses on the audiovisual memory of working women in Argentina.

Eduardo Elena is an assistant professor of history at the University of Miami. The author of multiple articles on mid-twentieth-century Argentina, he is currently finishing a book manuscript entitled *Consuming Dignity: The Politics of Citizenship and Consumption in Peronist Argentina*.

César Seveso recently completed his PhD at Indiana University and is an adjunct professor of history at the University of Houston. He has published articles on Argentine anticommunism, the relationship between communists and Peronists, and the history of political imprisonment after 1955. He is currently working on a book manuscript entitled *Violence, Mourning, and Memory: Political Rituals and Revolutionary Militancy in Argentina, 1955–1985*.

Mariano Ben Plotkin is a professor of history at the National University of Tres de Febrero in Argentina as well as a researcher at CONICET and at the Institute of Economic and Social Development in Buenos Aires. He has been a visiting scholar at several universities in the United States, as well as the recipient of international grants and awards. Among his publications are the books *Mañana Es San Perón: A Cultural History of Peronist Argentina* and *Freud in the Pampas: The Emergence and Development of a Psychoanalytic Culture in Argentina*.